Economic Policy
Beyond the Headlines

Economic Policy Beyond the Headlines

Second Edition

George P. Shultz
and Kenneth W. Dam

THE UNIVERSITY OF CHICAGO PRESS
Chicago and London

The first edition of this book was originally published in 1977 as a part of the The Portable Stanford, a series of books published by the Stanford Alumni Association, Stanford, California, and was reprinted in 1978 by W. W. Norton & Company, Inc.

The University of Chicago Press, Chicago 60637
The University of Chicago Press, Ltd., London
University of Chicago Press Edition 1998
Printed in the United States of America
04   03   02   01   99   98   6   5   4   3   2   1

Library of Congress Cataloging-in-Publication Data

Shultz, George Pratt, 1920–
    Economic policy beyond the headlines / George P. Shultz, and Kenneth W. Dam.—2nd ed.
        p.   cm.
    Previous ed. was published by Stanford Alumni Association, 1977.
    Includes bibliographical references and index.
    ISBN 0-226-75599-1 (alk. paper)
    1. United States—Economic policy—1971–1981.   2. United States—Economic policy—1981–1993.   3. United States—Economic policy—1993–   I. Dam, Kenneth W.   II. Title.
HC106.7.S37   1998
338.973—dc21
                                                            97-47077
                                                            CIP

⊗ The paper used in this publication meets the minimum requirements of the American National Standard for Information Sciences—Permanence of Paper for Printed Library Materials, ANSI Z39.48-1992.

Table of Contents

PREFACE TO THE SECOND EDITION ix

INTRODUCTION x

CHAPTER ONE   Themes   1

Inflation and Unemployment   20

CHAPTER TWO   The Myth of Budget Tuning   23

CHAPTER THREE   Tax Policy and the Taxpayer   43

CHAPTER FOUR   The Life Cycle of Wage and Price Controls   65

CHAPTER FIVE   Income Security: The Vital Trade-on   87

International Economic Policy   106

CHAPTER SIX   International Monetary Policy   109

CHAPTER SEVEN   International Trade Policy:
New Dimensions to Old Problems   133

Organizing for Problem Solving   152

CHAPTER EIGHT   Organizations and Reorganizations   155

CHAPTER NINE   Energy and the Marketplace   179

CHAPTER TEN   Tools for a Constructive Economic Policy   199

CHAPTER ELEVEN   A Changed World   207

READER'S GUIDE   224

NOTES ON SOURCES   227

INDEX   229

ABOUT THE AUTHORS   240

CREDITS

Acknowledgments

WE WISH TO EXPRESS OUR APPRECIATION to Phillip Areeda, G.L. Bach, Walter Blum, J.D. Bonney, Aaron Director, John Dunlop, Reginald Jones, Stanley Katz, Edmund Kitch, Harold Richman, Hugo Simens, Ezra Solomon, Herbert Stein, and James White. Each has read part or all of our manuscript at one stage or another of its development and all have given us valuable and constructive ideas and criticisms, though not necessarily approval. In addition, we thank Virginia Zinns, Rita Gallagher, and Maryelinor Sanders, who typed and retyped this manuscript, and Clara Ann Bowler, who assisted with verification of factual data. We extend special appreciation to our editor, Cynthia Fry Gunn, whose professional skill and conscientious effort have greatly helped strengthen and clarify our written words.

We claim responsibility for all errors and omissions.

G.P.S.
K.W.D.

Preface to the Second Edition

WE WROTE THIS BOOK in the late 1970s and explicitly based it on our government experiences in the early 1970s. Now, two decades after writing and a bit longer since those experiences, we thought it time to ask ourselves whether anything had changed. As our new closing chapter shows, we think the primary difference is not in how government operates, but in the nature of the problems—particularly the problems we see lying ahead as we turn the corner into a new century.

Since we first wrote, we returned to the well of government in the State Department in the 1980s, and perhaps that experience led us to place greater emphasis on the international side of issues. But our experiences in the business world teach us that globalization is not just a slogan but increasingly dominates the economic scene. Finally, we have also spent time in the 1990s at two great universities, Chicago and Stanford, reminding us that there is no substitute for writing down one's thoughts. We offer in our last chapter a summary of what we have to add to what we said before.

We should like to thank Martin Anderson, Michael Boskin, Robert Crow, Adele Hayutin, Ezra Solomon, and Marina Whitman for their comments on the new last chapter.

G.P.S.
K.W.D.

Introduction

OUR SUBJECT is economic policy. Economic policy issues can be discussed on several levels. One is the world of headlines. Newspaper stories, editorial columns, and television news are sometimes concerned with the broad economics of the issues, but more often they focus largely on the issues of the day, especially their political implications. At the other end of the spectrum, professional discussions in economics journals deal primarily with technical aspects of economic issues. Both levels of analysis are important: Economic policy cannot be made in an ethical or a political vacuum, and the concepts of the discipline of economics are crucial to sound policy.

But between these two levels—beyond the headlines and short of the technicalities—lies a neglected world of ideas and concepts, of organizational arrangements, of pressures and demands. This is the workaday world of economic policymaking and implementation.

In the essays that follow, we aspire to explore that world, using the large issues more as the stage than as the play itself. We have relied heavily on impressions gained in Washington, but we have also attempted to deal with some of these issues from a more general analytical perspective—without providing a technical economic analysis, for which there is already a vast literature available. Our objective is to present an additional framework for thought rather than to offer formulas or panaceas. We are in search of principles that can be applied in the future. Although we cannot pretend to have achieved that goal, we believe that we have gained certain insights from the government positions we have held over the past few decades.

Most of our examples will be taken from the years 1969-74. Our excuse for this restriction in time is twofold. First, we know more about those years than others. Second, we believe that the impressions, distilled by reflection, of those who were part of the economic policy process are themselves data from which the principles we seek can be derived. We do not believe that these impressions are a substitute for the results of serious economic and other social science research. But neither do we believe that they are of little consequence. While we therefore have provided facts and figures to illustrate our impressions, we do not use these facts and figures to "prove" their accuracy. It is the impressions themselves that we offer, sharpened we hope by thought and by the discipline of writing, but largely without the apparatus of the social scientist, the factual accumulation of historian, or the anecdotes of the autobiographer.

George P. Shultz
Kenneth W. Dam

Stanford, California
Chicago, Illinois

CHAPTER ONE

Themes

"WELL, MR. SECRETARY, what is going to happen to your professorial convictions now that you have responsibility for solving the practical problems of the world?" It was a good question, posed by members of the press to the new Secretary of Labor in January 1969.

I (Shultz) was on the printed record as believing that private collective bargaining could work well and that it was being subverted by too much government involvement; that potential crises from strikes tended to be overrated and overdramatized; that high officials should refuse to become involved and certainly should not attempt to force the parties to settle their disputes; and that the clear willingness of high administration officials to become involved resulted in their exploitation by labor or management in a process where "supply created its own demand." I had expressed this view to a group of lawyers, saying that if the President hangs out his shingle, he'll get all the business.

The labor situation in January 1969, however, hardly seemed propitious for implementation of such a self-denying strategy. A strike of East Coast longshoremen was well under way. Outgoing President Johnson had declared a national emergency and had invoked the Taft-Hartley injunction procedures on October 1, 1968, thereby postponing the strike until mid-December—just before the new administration came into office. Some three emergency boards were already dealing with railroad industry disputes. Still other railroad disputes were in the making, with the parties refusing to engage in bargaining because they expected the government to invoke an emergency board.

The concerns of the many enterprises and millions of workers indirectly affected by the longshoremen's strike manifested themselves in direct pleas, sometimes delivered forcibly by key members of Congress, to "do something." The shift to a less interventionist role of government created severe strain, but this test of the new policy at the outset of the incoming administration turned out to be fortunate. I stayed out of the dispute, as did the President. All labor disputes are settled eventually, and this one was no exception. The groundwork was thus laid for heading off public expectations of government intervention in subsequent labor disputes.

Only if expectations of government intervention and emergency procedures can be reduced will healthy collective bargaining be likely. In this regard, we note that there were no new emergency boards in operation as the Carter administration took office. Indeed, there were no major strikes on the docket, and the Taft-Hartley injunction procedures had been used only once during the eight years of the Nixon and Ford administrations.

Nevertheless, the pressure to "do something" is present at almost all times across all policy issues and is sometimes virtually irresistible. Of course there are many occasions when action *is* called for. But perhaps my two most important words during almost six years of government service were "Do nothing." This was an order to the commissioner of Internal Revenue, who came to me in September 1972 with a request from the President's counsel, John Dean, to start IRS investigations of a list of people (later dubbed the "enemies list") supplied to him by Dean. The need to use these words on that occasion was clear. But in many areas of public policy, including economic policy, the need is as great, though it is not necessarily clear to all concerned. Leadership is all too often equated with doing something and patience equated with indecision. Indeed, one of the most difficult problems for economic policy is finding ways to "do nothing" while waiting for the lagged effects of actions already initiated to work their way through the market process.

Four other major ideas or themes are frequently encountered in the workaday world of formulating and administering economic policy: the interplay between efficiency and equity as prime objectives, the growth of an advocacy system for making policy and the associated trend toward balkanization of government, the interconnections between policy issues traditionally treated as separate domains, and the importance of anticipations and expectations in the making of sound policy. Beyond these analytical themes, we offer four more subjective observations about policymakers themselves: the role of individuals in the policymaking process, the differences between professionals and politicians, the importance of work and homework, and the role of timing in making and implementing policy decisions. In exploring the world of economic policymaking beyond the headlines, we have found it helpful to think about these concepts and insights in their own terms.

Efficiency and Equity

A central idea in this book and perhaps the most recurrent theme confronted in economic policy decisions is the interplay and often apparent conflict between efficiency and equity. The efficient solution may be widely regarded as at least immediately unjust or inequitable, and what many regard as the equitable solution may turn out upon analysis to be hopelessly inefficient.

Economists, budgetmakers, and other financial officials must try to get the most possible for the resources placed in their hands by taxpayers, and that means seeking the most efficient solution to a problem—pursuing policies that take full advantage of the problem-solving capacity of the system of markets and enterprise. Limitations of resources demand no less. Within the private sector, competition forces efficiency on businessmen and financiers, whether they like it or not. Indeed, one can say that those in public or private life who have resources placed in their hands must— almost as a matter of trust on behalf of society—see that those resources are used as productively as possible. So the business and financial system marches to the drummer of efficiency.

But not the political system. Most politicians will nod to efficiency, but it is usually little more than a nod. The drummer that the politician marches to is equity. When a problem comes up, economic thinking says, "What is the efficient way to solve it?" Political thinking says, "What is the equitable solution?" In any exercise in political economy, these two distinct patterns of thought are interacting, and the task at hand is to see how they can be meshed.

That equity arguments are all too often used as a guise to support narrow self-interest does not alter the basic appeal to the body politic of the "fair shake." Certainly a key problem for policy is to recognize the legitimacy of the concern for the poor and the disadvantaged but to avoid having the rhetoric of poverty become the servant of well-placed interests. At any rate it is common to see economists and financially oriented government officials lined up behind a relatively efficient solution and the more politically inclined policy officials supporting what they regard—or at least what they believe Congress and the people regard—as the equitable solution.

This view of efficiency as something *opposed to* equity contains an element of truth, but in actual practice it is a gross oversimplification. In one sense, efficiency and equity may not be alternatives but rather the poles of a spectrum. The options realistically open to policymakers may lie somewhere along that spectrum. The concept of a trade-off between efficiency and equity neatly expresses this insight but may itself obscure more subtle interactions of these two objectives.

In fact, the pervasiveness of the trade-off concept in public policy discussions can blind us to the most desirable solutions. For example, it is frequently said that there is a trade-off between inflation and unemployment. That notion tends to obscure the possibility of dealing with the inequities of unemployment by welfare reform. If the human consequences of unemployment can be dealt with by direct cash payments to the unemployed that neither stigmatize nor humiliate the recipients and that at the same time preserve incentives to return to work, then more effective measures can be used to deal with inflation. In short, what policymakers should seek is *trade-ons* that permit the goals of efficiency and equity to be served simultaneously.

The Advocacy System and Balkanization of Government

One widespread view of public policymaking envisions a group of officials within the executive branch working together to achieve what is in the best interests of the nation as a whole, with the political process external to the executive branch characterized by competing groups attempting to obtain legislation favorable to themselves. This view, however, overlooks that these same competing interests are well-represented within the executive branch and that the making of policy involves a struggle between them.

That interest groups are represented within the legislative branch seems well understood, although citizens are sometimes shocked to realize to what extent the agriculture committees represent farmers rather than consumers, the armed services committees represent the military and defense contractors, and the interior committees Western interests. The same kind of representation is found in the executive branch. Based on long tradition and what seems to be nearly an "iron law" of politics, the Agriculture Department tends to represent farmers, the Department of Health, Education and Welfare the interests of professionals who provide health, education, and welfare services, and so forth. Some observers even say, sometimes with justification, that the State Department represents foreign governments.

This is government by advocacy. The chief danger is that policy will be made not so much by the weighing and balancing of alternatives but rather by collusion among various representatives of particular interest groups: the department, the legislative committee, and the organized group within the society. Not the least of the unfortunate consequences of the advocacy system has been the dramatic growth over the past three or four administrations of the Executive Office of the President. The Executive Office, influenced by its identification with a President elected by all the people, has generally been better able to analyze policy issues in a disinterested fashion than have advocacy agencies. But the size and the relative remoteness of most parts of the Executive Office from the political firing line have led to a further extension of the advocacy system. Recent Presidents have begun to appoint assistants and even to create bureaus within the Executive Office to represent these interest groups in policy discussions at the center.

So long as the advocacy principle reigns, the new cabinet officer of an advocacy department faces a major problem in defining the role he is to play. Most cabinet officers are content to represent their respective constituencies: agriculture, business, labor, and so forth. Since the departmental bureaucracy will already be fulfilling this representational role, this tendency of cabinet officers is sometimes decried with the comment that they have been captured by their bureaucracies. It is unnecessary for a cabinet officer to be the prisoner of the advocacy form of organization, but he must be prepared to recognize and understand the views of a constituency group when issues involving that constituency are presented for decision within the administration.

In defining my own role as Labor Secretary in 1969, I (Shultz) benefited from George Meany's commanding presence on the labor scene. In response to the press question, "Do you expect to be the spokesman for organized labor in the President's cabinet?" I could respond simply that I expected to represent the public interest on the broad range of subjects with which the Labor Department deals, and I looked to George Meany as the spokesman for organized labor. I added, however, that I would spare no effort to see that organized labor had a means to make its views known in the White House and elsewhere in the administration, and that I would take pains to understand those views and their rationale.

Since the advocacy system serves the interests of well-situated groups, it is not surprising that interest groups are vitally concerned with government organization. Organization is also important to any President, who must have some way of balancing competing interest groups against one another while at the same time building a policy structure that can take account of broader considerations.

The Departmental Reorganization Plan of 1971 attempted to reform advocacy government by submerging the more explicitly representative of the departments into ones that were larger and more functionally oriented. The plan was soundly defeated, or perhaps one should say "smothered," by a combination of the same interest groups and legislative committees (with implicit support from some of the representative departments themselves) that benefit from the advocacy system.

Continued efforts to subvert the concept of a single executive branch under a popularly elected President take a number of forms—all leading to further balkanization of the executive branch:

- the creation of so-called independent agencies that make policy without direction or even influence of the President;

- the subversion of the concept of a President's budget and the spread of the notion that independent agencies should submit their budgets directly to Congress;

- the growth of the idea that certain executive functions, such as the investigation and prosecution of crime, should be isolated from all presidential and Executive Office policy direction; and

- the tendency to turn to the judicial branch not only for the resolution of disputes between individuals and between well-defined groups but also for determining priorities between broad social, economic, and political interests.

This balkanization can be attributed to a variety of influences. The idealism of Americans leads to the espousal of causes, such as, in recent times, environmentalism. The political process initially deflects the cause by giving it a symbol of power, such as an agency bearing the cause's name rather than, at least immediately, the political outcome sought. Another source of balkanization is the success of traditional interest groups in the advocacy process. Following their model, newer interest groups, particularly those without well-defined economic objectives, are encouraged to establish organizations within government to fight for their causes.

The drive for independence from presidential leadership can also be traced to the widespread belief that better policies would be achieved by government if only better people were chosen and were shielded from the political process. A further stimulus to balkanization can be found in the "cult of law," an elitist view that righteous causes can be served better in a court of law presided over by a lifetime appointee than in the democratic political process.

Whatever its origins, presidential reliance on the advocacy process to assure that all sides are heard, coupled with the desire of economic and social interests both to gain recognition and to insulate themselves from the influence of competing interests, leads to balkanized government.

Interconnections

Early morning half hours at the White House are consumed by meetings.

Beginning in early 1973, one of these was a daily 8:00 a.m. meeting on economic policy. The top few economic policy officers of the executive branch attended. We used the 30 minutes to review leading events and problems and, when appropriate, to decide who would follow up on issues. A half hour is not long enough to discuss a problem in depth. Yet one advantage of short regular meetings was that it permitted us to identify the connections between different policy areas raised by a single subject.

It is a truism in policymaking that everything is related to everything else so that, in one sense, all interrelationships and subsequent effects should be taken into account before decisions are made. But some factors are obviously more relevant to a particular matter than others, and the task of the policymaker is to recognize the most relevant connections and harness them creatively in the solution of broad problems.

In the real world of time pressures and staff specialization, the internal links within a policy area are typically explored in great detail. For example, in pension reform discussions, the intimate relationships between funding and vesting have been matters of intense study and debate. But another level, the interconnections between policy areas—for example, in the relation of pension reform to developments in the fields of international trade and unemployment compensation—is often overlooked. The thrust of pension reform is to protect the worker's principal asset, the savings implicit in his pension, while unemployment compensation protects his income. When a worker loses his job, both his savings and his income are endangered and in a related way.

This connection between the pension and unemployment compensation systems transcends our national boundaries. A trade bill authorizing international negotiations for tariff reductions cannot be drafted without considering both systems for protecting workers against the consequences of the unemployment that would be created by increased imports. The interplay of trade legislation, pension reform, and unemployment compensation reform thus illustrates the importance of considering economic policy as a connected whole, rather than as simply a set of more or less independent parts.

The pervasiveness of these policy connections has organizational implications. Trade, pensions, and unemployment compensation have traditionally been handled in entirely different parts of the government. The need for an economic policy coordinating group, dealing with domestic and international matters, is clear. The Council on Economic Policy, which we organized, performed this role both in its formal and informal meetings and also through its task groups.

Economic policy must also be closely linked to social policy. The realities of a strong fight on inflation imply a higher level of unemployment than is desirable. At the same time, price problems involving scarce products will be dealt with more quickly and completely if the market is allowed to do its job of encouraging supply and restricting demand. If price stabilization and supply-expanding policies are to be pursued successfully, they must be accompanied by a satisfactory level of income maintenance for the poor. Although the relation between economic policy and welfare reform is obvious, it is seldom analyzed explicitly.

Anticipations and Expectations

The conventional way of looking at economic policy is to analyze the problems of the private sector and then propose governmental measures for solving those problems. This view of the government as a regulator of the private economy is too narrow a focus. A more useful way to look at the economy is to view it as having interacting private and government sectors. The government may regulate the private sector, but in many ways the economy regulates the government. This reverse effect is not primarily the result of any improper influence or even of political pressure from powerful business, farm, social, or labor groups. In a democratic society the government should and will be responsive to real or perceived ills in the private economy. To every government action the private sector reacts or accommodates, and the government further reacts as the private economy "talks back" to the government.

This policymaker's version of Newton's Law operates in a system in which most units in the private economy are relatively small but the federal government is large and its impact potentially great. This action and reaction results in frequent efforts to anticipate what the government may do and to act upon expectations of what such actions may bring about—all of which creates both problems and opportunities for the policymaker. Anticipations and expectations are, of course, problematic in the decisions of any organization, large or small, but because of the sheer size and importance of the government they may be of particular concern in public policy formation.

A few illustrations may clarify the anticipations phenomenon. In 1973 the rapid escalation of food prices was an urgent problem. The United States was a major exporter of grains and other food commodities; such exports were essential to pay for the imports of foreign products that U.S. consumers had increasingly come to view as essential to their life-style and their level of consumption. Nevertheless, the access of all comers to the U.S. free market led to foreign bids for U.S. commodities that dramatically raised the price of food to domestic consumers. As a result of crop shortfalls, the mysterious disappearance of anchovies (an important source of protein for animal foods) from the ocean off Peru, and other factors, foreign purchases of U.S. grains and soybeans accelerated. The resulting price rises led to a clamor for export controls. The rationale behind these increasingly insistent demands in the executive branch and Congress was that export controls would assure that the quantities of the commodities "needed" in the United States would be kept here and that domestic food prices would fall below world prices.

As a decision on export controls approached, it became apparent that little information existed on actual intentions to export. A natural and obvious reaction was to establish a statistical base for an informed decision by introducing a reporting program. Such statistics could be of assistance both in deciding whether or not to impose export controls and in designing the controls program itself. The policy decision could thus be based on anticipated events, not merely past events.

The very problem of anticipations, however, made it almost impossible to collect accurate information. Realizing that the information provided might at some point establish the base for export levels under any controls that might be introduced, exporters built up the stated volume of their export intentions. In many cases exports were reported as intended without any destination being given. Such reports could not be rejected, because export contracts with the destination stated at time of shipment were customary. But the volume of such contracts grew rapidly. The resulting set of statistics showed that the quantity of soybeans expected to be exported before the 1973 soybean crop harvest was greater than soybean stocks on hand.

These statistics led to the conclusion that export controls had to be instituted. Subsequent examination, however, showed that the reports filed on export intentions vastly inflated the probable level of exports. Fraud was not involved because the contracts actually existed. Both exporters and importers had a strong incentive to enter into such contracts so that if controls were instituted and the amounts of permissible exports were based on a formula tied to contracts (say, some percentage of the contracted amount), their interests would not be affected. If controls did not materialize, they could then reverse the transactions either by cancellation or by resale of the purchased commodities to domestic buyers. Costs might be incurred, but both exporters and importers regarded these costs as insurance premiums against future controls. This was an instance where the anticipation of government action made it extremely difficult for the government to collect the information on which a rational decision could be made. An efficient solution would have let the market operate. In the name of equity for U.S. consumers a process was initiated that produced a decision which, in operation, was neither efficient *nor* equitable.

Political, as opposed to economic, anticipations can also affect the making of presidential policy. Before instituting new measures, Presidents and their advisers usually wish to have wide consultations in order to gain a detailed understanding of the problems involved and a base of support for the President's eventual decision. But the process of consultation requires disclosure of the President's intention to reach a decision, and various clues are necessarily given in the course of consultation as to the probable direction of that decision. A group that feels the decision may be unfavorable to its interests can thereby launch a campaign to head off the presidential decision. Consultation may thus lead to political anticipations. The impact of a presidential decision may be diluted or the decision may even be foreclosed. Alternatively, if a President is on a potentially popular course, the political opposition may seize upon the idea and try to capture a policy position in the public mind before the President has a chance to announce his own policy.

Considerations such as these often lead Presidents to develop their policy proposals within a small group of advisers without public consultations. The new program is then proclaimed without the embarrassments of political anticipations but also without the substantive exploration required to avoid misjudgments and without the political support that could have been developed by consultation.

Closely held decisions may also be found in economic matters of less political significance. A decision whether or not to impose, say, export controls on commodities traded on an organized exchange, must necessarily be debated within a restricted group. A leak of the results of a decision meeting could mean wide price movements and vast profits for professionals. No government can afford to have generated profits for speculators. But such "closet decisions" can be based on misinformation and are thus often bad decisions.

The development of government subsidy programs provides a further example of anticipations. The most popular way to bring about more economic activity in a particular sector is to create a new subsidy program. In research and development, government subsidies have proved so attractive that more than half of all such activity in the economy is paid for by the federal government. Yet a prime difficulty is to assure that government funds do not simply substitute for private funds. The institution of a new subsidy program may even discourage private activity in the first place as private firms, seeking a subsidy, defer new projects while attempting to induce the government to put up the necessary funds.

Popular social programs present a different aspect of the anticipations phenomenon. Here a decision to begin in a small way creates expectations of program growth that are likely to be impossible to resist. It can certainly be argued on equity grounds, for example, that the government should provide school lunches for poor children. But the school lunch program proved to be so popular, particularly with agricultural interests, that each new expansion of the number of children fed was viewed as totally inadequate. Within a few years the program had far surpassed the objective of eliminating hunger among poor children and, through provision of school lunches to all children in many suburban schools, had also become a subsidy program for middle-class parents. The trade-off between the use of scarce budget funds for such lunches and their use for other social welfare programs was totally ignored in public discussions. These developments were probably anticipated by agricultural interests and budgeteers at the outset, but appealing causes are hard to oppose on the grounds of "where will this lead?"

The Role of Individuals

In addition to the major ideas that appear explicitly throughout our discussion of substantive issues, several more subjective aspects of economic policymaking warrant attention; these concern the decision makers themselves and the way they work to reach decisions.

Economic policy is formed and implemented by people who work within a political environment. Some of the people with whom the policymaker works will have little interest in the economic dimensions of economic policy. Some may have primarily a political orientation. Others may be substantively oriented, but their interest may lie in some other area of government concern, such as national security policy. The emphasis of this book is on the primacy of ideas and institutions and the flow of events. The quality of public appointments is surely important. But the proposition so often found in popular journalism and everyday discussion that problems would go away if only a new and better group of people could be attracted to government service must as surely be rejected.

Nevertheless, individuals can be crucial to the execution of policy decisions. Few people believe that the history of U.S. foreign relations in the early 1970s would have been quite the same if Henry Kissinger had never moved from Cambridge to Foggy Bottom. At any time in any administration there will be a few individuals who have a preeminence transcending their official post. This commanding position depends largely on their perceived influence with the President, though ability, ambition, stamina, and determination also play a role. These individuals must be taken into account in policy formation and execution when individuals holding the same positions but lacking this special "clout" could be ignored.

For some years in the Nixon and Ford administrations, Kissinger had that preeminence. Though he took no special interest in economic questions, any policy decision with foreign policy implications had to be accepted by Kissinger. A failure to obtain this acceptance could easily doom the policy decision. For example, in 1971 Secretary of the Treasury John Connally, then the chief economic official of the administration, was pursuing an extremely hard line toward European governments on the issue of the proper exchange rate for the dollar. When this economic policy began to create political fallout, Kissinger began to take an interest. Because of the political implications of the policy, Kissinger concluded that the Connally policy was too costly to pursue unbendingly. In several bilateral summit meetings, arranged by Kissinger, between the President and individual European heads of government, the need for good political relations and for a successful conclusion to the meeting led to a partial abandonment of the Connally hard-line position.

Whoever the key individuals may be and whatever their talents, good personal relationships among them, though far from assuring desirable outcomes, certainly help to bring them about. This is true not only within government but also between governments. Helmut Schmidt of West Germany, for example, has worked hard at developing good personal relationships with his counterparts—first as Minister of Defense, then as Minister of Finance, and most recently as Chancellor. Schmidt became Minister of Finance shortly after I (Shultz) assumed the roughly comparable post of Secretary of the Treasury. We first met in 1972 in my new office at the Treasury. We had a lengthy talk about world economic problems. He is an easy man to like and to admire—bright, well-informed, and, to put it mildly, forthright with his views. He listens to counterarguments and is prepared to change his mind when new information or new ideas cast a subject in a new light, but he also has strong ideas of his own.

We developed a strong friendship, starting with this first meeting and carrying through innumerable meetings of finance ministers. In part through Schmidt's good offices, a small group (dubbed "The Group of Five" by the press) was formed involving Schmidt, myself, Valéry Giscard d'Estaing, French Minister of Finance, and Anthony Barber, British Chancellor of the Exchequer, later joined by Kiichi Aichi and subsequently Takeo Fukuda, Japanese Ministers of Finance. This group first met for a day in April 1973 when all were in Washington for larger international monetary meetings. This and subsequent gatherings of the Group of Five played a crucial role in the international monetary reform discussions then under way.

My relationship with Schmidt and Giscard continued after I left government in May 1974 and after both Schmidt and Giscard became heads of their governments. In 1975 Giscard proposed a summit meeting on economic matters, a suggestion viewed with considerable skepticism in U.S. government circles. In September 1975, President Ford asked if I would meet with Chancellor Schmidt and President Giscard, as well as British Prime Minister Harold Wilson, to find out what they had in mind and to help evaluate whether such a meeting could be constructive.

I met first with Helmut Schmidt. After conversations Saturday afternoon and evening and the next morning, we both felt that a summit could be quite constructive. Knowing that my schedule was to go from Bonn directly to Chequers for a meeting with Wilson and then on to Paris on Monday for a luncheon meeting with Giscard, Schmidt suggested that he come to Paris after my meeting with Giscard for a dinner Monday evening among the three of us. When I advised Wilson of this plan, he was eager to be informed of the outcome of the dinner and arranged for Sir John Hunt, his cabinet secretary, to join me for breakfast on Tuesday morning before I left for Washington. As discussions proceeded, the breakfast group expanded to include Schmidt's key monetary representative, Karl Otto Pöhl, and Raymond Barre, later French Prime Minister.

By the conclusion of the noon meeting with Giscard, the idea of a summit conference had acquired considerable momentum, with all three European heads of government prepared to be enthusiastic about it. I then telephoned my evaluation to Secretary of State Kissinger and through Kissinger to President Ford. The approaching dinner presented an opportunity to explore the matter in an encouraging and positive manner with Schmidt and Giscard without committing the President. Until then I had been operating under neutral instructions and the dinner created an opportunity to move further, if the President chose. Word came back within the hour that, on the basis of this information, the President had a quite positive attitude.

The dinner was held at Marly, a house reserved for the President of France on a large estate near Versailles. The discussion, which centered on the prospects for international monetary reform, was informal but substantive. That these two chiefs of government could meet with a friend from the United States for a four-hour discussion over dinner without the event being reported or perhaps even known by the world press is remarkable. It is difficult to imagine the President going, let us say, to Canada for dinner with the Prime Minister without press comment.

These conversations were expanded at next morning's breakfast and at subsequent meetings of this group, joined by former Ambassador Nobuhiko Ushiba of Japan. These discussions at the least provided encouragement to the creative efforts of Edwin Yeo of the U.S. Treasury Department and his French counterpart, Jacques de Larosière, who prepared the way for agreement at the six-nation Rambouillet summit in November 1975 and the resulting Jamaica agreement of January 1976, amending the Bretton Woods agreement that had governed international monetary relations since World War II and setting out rules for the more flexible monetary system now in place.

It is possible that events would have unfolded in roughly the same way without the benefit of good personal relationships. But that conclusion seems not entirely plausible in view of the fact that *all* of the national bureaucracies were opposed to holding a summit meeting. Without the Rambouillet summit, the detailed work reflected in the Jamaica agreement would have taken much longer. In any event, Ford, Schmidt, and Giscard have all remarked that they felt that the personal relationships developed during the summit meetings and during bilateral meetings proved invaluable in the conduct of their intercountry discussions.

The importance of good personal relationships in situations of potential conflict has wide applicability. This said, it is also true that personal relationships will in fact deteriorate if one of the representatives gives way to the temptation to sacrifice the interests he represents in order to preserve good relations. This point is fundamental in any negotiation. French negotiators, for example, simply do not give way in tough negotiations in order to maintain good relationships. They usually remain charming but are quite willing, in pursuing French interests, to incur the wrath that falls on the obstinate member in a negotiating session. It is a good lesson for everyone.

Professionals and Politicians

A helpful distinction in analyzing the role of particular individuals is one between professionals and politicians. By professionals we mean policy officials who have some independent professional status in the society (as lawyers, economists, businessmen, investment bankers, and the like) and who come to policy positions for a limited period of time with the intention of returning to their professions. By politicians we mean officials whose career ambitions involve future elective or high appointive office. Politicians, of course, have a profession—politics. But it is useful for these purposes to think of that profession in a separate category.

The twin categories of professionals and politicians obviously do not exhaust the ranks of policy officials. Civil servants elevated to policy positions do not clearly fall in either group. Moreover, the line between professionals and politicians is an uncertain one because many professionals develop political ambitions—"Potomac fever"—when they experience the excitement and challenge of dealing with great public issues. Despite the imprecision of this definition, it can nonetheless be useful in understanding how various types of individuals can work together to produce better policy than could any one type alone.

A professional in a key position is more likely to accept a policy decision

and give it active public support if it reflects the standards and aspirations of his profession. Scientists in government uphold the importance of basic research and rarely give wholehearted support to reductions in funding for science. Economists are unlikely to support regulation that merely entrenches the position of some economic interest, regardless of how politically crucial the support of that economic interest may be to some important policy objective.

A politician in a key position, as we have already suggested, will place emphasis on the "art of the possible." As the late Senator Everett Dirksen was fond of saying, "I am a man of principle, and the first principle is flexibility." Both politicians and professionals certainly consider the effect of their public statements on their future careers, but the audiences they seek to please are quite different.

The role of an individual as professional or politician and his role as an agency official in the advocacy process should sometimes be in conflict. Surprisingly, however, this is all too often not the case. Like chameleons, too many officials quickly take on the coloration of their agency and play the advocacy role to the hilt. Not all do so and, interestingly, politicians are often less likely to do so than professionals. Politicians may be instinctively more sophisticated about government, but personal ambition also plays a role. The politician with his eye on future governmental positions is more likely to be torn between institutional and personal views. Secretary of Defense Melvin Laird was required by his office to be a hawk on Vietnam, but he labored strenuously behind the scenes to resist decisions that might expand the war or slow U.S. withdrawal. Secretary of Health, Education and Welfare Caspar Weinberger had to support the spending programs of his department but worked hard to trim HEW spending and to introduce basic reforms in welfare programs that were opposed by most of the professional groups associated with HEW.

Whether a top official is a professional or a politician, self-selection plays a great role in determining where he will work within the executive branch. A person who desires a highly visible public role tends to seek major departmental appointments, whereas a person who prefers a lower-visibility position, yet one perhaps more internally influential, is likely to end up in the Executive Office or the White House proper. The choice of position has a number of implications. Especially within the White House, an official may easily develop the ambition (if he did not already have it) to be in the inner circle of presidential advisers. Access to the President is a key to power in the executive branch. Without power great objectives cannot be achieved. But the result is the creation of a structure and operating procedures at the very center of the executive branch that are quite different from those of the advocacy system found in the interdepartmental arena and the more impartial analytical system found in parts of the Executive Office.

The White House has many of the attributes of a royal court. Access to the President can easily become an end in itself. Intrigue can too easily replace analysis in policy formation and execution. On the other hand, White House officials are relatively free of the compulsion to advocate the interests of particular governmental institutions and can thus devote themselves more singlemindedly to the substance of policy problems. In our experience, logic, substantive argument, and reason, as instruments in making policy and gaining its acceptance, have their greatest value at the center of the executive branch and become relatively less important as one moves out into an interdepartmental arena or into the complex committee world of Capitol Hill. We do not mean to impugn either the importance or integrity of debates in these circles, but rather to suggest that candor suffers while symbolism and strategic maneuver take on greater significance there; within the privacy of a particular department or of a particular legislator's staff, candor and directness are much more prevalent than in public pronouncements.

The tendency for all Washington officials to act like politicians compounds these problems. Many economists are so deeply committed to such goals as the redistribution of income and wealth or so confident in their ability to outguess the political process that they behave in government less as professional economists than as political officials. Politicans, who are inevitably closer to the people and are more familiar with the receiving end of public policy decisions, often see aspects of a public policy issue that are not well sensed by more professionally oriented officials. If both are playing their proper roles, the inevitable exchange of views that precedes a presidential decision can substantially improve its quality.

Work and Homework

Hard work pays off in government as elsewhere. But it is surprising how often appointees to top offices underestimate the grinding work necessary to get astride the manifold issues and problems that face any government agency. Few are prepared by prior experience or study for the enormous variety of issues that confronts even a single department. It is not sufficient to have substantive views. The views of a new top-level official must be backed by facts and insight if he is to persuade the diverse constituencies he faces every week (congressional committees, the press, the White House staff) and avoid becoming the captive of his departmental bureaucracy or private sector groups to which his department most closely relates. Much more than the professor in his class or the business executive in his corporate meetings, the cabinet member or other top-level official is out front, exposed in a variety of forums. If he does not command his subject, his views will soon carry little weight.

It is not enough to spend the days going from meeting to meeting, from press conference to committee hearing, from speech to television interview. What makes the difference is homework—the long hours with the staff and with the black looseleaf books they habitually prepare. It is, moreover, not enough to be a spokesman, reciting a brief prepared by others. The key is the ability to interpret the public interest in the midst of controversy through an informed and objective understanding of the issues.

The combination of a willingness to do homework with a lifetime of study of the issues is what has produced superlative public servants like Arthur Burns and Henry Kissinger and, in earlier administrations, Dean Acheson and Douglas Dillon. Even without the historically rooted, balanced understanding that comes from long exposure to the issues, many appointees have had highly successful government careers as a consequence of personal qualities, luck, and—in every such case, we suspect—homework.

Timing

One of the most important factors affecting the success of a policy decision is timing. The right decision at the wrong time may permanently ruin the chances of a constructive proposal. At the very least, the energy that goes into supporting a decision that cannot be implemented will be wasted.

Some issues are best dealt with by a "bold, imaginative program," launched with maximum publicity and given top presidential priority. These are the programs that attract the most attention and have particular appeal to politicians. But not all issues lend themselves to the bold stroke. Assuming that a problem has been properly analyzed so that the objectives to be pursued are clearly in mind, progress is often best made by an incremental approach. Progress often depends on adding one small piece at a time to an existing policy structure, sometimes by moving the issue to the professional level. In government this can only be done by treating the issue as unimportant, at least politically. Politically unimportant issues can often be resolved on an objective, professional basis—thereby illustrating the occasional importance of being unimportant.

Most decisions in government, however, are made not in the process of designing new programs nor even in incrementally improving existing programs but rather in the day-to-day process of responding to crises of the moment. The danger is that this daily firefighting leaves the policymaker further and further from his goal. But if one has a clear sense of strategy, it is possible to move in the desired direction in the unending process of contending with the issues of the day. The trick is to deal with them in a manner consistent with the long-term policy objective. As particular short-range problems are solved, none of which are major in themselves, successful coping requires that the direction of the solution be consistent with the long-term goal. Many of the failures of government in dealing with the economy can be traced to an attempt to solve minor problems piecemeal. Since many problems of this sort arise from demands of particular groups for special government assistance or for government regulation, the resulting patchwork of ad hoc solutions and quick fixes often makes such fundamental goals as price stability and economic growth more difficult to achieve.

Another critical aspect of timing is preparation. The best of ideas may be impossible to implement unless the political and economic environment is favorable. The fertile moment may come suddenly and evaporate as quickly. The government official who is well prepared and ready to move is the person able to achieve something constructive at the critical moment.

The removal of controls on the outflow of capital from the U.S. in early 1974 illustrates this point. Instituted in the 1960s to reduce balance-of-payments deficits, those controls—including the interest equalization tax (on purchases of foreign securities by Americans), the foreign direct investment program (regulating direct investment abroad by U.S. corporations), and the voluntary foreign credit restraints program (restricting expansion of foreign loans by U.S. banks)—were universally acknowledged to be bad in the long run because they hurt U.S. business and reduced the efficiency of the international financial system. But key officials in the executive branch and many private experts took the position that, bad as the controls were, the time was not quite ripe for their removal because their elimination might worsen the U.S. balance of payments and anger foreign governments. Years passed, but the time never seemed right. As we felt strongly that the controls should be removed, our inability to do the "right" thing was particularly frustrating.

It proved worthwhile, nevertheless, to keep repeating that the controls would eventually be eliminated and, more important, to have available a program for eliminating them if the situation ever arose when no one could convincingly argue that the timing was wrong. When the dollar moved strongly on international exchange markets in early 1971 and concern began to be expressed in world financial circles that the dollar would become too strong, the time to act arrived.

All the prior work then paid off, and it was possible to terminate all capital controls programs in a matter of days. This move strengthened U.S. financial markets by helping New York City to begin to recoup its former position as the center of the world financial community and indirectly improved worldwide access to capital as well.

Timing, work, personal relationships, and prepared positions open up tactical options in the development of economic policy, just as the advocacy process, the balkanization of government, and the problem of anticipations characterize the setting for and constrain the process of policy formulation. Any good strategy for economic policy must recognize the connections between subjects; this point is especially important because organizational arrangements tend to obscure them and because these interrelationships present opportunities for creative thought and action.

With all this said, we return to the idea of the interplay between the objectives of efficiency and equity. In its broadest sense, this interplay expresses the essence of the social compact so necessary for a stable economy that is both effective and fair. And within issue after issue, the interplay between equity and efficiency provides a way of analyzing and reconciling competing aspects of the problem. This is nowhere more true than in the four issues in the next section. Thus, while each chapter stands on its own, they are inextricably intertwined. Each is in a particular way related to the problems of inflation and unemployment.

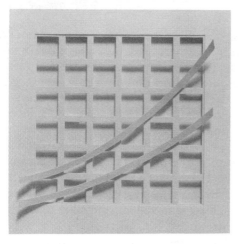

Inflation and Unemployment

NEARLY EVERYONE—economists, pundits, politicians, even policymakers themselves—would like to think it possible to achieve high employment with stable prices and to adjust the economy continuously to maintain that objective. The primary tools available are fiscal policy and monetary policy. We shall be concerned here almost exclusively with fiscal policy because that is where our own experience has been concentrated.

Nevertheless, we recognize the great, perhaps dominant, importance of monetary policy for achieving stabilization goals. The Federal Reserve is an "independent" agency, and therefore monetary policy should be expected to be free of some of the institutional and political constraints that plague fiscal policy. Independence is, however, a relative matter. The Federal Reserve is part of the government. The chairman meets with the President and with fiscal policy officials, seeking to gain acceptance for policies the Fed favors. It is questionable whether the Federal Reserve can remain entirely independent of administration views about domestic monetary policy; and, of course, the Fed takes direction from the President, through the Treasury Department, on international monetary affairs.

The chairman of the Federal Reserve is in regular contact with Congress. He testifies many times a year and is forced to justify the Fed's policies, if only to prevent Congress from passing legislation that would directly compromise the Federal Reserve's independence. It would be extraordinary if congressional views did not also influence Federal Reserve Board policies. Congressional pressures are almost always in the direction of increasing the money supply.

The independence of the Federal Reserve, however relative, is nevertheless real and is a prime example of the balkanization of government. Monetary policy is, in principle, not even subject to presidential decision. In short, no one is ultimately in charge, either in the executive branch or in Congress. When the economy is going badly, fiscal officials tend to look to monetary policy for relief, and the Fed preaches the importance of better fiscal decisions or calls for an "incomes policy."

In discussing fiscal policy, we shall not address the question, often debated by economists, does fiscal policy actually "work"? Let us assume, for the sake of argument, that it could work with considerable precision if policymakers were in a position to make full use of it. We shall focus on the political and institutional constraints on fiscal policy—on the reasons it is difficult in practice to manipulate the flow of outlays and, to a lesser extent, tax revenues with the ease that even broad-tuning of the economy presupposes.

If, as we suggest, fiscal policy is a blunt tool for stabilization purposes, then the conclusion is not so much that government, here as elsewhere, tends to promise far more than it delivers but, more important, that the focus on short-term stabilization diverts attention from more significant long-range questions. On the outlay side, issues such as the role of government and the effectiveness of federal programs tend to take a back seat. And on the revenue side, macroeconomic concerns about inflation and unemployment tend to swamp consideration of the design and fairness of the tax system. What is required is more steadiness at the throttle and fewer attempts to gun the engine.

We discuss wage and price controls and income security (welfare, unemployment insurance, etc.) together with fiscal policy because most people either do not see or misperceive the interconnections between these topics. The great vice of wage and price controls is not so much that they work poorly or that they are an inappropriate response to inflation as it actually occurs in our economy, but rather that they induce government to relax monetary and fiscal policy. The income security question, popularly known as the welfare issue, goes to the heart of what is often called the trade-off between inflation and unemployment. A comprehensive restructuring of our vast array of social programs is our best hope for solving the inflation problem while maintaining the incomes of the unemployed in ways that do not actually contribute to unemployment—which far too many such programs in fact do today.

CHAPTER TWO

The Myth of Budget Tuning

FISCAL POLICY is universally regarded as a cornerstone of economic policy. For many economists, fiscal policy is the essence of stabilization—a view held even more widely among politicians and government officials. Not many years ago, the notion was that policymakers could calibrate the exact amount of the budget deficit or surplus to fine-tune the economy. Theories fade in the face of overwhelming evidence, but the widespread view in Washington is still that the economy can at least be broadly tuned by varying the degree of fiscal ease or stringency. Whatever the economics of the matter, nothing could be further from the truth.

Fiscal policy is not a valve that can be readily adjusted to determine the amount of stimulus or restraint to apply to the economy. In the United States fiscal policy is an unwieldy tool that can be applied to the economic machine only with the greatest clumsiness, however refined the mental processes of the policymakers. Perhaps in the land of Keynes a Chancellor of the Exchequer can execute spending and taxing decisions with precision and promptness. If so, the explanation lies in the structure of British institutions, where the "budget" (which includes both spending decisions and tax changes) will normally be enacted within a few months of submission and without substantial change, thanks to the parliamentary system and party discipline.

In the United States both the theory and the reality are different. The

President proposes but can hardly dispose. Spending and taxing decisions go forward independently, both in the executive branch and in Congress. Party discipline is the exception, not the rule. Spending decisions are fragmented, particularly in Congress, and many important taxing decisions, notably concerning the social security tax, are made with only the most perfunctory bow to fiscal policy considerations.

Under these circumstances fine-tuning is out of the question. Even a rough-hewn countercyclical fiscal policy is often beyond the government's grasp, at least when such a policy calls for a surplus rather than a deficit. And to the extent that fiscal policy decisions are translated into spending and taxing flows, the impact on the economy is more often than not too late, sometimes coming half a cycle too late and exacerbating rather than moderating swings in economic activity.

In order to explain these limitations on fiscal policy, it is first necessary to take a closer look at the complexity of the budget process. Budget totals are just that—totals—and they are made up of thousands of individual items. The President's budget, as submitted to Congress in the annual Budget Appendix, runs over 1,000 telephone book-sized pages in small type. The process of determining the components, and thereby the totals, begins in the executive branch more than a year before the commencement of the fiscal year and has often not ended in Congress until well into the fiscal year itself.

The 1974 Congressional Budget and Impoundment Control Act altered the fiscal year and changed the congressional half of the budget process. Because it is not yet clear how much the new law, which did not become fully effective until mid-1976, will change budget reality and because the changes can only be understood against the background of the existing system, we shall briefly sketch the sequence of events in the prereform annual budget cycle.

The Annual Cycle

In May of each year Conference Room 248 of the Old Executive Office Building, across the street from the White House, is the scene of the Office of Management and Budget's Spring Preview. The director of the OMB or his deputy presides, as OMB officials and a few invited guests from other Executive Office organizations take their first comprehensive look at the fiscal year to commence more than a year later. After an overall look at the prospective revenue and outlay totals and the prospective economic situation they then examine the probable expenditures by department more closely and take a first pass at fitting the pieces into the total.

After the Spring Preview and subsequent discussions with the President, the OMB sends planning numbers to the departments. On the basis of these OMB figures the departments submit their proposed budgets to the OMB in late summer or early autumn. Because these planning numbers usually served only as a base to which the departments added a number of percentage points worth of proposed spending, the OMB several years ago started calling those planning figures "ceilings," implying that the departments had to come in with a submission below the ceiling figure. Reality has not changed, and the department submissions regularly sum to many billions of dollars more than the OMB's overall planning total.

Squeezing these billions of dollars out of the departmental submissions occupies the OMB from October to the last moment at which changes can be made in page proofs of the President's budget submitted to Congress in January. The first act in this high budget season drama is the autumn Director's Review. Again Conference Room 248 is the scene and, as before, the stage is limited to OMB officials and a few others from the Executive Office. Out of these meetings come the "marks" sent to the departments. The sum of these marks equals the latest OMB overall planning total minus a small allowance for subsequent negotiations with the departments. If the marks exceed the OMB planning total, that is a sign that the OMB has already been defeated and that spending will be larger than hoped for.

After recoiling with real or feigned horror at the severity of the OMB reductions, the departments uniformly "appeal" the OMB marks. The first appeal is normally to the deputy director of the OMB, who meets with the appealing cabinet officer and either stands his ground or adds back a small amount in the attempt to shut off the appellate process at that point. From then on the appellate process becomes an illusive struggle in which the rules are not well known and in which each side attempts to change any unfavorable rules. The OMB director is the next stop on the appellate route, if indeed he was not already involved in the first stage. After further negotiation large budget issues reach the President for final resolution.

Because these remaining issues are inevitably of the greatest importance to the OMB and to departmental participants and often involve major political questions, the last stages of the process are often unruly and unstructured. But by Christmas Eve nearly every decision will have been made, though it is not uncommon for decisions to become unstuck and for new adjustments to be made as late as the first week of January. Late in January the President's budget appears. The preceding description is only a general outline. For every rule there are exceptions. The Defense Department budget is an exception to the entire process on two counts: Since 1951 a joint review has been held in the Pentagon at which both OMB and Department of Defense officials participate; furthermore, National Security Council officials play a major role in resolving OMB-DOD differences.

Once the President submits his budget, the congressional half of the budget process begins in earnest. The President's budget is only a proposal and thousands of changes will be made in the months of congressional deliberations still ahead. After an initial round of hearings before the full appropriations committees of the House and Senate and the Joint Economic Committee, the congressional committees (normally meeting in subcommittees) will begin looking at each department's budget line by line. First the substantive committees (Education and Labor, Armed Services, etc.) must report out bills authorizing expenditures, followed by congressional passage of the authorization bills, with eventual presidential approval or disapproval. The appropriations committees must work on bills that appropriate funds within the amounts authorized, and again these bills must go through both houses and be signed by the President. As in the case of executive branch treatment of the budget, there are many exceptions to this simplified sketch of the process. One that we shall examine in a moment is the bypassing of the appropriations committees by back-door spending techniques.

Prior to the reform of congressional budget procedures in 1974, Congress rarely completed its work on the budget by the beginning of the fiscal year (then July 1) and hence stopgap continuing resolutions were necessary to keep some departments in operation pending eventual congressional action. In the end, however, Congress does act, and it will be up to the departments to spend.

The relationship between the amounts the President proposes in his budget and the amounts Congress eventually appropriates is complex; there are often large differences, both in total amount and, especially, in particular budget categories. For many years Congress has cut the Defense budget and supplemented social welfare budgets—with the supplements usually greatly outrunning the cuts.

Equally interesting from a fiscal policy viewpoint is the discrepancy between amounts appropriated and amounts spent. Even if the President does not attempt to "impound" certain appropriations, the departments may not spend all that is appropriated. Underspending is, if not the rule, at least not exceptional. Departments that felt their vital interests compromised in OMB and congressional cuts will often be unable to spend the amounts appropriated. Overspending also occurs, requiring supplemental appropriations. Consequently the spending totals for a fiscal year will fluctuate throughout the year, but rarely in response to the felt needs of fiscal policy. Although the President, through his advisers, may try to accelerate or slow down the spending of appropriated amounts in response to economic policy decisions, the effects are regularly swamped by the cumulative vicissitudes of individual spending programs.

The 1974 Act

The 1974 Congressional Budget and Impoundment Control Act changed this chronology in two ways. First, it changed the fiscal year from July-June to October-September, though the President must still submit his budget in January (more precisely, 15 days after Congress convenes). The reform thus forces fiscal policy decisions to be made an additional three months further from the event. The consequence may be like trying to steer a modern oceangoing oil tanker down an uncharted, meandering river. From the helm at the rear of the ship one can hardly see the bow and yet momentum limits maneuverability. Fortunately, it is possible to bend the fiscal ship somewhat in midstream.

Second, the new statute creates the opportunity and imposes something of an obligation on Congress to make a judgment on the overall spending totals. Several concurrent resolutions on spending totals are required of Congress, with procedures for allocations to particular committees and for reconciliation of discrepancies between the actual total and the intended total.

How well the reform of the congressional half of the budget process will work remains to be seen. If it works well, the use of fiscal policy will become more feasible and a far greater measure of control over spending will have been achieved. But this is not the first time reforms have been passed. "Legislative budgets" resembling the proposed concurrent resolutions were attempted in 1947 and 1948. In 1947 Congress could not agree on the total, and in 1948 the agreed total was simply ignored in the later appropriations process. Although the new procedures are more sophisticated than those invoked in 1947 and 1948, the exemption of the social security and highway trust funds, general revenue sharing, entitlement programs, and other popular forms of back-door spending from the full rigors of the budget reform act suggests a wait-and-see attitude. It will be all too easy simply to raise the allowed total if the parts add up to more than originally planned. And when it comes to controlling the spending instinct, as OMB hands we remember getting the word, "I don't care what you think as long as you give a dam—in my congressional district."

Although the new act may assure more deliberate congressional action, it may also dilute the ability of executive branch decision makers to carry out their views of appropriate fiscal policy. Under the prior system the President's budget set the parameters of the public fiscal policy debate. The critics of the fiscal policy as set forth in the budget and its accompanying message had no alternative document around which to coalesce. The congressional concurrent resolutions under the new act provide such a focus and give Congress an opportunity to set parameters. Although the reform should improve public dialogue, the fiscal result may become more of a compromise between executive and legislative views than a reflection of a consistent view of the economy. That danger is less to be feared, however, than the mindless compromises that resulted from the disjointed and unfocused congressional budget process that preceded the new act.

The Uncontrollable Budget

Against the background of this summary description of the budget process, we can now discuss the constraints on budget policy more concretely. Perhaps the major constraint is that so much of the budget is beyond the reach of the normal budget process. In fiscal 1977, 73 percent of the President's budget is virtually uncontrollable. Of the $411 billion of estimated outlays, only $115 billion is controllable. Of this amount $69 billion is in the Defense budget, leaving only $46 billion of controllable civilian outlays, little more than 10 percent of the total budget. Here we are talking of uncontrollability as a matter of law; as a political matter, many controllable programs have a sacred cow aspect that renders them off limits to those who worry about fiscal policy. Still other outlay savings are difficult to achieve in any particular fiscal year. Reduction of federal employment, for example, is a favorite budget-cutting tool but it takes time, and termination payments eat up much of the first-year savings. Defense bases can be closed, but projected first-year savings usually prove illusory.

Budget outlays may be legally uncontrollable for any of several reasons. First, the decisive event in the spending process is the obligation of funds. The actual expenditure of the funds—the outlays—may come much later. For construction and procurement expenditures, the outlays will necessarily be spread over a number of years as the dam or weapons system or whatever the item to be purchased is built. In fiscal 1977 outlays resulting from prior-year obligations and contracts are expected to total $61 billion, not including trust funds. Although some of these expenditures can be avoided if required for fiscal policy, the *deobligation* of funds often results in substantial termination costs, the complete waste of funds expended to date, and, of course, the frustration of the public policy being carried out under the spending program. And deobligation may involve the impoundment of funds by the President, which has been made more difficult, if not in some cases impossible, by the 1974 Budget and Impoundment Control Act.

Another category of uncontrollable outlays stems from the use of trust funds. The largest of these, the social security trust fund, has more than $83 billion in estimated outlays for fiscal 1977. Lumping together trust funds and other forms of entitlements to individuals, which under existing law are outside the control of either the executive branch or the appropriations committees, some $192 billion in outlays—nearly half the budget—is beyond the reach of fiscal policy. Interest paid by the government on the national debt, hardly controllable in the name of fiscal policy, has been running about $30 billion per year. In all, the uncontrollable portion of the $411 billion in outlays for fiscal 1977 comes to $301 billion.

Why has so much of the budget become uncontrollable? The prime reason is that advocates of particular programs want to place their outlays beyond the reach of the annual budget process. They believe strongly in their programs and want to keep money grubbers in the OMB or on the appropriations committees from chiseling away at the program in order to achieve some arbitrary spending total completely unrelated to the merits of the program. Pious talk about fiscal policy is either dismissed as an irrelevant abstraction or, if taken seriously, is thought best directed at someone else's program. The blame is equally shared by the legislative and executive branches. Legislative committees seek protection from appropriations committees, and departments seek protection from the President's budgetary apparatus. Even a President may be an advocate who seeks to protect a favored program by making it uncontrollable.

When President Nixon proposed general revenue sharing to implement his vision of the "New Federalism," he advocated that it be enacted as a "permanent appropriation" of a "designated percentage of the nation's taxable personal income" in order to "relieve the States and localities of the uncertainty which comes when a new level of support must be debated each year." However worthy this objective, that decision made about two more percentage points of the budget uncontrollable. In this case Congress reduced the period of the appropriation to five years and fixed the amount at $5 billion per year.

Within the legislature, back-door spending—the bypassing of the appropriations committees—is a favorite technique for insulating a program. Contract authority, which permits government agencies to enter into construction contracts, relegates the appropriations committees to the clerical function of "paying the bills." Entitlement programs create rights in individual citizens, and the principal budgeting function in both the executive branch and Congress is to estimate the funds that will be necessary. The entitlement or right, say, to food stamps or welfare payments means that Congress has no option but to make the appropriations available. "Permanent" appropriations generate spending authority year after year without new congressional action. Through trust funds, permanent appropriations, and other devices some program advocates have succeeded in bypassing not only the appropriations committees but even

Congress itself. Over 40 percent of the budget now becomes effective without any congressional review.

A more drastic way to insulate a favored program is to take it out of the budget entirely. The impact of the program's spending or lending on the economy is in no way affected by taking it out of the budget, but the authority of those in the executive and legislative branches interested in fiscal policy is decisively weakened. In 1971 the Export-Import Bank was taken out of the budget, and in 1973 the Rural Electrification Administration and the Rural Telephone Bank were also removed from the budget rolls. By fiscal 1975 the outlay-hiding effect for the Export-Import Bank alone was estimated at $1.6 billion. For the Rural Electrification Administration and the Rural Telephone Bank the outlay-hiding effects for fiscal 1977 were estimated at $0.5 billion and $0.1 billion, respectively. The technique of moving outlays off the budget has not been limited to lending programs. Although the annual federal subsidy to the Postal Service remains in the budget, outlays from the Postal Service fund no longer appear.

The motives of the proponents of off-budget legislation have been to protect their programs, but the result has been to reduce the comprehensiveness of the budget as a statement of the government's effect on the economy. In fiscal 1977, off-budget outlays for government-owned institutions are estimated at $10.8 billion. The trend has not ended, although the Export-Import Bank was restored to the budget in 1976. In the past few years Congress voted to create the United States Railway Association and the Pension Benefit Guaranty Corporation, both as off-budget institutions.

These off-budget figures do not include much more significant effects from treating certain government-sponsored agencies—such as the Federal National Mortgage Association, the Banks for Cooperatives, and the Federal Intermediate Credit Banks—as outside the government sector. These credit institutions were removed from the budget in fiscal 1969. Again, whether or not the government-sponsored institutions appear in the budget, the fiscal impact remains the same. The net outlays of these and other government-sponsored institutions are estimated at another $11 billion in fiscal 1977. Taking government-owned and government-sponsored institutions together, off-budget outlays were estimated at over $21.8 billion in fiscal 1977, roughly 5 percent of on-budget outlays and more than 1 percent of the Gross National Product (GNP).

The Budget as an Outcome

This description of the budget process is oversimplified. The President's budget is not like a court decision—the result of the application of fiscal criteria to the pleas of advocates. Rather it is the outcome of a process in which the President and his associates make political choices among alternatives. One, but only one, interest will be the impact of the budget on the economy. The decisions that underpin the budget will also reflect foreign, military, social, and health policy concerns, to mention just a few of the important influences on the overall budget. The budget also reflects presidential compromises with advocates in the departments, with outside interest groups, and with congressional leaders. The wonder is that fiscal policy concerns play as large a role as they do in shaping the proposed deficit or (rarely) surplus.

This description of the budget process also suggests that the budget is made up only once a year. In fact, the budget changes every time the President makes a new legislative proposal. Most new legislative proposals for the year will be contained in the budget; the appearance of the President's budget, the Economic Report of the President, and the State of the Union Message within a few weeks of one another helps to assure that result. But in fiscal 1973, for example, the President made 99 legislative proposals for new or expanded programs, only 45 of which were in the January budget. The other 44 emerged during the course of the year either in response to new problems or as an outlet for the fertile creativity of the federal bureaucracy.

Countless more proposals were generated on the legislative end of Constitution Avenue, and some of those made the statute books. To be sure, even the proposals that became law did not necessarily increase the budget because, though the legislation may have authorized expenditures, the appropriations may not have been forthcoming for another year. But many proposals involved back-door spending and generated increased expenditures immediately. Of the 99 presidential initiatives in the fiscal 1973 budget, 11 involved mandatory or back-door spending.

The Budget as a Cosmetic Document

Although the President submits his budget to Congress, he does not direct it solely to the senators and representatives. The budget is addressed to the public at large. The financial community scrutinizes it carefully. So do defense contractors, social welfare organizations, foreign aid recipients, and other special-interest groups. An administration wishes to speak to all of these audiences.

One of the messages the President transmits is his attitude toward spending. In times of inflation, for example, a President will want to strike a tough public stance. If the momentum of spending prevents him from presenting a balanced budget, he will nonetheless usually want to project as small a deficit as possible. When the economy is sluggish, he may choose to strike an expansionary stance. What he will do when *both* conditions are present is more complicated.

Even if all of the constraints we have catalogued prevent a President from altering the path of public spending much in a particular year (even increased spending occurs with a lag), he has some flexibility to show a higher or lower rate of spending in the budget. The budget's joints are so loose that this flexibility need not involve any misrepresentation.

Much of the budget, perhaps most of it, is less a plan than an estimate of what will in any event happen. Expenditures on all entitlement programs, on most grants-in-aid, and indeed on any program in which only those who apply for government funds receive them cannot be much influenced by the budget process. Budgeting becomes more of an exercise in estimating than in planning. Even in procurement and construction programs, the date of contract letting and of construction starts must be projected and the rate of outlays thereafter is an estimate. Certain conventions are of course used by professional budget analysts to allocate how much of a particular year's obligations will be spent in that year and how much in each subsequent year, but these are no more than conventions, subject to change if better evidence comes along. A desire to alter outlay estimates may furnish someone the incentive to dig out that evidence.

The unremarkable fact that one fiscal year ends on one evening and another begins bright and early the next morning provides additional flexibility. A decision to pay a bill on one day rather than another can have an effect on a fiscal year's budget totals unrelated to its impact on the economy. A swing of up to about $3 billion (that is, $1.5 billion from "neutral") is possible in the Defense budget in the process of closing the books. By shifting the date of payment of grants-in-aid or social welfare grants, a similar effect may be generated. The more of this discretion that is used up in one year the less remains for the next year, but perhaps the next year the desire will be to reverse the process to show the opposite result.

Since receipts from offshore lease sales are counted as negative outlays in the budget, the acceleration or deferral of a lease sale can have an impact of more than $1 billion in a single year. Yet a sale in May or June rather than July or August can hardly have a substantial impact on the level of economic activity.

Similarly, the sale of assets may provide opportunities for altering the printed outlay figures. A standard device in some years has been the sale of loans from loan portfolios. The receipts count as negative outlays, but the economic effect may be quite different from that caused by a reduction in spending. Sales of loans are currently running above $10 billion per year.

The reduction of fiscal 1973 outlays from $261 billion to $249.8 billion as a result of decisions announced midway through the fiscal year provides an example of what kinds of flexibility are available in the budget. Of the $11.2 billion in savings, $1 billion stemmed from additional offshore oil receipts, $1.5 billion from deferral of general revenue sharing payments, $0.5 billion from deferral of other payments, $0.4 billion from the sale of federal stockpiles, $1.1 billion from additional nonfederal financing for federal credit programs ("sales of loans"), and $0.2 billion from proposed "increases in user charges and other actions." None of this $4.7 billion involved any diminution in the flow of federal spending, though some of the steps (such as the sale of stockpiles) were sound public policy. The remaining $6.5 billion in savings was to be the result of "program reductions and terminations." Some $2.3 billion of this $6.5 billion was already in hand through the congressional enactment of a ceiling on social services grants. The remaining $4.2 billion was spread out over many dozens of separate programs, and these changes—to the extent not reversed by Congress or by the courts in impoundment cases—did in most instances involve a reduction of the flow of federal spending. That $4.2 billion in savings actually grew—by the natural momentum of the budget (here a negative momentum since spending was being cut)—to $17 billion by fiscal 1975. Yet the extreme difficulty of making major cuts in the budget in order to achieve short-term stabilizing objectives is clear.

One moral of the story is that substantial cuts in spending are more difficult in the short run than in the long run. Yet it is in the short run that any adjustments for fiscal policy purposes must be made. Another lesson is that small short-term adjustments can have large long-term effects. However, if short-term reductions are resisted because of concern about their impact on the rate of economic activity, a reduction in the size of government or elimination of ineffective programs cannot be expected.

And what of the aftermath of the great budget-cutting exercise of fiscal 1973? Despite nearly total disbelief in Washington that the announced objective of a $250 billion budget could be achieved, actual spending was only $246.5 billion. Credit for further reduction, however, could not really be claimed by the budget cutters in OMB. As a result of a variety of coincidences, agency estimates of spending in uncontrollable entitlement programs in the last months of the fiscal year were much too high, and other agencies, having fiercely guarded their budgets during the reduction exercise, simply failed to carry on their activities at the budgeted level. Perhaps an atmosphere had been created that dampened the general tendency to spend as much as had been appropriated. In the third quarter of 1976, another shortfall of outlays below projections (this time of considerably larger dimensions) showed that the great efforts of agencies to obtain appropriations are not always matched by a similar ability actually to expend appropriated funds.

The Short-Term Economic Effect of the Budget

Even assuming that the budget contains the requisite flexibility to permit the use of fiscal policy for stabilization, no serious attempt is made to measure the budget's effect on economic activity other than by the amount of the surplus or deficit. A dollar is a dollar in the budget, but different kinds of expenditures can have widely different impacts on the economy.

A fundamental distinction should be made between government purchases of goods or services and government transfer payments. Although estimates differ as to the degree of stimulus of the two kinds of expenditures, purchases are considerably more stimulating than are transfer payments. Transfer payments merely transfer funds to a citizen from a taxpayer (who would otherwise spend) or from a lender (who would otherwise lend to someone who would spend on consumption or investment). Even government purchases of goods and services differ in their impact on the economy, depending on whether or not they are financed by taxing (though the degree of this difference is largely unknown). Still another category of government outlays involves federal grants-in-aid to states. The economic impact here depends on, among other things, how these grants-in-aid affect state purchases and transfer programs. All three of these categories—purchases, transfers, and grants-in-aid—are treated equally in the budget.

This tripartite distinction is particularly important if for no other reason than that transfer payments have been growing much more rapidly than purchases. Between fiscal 1969 and fiscal 1977 government purchases grew $47 billion (from $98 billion to $145 billion). Meanwhile, transfer payments passed purchases in total size, growing $120 billion (from $51 billion to $171 billion). Transfer payments more than quadrupled in the decade between 1967 and 1977. Grants-in-aid, the third category, have been increasing at about the same rate as transfer payments, though at a lower level. Much of this money is indeed transferred by the recipient states to individuals. Between fiscal 1969 and fiscal 1977 grants-in-aid increased $51 billion (from $19 billion to $70 billion).

Government purchases, transfer payments, and grants-in-aid do not exhaust the range of government outlays. We have already mentioned government lending programs. One particularly potent form of fiscal stimulus has been used in housing programs, in which the government has undertaken to pay future interest payments—for up to 40 years—on new housing. Such an arrangement, of course, renders the budget more uncon-

"*. . . and so it is with some degree of pride that I say there is no fat in the budget.*"

trollable in future years. From an economic perspective, however, the crucial point is that in such an action the government is essentially purchasing a portion of the house itself—to the extent of the present value of the future interest subsidies. Yet only the current year's interest subsidy is included as an outlay in the budget. If the future interest payments are merely guaranteed, the program does not appear in the budget at all. Thus, even a balanced budget containing a substantial volume of such interest subsidies could be highly stimulative. The amounts involved are not negligible. From fiscal 1973 through fiscal 1975 the present value of future interest subsidies newly committed in each year ranged between $5 billion and $7 billion.

The Momentum of the Budget

We have emphasized the limitations of the budget as a device for stabilizing the economy. The essence of our argument is that although cosmetic changes can be made in the short run, it is extremely difficult to make real changes, either expansionary or contractionary (the latter obviously being more difficult). This does not mean that a countercyclical fiscal policy is impossible, but it does lead one to abandon any notion of steering the economy through fiscal policy.

This pessimism is reinforced by two other facts of life. First, short-term economic forecasting is an uncommonly hazardous occupation. In recent years, both private and government forecasters have missed many of the changes in the economy, particularly in the rate of price increase. Second, even if forecasting could be made more precise, any forecast must be based on an understanding of where the economy is at any given time. Our statistical collection and reporting programs, however, are not good enough to let one know where the economy was even a month ago, much less at present. As more data become available, the initial figures on important statistical series may be corrected substantially one or two months later, often to such an extent as to make short-term policies based upon the initial figures simply mistaken. These corrections are usually largest just when new developments in the economy are emerging.

Skeptics might argue that we have overemphasized the difficulty of making short-term reductions in the budget because we have failed to consider the possibility of delaying the introduction of new spending programs. Surely it is possible, they argue, to balance the government's books, just like household budgets, by deferring major new purchases. One answer is that the courts in the impoundment cases and Congress in the 1974 Budget and Impoundment Control Act have greatly reduced the President's discretion in this regard. But another answer is that the image of a constantly growing federal budget is misleading in one important

respect: Merely maintaining present programs at existing levels now consumes almost the entire increment in tax receipts from one fiscal year to
another. If a presidential budget proposes major new programs, it must
either reduce existing programs—with all that that implies in bureaucratic
resistance and political rancor—or the President must propose a tax
increase or, perhaps more likely, simply accept a larger deficit.

An instructive chart in the 1975 budget showed that the programs in the
fiscal 1975 budget, there estimated at $303 billion, would automatically
grow to $329 billion in fiscal 1976, a difference of $26 billion. Meanwhile,
the existing tax base would have generated only $28 billion more in
receipts. (Indeed, the $28 billion estimate was a "full-employment re-
ceipts" estimate; hence, as the economy softened in fiscal 1975, the increase in actual receipts fell short of the increase in outlays.) Since it is
politically unrealistic to believe that Congress will not add new programs
or expand existing ones during the fiscal year, there is little presidential
discretion to reduce outlays by delaying the introduction of new programs.

One may ask how it is possible that a growing economy no longer
generates a fiscal dividend as it did in the 1960s. The answer is that these
additional revenues from growth have been spent before they are received.
To some extent this is a result of uncontrollable entitlement programs,
such as food stamps, where the proportion of applicants from those legally
eligible to receive benefits grows steadily.

Another explanation can be referred to as the camel's nose phenomenon. Proponents of new procurement programs are most likely to succeed
in winning a place for such programs in the budget if they can focus
attention in the White House and Congress on the initial year when outlays
are low. By the time outlays have grown large enough to become visible in a
budget-cutting exercise, the program has acquired a political clientele in
Congress, and any termination would involve an obvious waste of earlier
expenditures. One need not make a complete list of these causes of built-in
growth to see that, in the absence of a presidential impoundment power,
short-term downward adjustments in spending cannot be made without
taking on major political battles—battles that will take too long to resolve
to make fine tuning possible.

The Long-Term Effect of the Budget

The limitations of the budget as a short-term instrument for stabilizing the economy do not reduce its long-term usefulness as a device
for allocating resources in the economy. Over 20 percent of the GNP
flows through the federal treasury. Although much of the budget goes
for transfer payments and thus does not involve government claims
on resources, even transfer payments alter the way income is spent and

"Oh, it's great here, all right, but I sort of feel uncomfortable in a place with no budget at <u>all</u>."

hence the composition of national output. Moreover, the raw budget totals do not reflect the genuine impact of the budget on the economy. Federal outlays decisively influence the size and development of whole sectors of the economy—health, atomic energy, and housing, to name just a few.

The budget also affects the allocation of resources by marking off two of the most decisive boundaries in our political life: the boundary between the public and private sectors and the boundary between federal and state responsibility. The role of the federal government in research and development, for instance, will be affected for decades to come by the nature and amount of outlays for energy research and development, one of the greatest budgetary growth sectors in the mid-1970s. And general revenue sharing is an example of what may prove to be a major step toward the decentralization of spending power from the federal government to the states, coupled with retention of the federal advantage in tax collection. This decentralization will surely influence the purposes for which the funds will be spent. These examples could be multiplied to the point where the obvious truism would emerge—nearly all major decisions about the economy are reflected in the budget. What is perhaps surprising, however, is how many of these broad decisions are presented and actually made in the annual budget cycle.

Because these decisions are made as budget decisions, the goals of short-term economic stabilization and long-term allocation of resources are often in conflict. And since the budgetary process is at base a political process, the confusion is used by all sides to achieve their purposes. Opponents of new programs will attempt to exclude them from the budget on the ground, for example, that they would increase the deficit and thereby contribute to inflation. Proponents of a new program will obviously be in a stronger position when there is substantial unemployment and increased spending would seem to serve the stabilization goal. Thus, decisions ostensibly made in one context are often far more important in another context.

These battles are fought in both the executive and legislative branches. The procedural rules governing the budget process may nevertheless be an important determinant of the relative influence of the President and Congress on the allocation of national resources. As we have seen, the 1974 budget reform act gives Congress an opportunity to share with the President the function of setting budget parameters. And the movement toward trust funds, entitlement programs, and other uncontrollable programs shifts power to the legislative committees of Congress (where the advocates of particular interests are likely to sit) and away from the more broadly focused appropriations committees and the President.

The perennial battle over the Defense budget illustrates how the legislative committees have gained power. Since recent Presidents have been more interested in a strong defense establishment than has Congress and since they have known that any Defense budget sent to Congress would be cut, the natural result has been for the President to send Congress a larger Defense budget than he expects to receive. The reduction in some years has been on the order of $5 billion in budget authority (which, because of the slow-spending nature of Defense programs, has come to no more than $2 billion in outlays).

The legislative committees interested in social programs have succeeded in grasping the opportunity presented to redirect the Defense funds toward their programs—many of which have been made uncontrollable, thereby locking them into future budgets. A dollar of budget authority gained for social programs by trimming a dollar from the Defense budget may in fact be spent faster. The result is a greater deficit in the fiscal year. In fiscal 1973 Congress cut $6.1 billion in Defense budget authority, but the effect was only a $1.4 billion reduction in outlays. At the same time, Congress added $15 billion in budget authority for back-door and mandatory spending programs, and this increased outlays by $7.8 billion.

Not only has the ability of Congress to control the budget been greatly enhanced by the 1974 budget reform act, but also its will to exercise this control seems to have improved. Although Congress in 1975 rejected President Ford's request for a $28 billion reduction in outlays below $423 billion (which was then projected to be, according to President Ford, what "we will spend if we just stand still and let the train run over us"), Congress—largely as a result of the efforts of the new House and Senate budget committees—in fact reduced outlays by about $12 billion to an amount (estimated in January 1977) of $411 billion for fiscal 1977.

The newfound congressional ability and willingness to control expenditures does not, however, mean that expenditure levels can be reduced or even increased as quickly as most of the discussion, both in the headlines and in the economic literature, assumes. Almost all public discussion of the budget continues to revolve around the latest unemployment and inflation statistics. Meanwhile, little public attention is given to the long-run function of the budget as a device for allocating resources. In short, public discussion is directed away from what the budget can unquestionably do toward what the budget can, at best, do only in part—and with too great a lag.

Keeping in mind the importance of shifting the budget focus from short-term preoccupations to questions of long-term allocation of resources, we turned to the concept of a "full-employment budget," introducing it formally into the budget for the first time in 1972. The full-employment budget technique projects revenues as they would be if the economy were operating at a full-employment level, when the higher levels of economic activity would generate more tax revenues. Outlays can then be budgeted so that at full employment (taking into account the reduced outlays for items such as unemployment insurance) the budget is in balance.

If the full-employment budget is balanced, the actual budget would then automatically be in deficit when the economy is operating below full-employment levels. The deficit is roughly proportional to the shortfall of the economy from the full-employment level. When the economy reaches full employment, the deficit disappears. Some stabilization is thus "built in" to a full-employment budget approach, and the attention of budgeteers and the public can be focused on the budget's long-term allocation function.

The hypnotic effect that short-term unemployment and inflation problems exercise on the public and political imagination has been so strong that since 1972 interest in the full-employment concept has waned even among those concerned about the budget's allocation function. The temptation has been to treat the deficit arising from the full-employment budget technique as a base from which new expenditures can be made to "stimulate" the economy. By fiscal 1977 the budget, even calculated on a full-employment basis, was some $26 billion in deficit and still there was a strong consensus in the incoming administration and Congress for an increase in outlays (and reduction in taxes) to reduce unemployment.

Without taking sides in the economic debates between monetarists and fiscalists, a close observer of the budget process is driven to conclude that the ability of policymakers to steer the economy through variations in rates of government spending is severely limited. Although this conclusion would have been controversial as late as the early 1970s, it has become increasingly accepted in public discussions in the past few years. The main reason for this shift in public attitudes has been, to be sure, the perceived inability or unwillingness of Congress to submit spending for social programs to the control that would be required to cool off an overheated economy.

The public has correctly perceived that the budget is in practice a weak reed for short-term stabilization of the economy even if it has not understood all of the reasons for that conclusion. With this new perception has come a growing interest in using the other side of the fiscal coin—revenues—to achieve the same objectives. Control of revenues can only be exercised through the tax system which, as will be seen in the next chapter, presents an entirely different set of conceptual and institutional considerations.

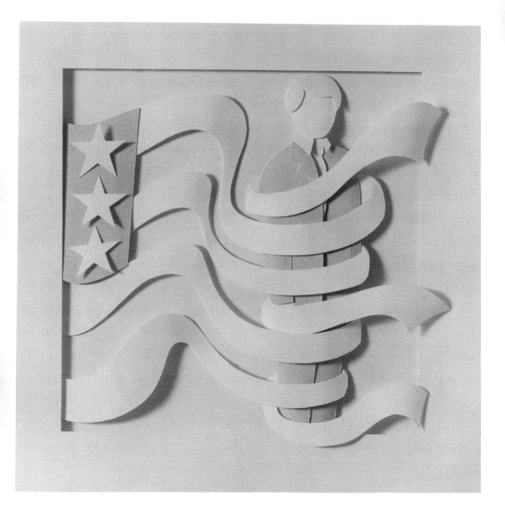

CHAPTER THREE

Tax Policy and the Taxpayer

WE ALL PAY TAXES, but the field of tax policy is dominated by the specialist and the interest group. The scene is populated with individuals and groups representing particular industries, economic objectives, or social goals. To hear most of their discussion of taxes, one would think the job of collecting revenues in a simple and effective way had little connection with tax policy. And to the frustration of the economist, the essence of a tax question moves swiftly from general principle to the excruciating detail of legal distinctions between potential cases. Tax policy is thus preeminently a field for the lawyer and, beyond that, the lawyer who specializes in taxation. Nevertheless, everyone worries and talks about taxes, for the power to tax is the power to destroy, to encourage one economic activity over another, to redistribute income, and to rearrange everything from corporate finance to family relations.

We have worked in this field on such diverse subjects as tax reform, tax simplification, audits and enforcement, and tax reduction for economic stimulation. But before tackling these individual issues, it is worth taking a look at tax policy from several contrasting economic and social perspectives.

Tax Policy as Macroeconomic Policy

In principle, taxes should be much more flexible than outlays as instruments of economic policy. Because it takes time to spend money, the budget is limited as a tool of antirecession policy; but once Congress acts on a tax proposal, tax increases or reductions can be implemented almost immediately. Withholding rates, for example, can be changed in the time it takes to print and distribute new withholding tables to employers. Most taxpayers whose income is not withheld will pay quarterly and will respond in their own economic behavior even before they file their tax return. To be sure, there is a serious question whether or not taxpayers will change spending and saving patterns substantially if they expect the tax change to be temporary, but whatever effects tax changes do have will be felt promptly.

Why then has the tax system not been used more effectively as a tool of stabilization policy? One reason is that tax bills take a long time to pass. The Johnson administration tax surcharge was debated for over a year within the administration and was proposed to Congress in August 1967, but it was not enacted until June 1968. The 1975 tax rebate was passed in record time, but even that took three and a half months. The delays stem from at least two institutional considerations. First, all revenue bills must originate, by command of the Constitution, in the House of Representatives. There, they must be considered first by the House Ways and Means Committee, perhaps the busiest committee in Congress (in addition to tax bills, Ways and Means must deal with trade, pensions, health insurance, unemployment insurance, and welfare, as well as bills on any subject that contains tax elements). Second, any tax bill tends to open up a full range of tax issues. A proposal to increase or to reduce taxes raises important questions as to who should bear the burden or enjoy the relief. Consequently, the Ways and Means Committee tends to permit testimony on a wide variety of tax issues, and there are no procedures to separate questions concerning tax rates from questions involving the base to which those rates are to be applied.

A second limitation of tax policy as a stabilization tool is that peacetime tax bills almost invariably become tax reduction bills. Every general tax statute since 1954 has reduced revenues—with the sole exception of the Johnson administration surcharge to pay the escalating costs of the Vietnam War. The President's 1969 tax reform proposals would have increased revenues by $540 million per year on a long-term basis, but the bill Congress enacted instead reduced revenues (calculated on the same basis) by about $5 billion per year. In 1971 the President's proposals would have reduced revenues by $4.1 billion in fiscal 1973, but congressional action widened this reduction to $6.9 billion.

Without tax reduction, the percentage of GNP going to taxes would, because of inflation, increase year after year. In the personal income tax system, for example, rising nominal incomes push taxpayers into higher and higher tax brackets. According to a 1975 estimate of the Advisory Commission on Intergovernmental Relations, the average family in 1953 earning $5,000 in current dollars paid 7.6 percent of that income in federal income taxes; in 1974 the comparable figures were $13,000 and 10.2 percent, a 34 percent increase in the effective tax rate. Some of the increase in income reflects greater productivity, but much more represents inflation. The escalating effects of inflation could be offset by indexing the tax brackets (having the range of incomes within each tax bracket expand in pace with inflation), but Congress has preferred to reduce rates from time to time on an ad hoc basis. Such periodic tax reductions served to maintain the effective rate of federal income tax on taxable personal incomes virtually unchanged between 1960 and 1971, but from 1971 to early 1975 the rate of inflation increased and there were no tax reductions. In addition, throughout the 1960-75 period, social security taxes and state taxes were rapidly increasing.

The inability of Congress to act promptly on proposals for tax rate changes has led to proposals for delegating to the executive branch the power to vary rates for stabilization purposes. President Kennedy proposed that the President be given standby authority to lower taxes up to 5 percent for a six-month period, subject to congressional veto. But Congress rejected the proposal without serious consideration. It is unlikely that any such proposal would be adopted by Congress, whatever its abstract merit. Congress wants the credit for tax reductions and will not easily allow that credit to be claimed by the executive branch. This understandable desire is stronger when Congress and the presidency are controlled by different parties, but it exists at all times. A proposal to allow the President to increase (but not reduce) taxes might be more palatable to Congress, since many congressmen do not want to be accountable for tax increases. But the natural congressional distrust of the executive branch would probably be a barrier to even such one-way discretion. Moreover, such a proposal might be construed to be a levy of taxes by the President, a function allocated by the Constitution to Congress.

Another possibility for tax reform is setting tax rates by a formula based on the rate of inflation, the rate of unemployment, or some other variable. However, neither Congress nor the executive branch is likely to support a formula approach: No one gets the credit for tax reduction when a formula is used. Advocates of higher government spending would object to any formula that prevented revenues from rising automatically with inflation, because under such circumstances an increase in revenues would have to stand the political test of a positive vote to raise taxes.

Thus far we have discussed only the *levels* of revenues as a component of fiscal policy. But the *composition* of revenues can also have important macroeconomic consequences. In particular, the tax system can affect the rate of investment and savings (as opposed to current consumption). Several administrations have experimented with variations in the investment tax credit (which gives favorable tax treatment to expenditures on plant and equipment) as a device for stimulating the economy in times of recession or for cooling off the economy in times of inflation. But varying the composition of revenues is normally thought of as a tool of microeconomic policy, affecting the fortunes of particular industries and the direction of the future economy, rather than as a tool of macroeconomic policy directed to stabilization of the economy in the short term.

Tax Policy as a Tool of Microeconomic Policy

Review of a few sectors where tax policy has been utilized to favor or discourage specific economic activities demonstrates the pervasive reach of microeconomic considerations in tax policy. The housing sector, for example, has been a particular favorite of tax policymakers. Homeowner deductions for mortgage interest and property taxes reduced revenues in fiscal 1977 more than $10 billion below what they would have been without those deductions. Similarly, accelerated depreciation on rental housing reduced revenues by more than $500 million. The fact that the rental value of an owner-occupied house is not considered gross income— even though the exclusion of that rental value from the tax base is an important incentive to home ownership—can be considered a further use of tax policy to promote home ownership and housing construction. (The difficulties of computing and enforcing a tax on this imputed income, however, might lead to its exclusion from the tax base in any event.) Homeowner deductions obviously reflect social policy objectives, but the notion has been widely accepted that an expanding homebuilding industry is indispensable to economic prosperity. The influence of the homebuilders, one of Washington's most powerful lobbies, cannot be underestimated in making politically effective the idea that home construction is more important to the economy than other industries of comparable size.

Energy is another area where tax policy has played an important role. Until the 1975 tax reduction act provided for partial phaseout of the percentage depletion allowance for oil (the excess of percentage depletion over cost depletion), that allowance reduced revenues by over $2.5 billion per year. The expensing of exploration, development, and intangible drilling costs (as opposed to treating them as capital items to be recovered over a period of years) reduced revenues in fiscal 1977 by more than $700 million. The prime justification of both of these tax preferences has been their stimulative effect on the development of energy resources; it is ironic in this regard that attacks on them sharpened as the country's need for energy increased. Tax policy toward energy has also had its revenue-increasing side. In 1975 President Ford imposed a tax on imported oil under powers delegated by Congress, presumably for the purpose of raising its price and thereby discouraging consumption.

Many other examples of the use of the tax system to achieve microeconomic goals can be given. For instance, the ability to expense research and development expenditures in the current year, rather than treating them as capital items, is an important incentive to technological innovation. In fiscal 1977 this provision reduced revenues by more than $1.4 billion.

Tax Policy as Social Policy

Perhaps more important than the use of tax policy as a microeconomic tool is its use in pursuit of social goals, such as the redistribution of income and wealth. Most people still regard the progressive income tax as the principal instrument for redistributing income even though, given the growth of transfer payments as a percentage of the budget, outlays are probably more important quantitatively. Whenever Congress considers a tax bill, great attention is paid to the appropriate degree of "progressivity" of the tax system, however difficult that concept may be to define. Even when progressivity is not discussed as such, the desire to lift tax burdens from the poor or from middle-income taxpayers has an important impact on the structure of the tax system. The 1969 and 1971 tax acts removed more than 12 million taxpayers from the tax rolls. These same statutes decreased taxes on incomes between $10,000 and $15,000 by 13 percent and increased taxes on incomes over $100,000 by 7 percent. And the 1975 tax rebate gave larger rebates, measured in absolute dollars, to middle-income taxpayers than to upper-income taxpayers.

Quite specific social goals have also been pursued through tax policy. Homeowner deductions for mortgage interest and property taxes constitute what might be called a middle-class social policy, encouraging home ownership rather than home rental. Other tax provisions are designed to enhance the independence of particular types of individuals, especially the aged who do not want to be dependent on children or direct government assistance. For example, tax laws presently favor the aged through the retirement income credit and the double personal exemption. President Nixon was strongly committed to property tax relief for the aged in order to permit them to continue to live in their homes after retirement. In April 1973 he proposed an income tax credit for property taxes paid to state and local governments by persons aged 65 or over, to the extent that such taxes exceeded 5 percent of their income. This credit, limited to a maximum of $500, would have been refundable in cash to those who would not otherwise pay sufficient income tax to use the credit. Congress did not act on this proposal. But the refundable feature was as widely noted in tax circles as was the political punch of the proposal for the aged. It would have been a first step toward using the tax system to distribute money as well as collect it.

The Nixon administration also considered a value-added tax (a variation of the sales tax that is imposed on every sale of a raw material, machine, or product rather than just on retail sales to consumers) that would be used to finance property tax relief for the young and old alike, as well as to finance assumption by the states of local governments' responsibilities for financing schools. No proposal was made, however, largely because a 1973 study of the Advisory Commission on Intergovernmental Relations disclosed that the states themselves were accomplishing the goal of property tax relief to the aged through various types of exemptions in their own property tax statutes.

The social security system can also be viewed as a tax instrument used to accomplish a social goal—income security for the aged and disabled and for survivors of deceased workers. The system today is based upon a social insurance concept in which all who pay social security taxes are entitled to receive social security payments upon reaching retirement age, whatever their income may have been. Consciously or not, however, the social security system is being changed, since benefit payments already scheduled to be paid in the future must almost surely be met in part from general revenues. This change would increase the progressivity of the total tax system because the personal income tax, one of the principal sources of general revenues, is progressive whereas the social security tax is not. Eliminating the public's perception that social security benefits are tied to social security taxes would make it easier for Congress to raise benefits without worrying about who is going to bear the cost. For the recipient, such a step would make social security benefits seem more like welfare payments instead of payments that have been earned. Thus, because the method of taxation influences the level and composition of outlays, the social security program, although preeminently a social program, raises important issues of both tax and budget policy.

Social security is only one example of the use of an important fiscal device, the trust fund, to accomplish social ends. Over the years a number of trust funds have been created to shelter particular social outlays from competition with other expenditure programs in the normal budget process. The trust fund has thus been one of the favorite forms of back-door spending, but it has been more than that. Trust fund receipts are also exempt from the conventional OMB policy against the earmarking of revenues for particular spending programs. Under the normal policy all revenues flow into the Treasury to finance whatever outlays survive the budget process. Today some one-third of the entire "unified" budget is composed of trust funds, and the conventional rules apply to only the other two-thirds of that budget. Trust funds are used not only for such general social purposes as social security ($85 billion in fiscal 1977), health insurance ($22 billion), federal employee retirement ($10 billion), and unemployment insurance ($15 billion), but also for such specific economic uses as highways ($6 billion) and airports ($1 billion).

As the use of trust funds grew, it became increasingly apparent that the balance between revenues and outlays in the rest of the budget (known as federal funds) was no longer a good measure of the impact of the budget on the economy. As the result of a recommendation of President Johnson's Commission on Budget Concepts, trust funds and federal funds are now unified in the revenue and outlay totals in the President's budget. Nevertheless some people, particularly critics of federal spending, have continued to place emphasis on federal funds because for some years that portion of the budget has shown a larger deficit than the unified budget. A favorite charge of these critics has been that surpluses in the trust funds are used to subsidize federal funds deficits. This allegation confuses the true state of affairs.

Because trust funds are invested in U.S. government securities, the federal funds used to pay interest on the national debt constitute *outlays* for the federal funds portion of the budget and *receipts* for the trust funds. For fiscal 1977, for example, the OMB estimated that trust funds would show a deficit of $21.6 billion in transactions with the public, but would receive $30.1 billion from federal funds, leaving a net trust fund surplus of $8.5 billion. It would thus be closer to the mark to say that federal funds subsidize trust funds.

In recent years the surplus in trust funds has begun to narrow, and some individual trust funds are, or shortly will be, showing a deficit even when interest receipts are included. The social security trust fund slipped into deficit for the first time in fiscal 1976, and the annual deficit will not be eliminated under current law. If trust funds as a whole were to slip into deficit, the burden on federal funds and hence on general revenues would be clear to all. When this happens, the demand can be anticipated to supplement trust fund receipts by appropriations out of general revenues. Since general revenues are raised largely by individual and corporate income taxes—whereas the trust funds are financed by social security taxes, gasoline taxes, and the like—growing cash trust fund deficits and increasing demands for direct supplements from general revenues will create pressures for higher corporate and personal income tax rates.

Revenue Collection and Other Functions

Perhaps the most fundamental tension in tax policy arises from the fact that the tax system is used simultaneously to collect revenues and to perform the social and economic functions that we have surveyed. One important school of thought holds that the tax system should be used only to collect revenues and that the attempt to use the tax system to achieve other goals is unwise. According to this view, the base for income taxation should be as comprehensive as possible, and exclusions, credits, and deductions designed to induce particular economic behavior or to further social goals should be eliminated. This revenue collection approach has a great deal to be said for it. Full implementation would greatly simplify tax law and would permit a major lowering of marginal tax rates, thereby eliminating many tax disincentives that reduce economic efficiency and growth. We strongly support this comprehensive approach to drastic overhaul of the personal income tax system.

The use of the income tax system to further economic and social goals has a long history. Interest income from state and municipal bonds has been exempt since the beginning of the federal income tax in 1913. The deduction for interest payments, including interest on home mortgages, also dates back to 1913. Charitable contributions became deductible in 1917, and the special rate for capital gains was inserted in the tax code in 1921. To be sure, some of these early tax preferences may have been initially included because of supposed constitutional constraints (for example, the state and municipal bond exemption) or as a way of equitably measuring income for tax purposes. Whatever their origins, their influence on the economy and society soon became a principal justification for their continuation.

Why have both the executive and legislative branches found themselves supporting the use of the tax system to further particular social and economic goals? Several possible advantages to those involved in the lawmaking process in the two branches can be discerned. First, these tax preferences are a powerful policy tool available to those seeking some social or economic goal. Certainly direct budgetary subsidies, the principal alternative, have many undesirable characteristics—perhaps the greatest, from the proponents' point of view, being the continued visibility of such a subsidy. Second, tax measures are one means for both the President and Congress to show that they are taking positive steps to deal with what are publicly conceived to be important problems, and in a way that doesn't cost (in budget outlays) anything. Public insistence on bold government action, so much a part of the policy environment in an era of instant public communications, thus has important implications for tax policy. Finally, for a variety of institutional reasons, interest groups may find it easier to obtain their ends through the tax system than by other means. For example, the closed rule (stipulating that a bill must be voted up or down without amendment) under which the House of Representatives traditionally debated tax bills tended to protect whatever preferences were decided upon by the Ways and Means Committee.

Whatever the tactical advantages of using tax policy to achieve particular economic and social objectives, there are important disadvantages—both for revenue collection and for the sensible conduct of economic policy. From a revenue standpoint, tax preferences inevitably contract the tax base, requiring higher tax rates on income that does not enjoy the preference. The natural response of taxpayers subject to high marginal rates of tax is to seek refuge in tax avoidance schemes to shelter this remaining income.

Tax preferences in turn lead to political demands for tax reform to eliminate both the preferences and the tax avoidance measures fostered by the correspondingly higher rates on other income. For example, real estate tax shelters designed to shelter nonrealty income are understandably popular with taxpayers subject to high rates of taxation, but they also lead other taxpayers to feel, equally understandably, that these taxpayers are flagrantly avoiding their tax responsibilities. The result is a deterioration in public confidence that the tax system is fair.

The demand for reform not only clashes with whatever economic and social goals the tax preferences were designed to achieve, but also tends further to politicize tax policy—already a highly political subject. Tax preferences turn out to be quite difficult to eliminate, even after priorities change and goals originally pursued are no longer thought so important. The value of the preference becomes part of property or business values, and eliminating the preference not only takes away the tax benefit but also causes capital losses to those who bought assets at values that reflected the tax advantage. An investor who bought a commercial building expecting to enjoy accelerated depreciation would be hard put to sell it for what he paid if accelerated depreciation were eliminated the next day.

Even when capital losses are not imposed by the elimination of tax preferences, workers may find themselves out of jobs as the preferred activity diminishes (for instance, some copper miners would lose their jobs if the percentage depletion allowance for copper were eliminated). Moreover, reasonable expectations of particular taxpayers may be destroyed. Advocacy groups fighting hard to retain their tax advantages will play upon the resentment engendered by the frustration of these expectations. Such advocacy groups may thus be even more effective in resisting the elimination of their tax preferences than they were in obtaining the preferences in the first place.

The use of tax preferences thus alters the balance of power between economic policymakers and advocacy groups, compared to what the balance would be if outlays, rather than revenues, were the means of obtaining their social and economic goals. However difficult it may be to eliminate or even reduce a budget item when priorities change, the funds have to be appropriated each year (assuming some back-door spending technique is not involved). A tax preference, on the other hand, may lie unexamined for years. When the drive for tax reform does call a preference into question, it may be more difficult, perhaps even unfair or unwise, to eliminate the preference rather than a corresponding outlay item. If the municipal bond exemption were repealed, for example, it would be manifestly unfair to eliminate it for outstanding bonds where the price paid by the investor reflected the tax advantage of the municipal bond exemption.

Tax Reform

Even if Congress enacts no new tax preferences, tax reform will continue to be a perennial subject for tax policymakers. Nobody likes to pay taxes, and everyone believes that he pays more than his fair share. Nearly everyone, however slight his technical knowledge of the tax law, has his own ideas about how to reform the tax system, if only by lowering his own rates or raising those of other kinds of taxpayers.

But if tax reform is politically popular, it is also greatly misunderstood. In the first place, one person's loophole is another person's social or economic policy. In particular, the familiar refrain that sums ranging from $50 billion to $100 billion annually could be raised by tax reform reflects a basic misconception of what is involved. These figures come from tables of so-called tax expenditures published annually in the President's budget. A glance at a tax expenditure table reveals that deeply held social objectives support large preference items—homeowner deductions (a reduction of $10 billion in tax revenues in fiscal 1977), pension and insurance provisions ($12 billion), and charitable contribution deductions ($6 billion) are examples. Economic objectives supported by tax preferences include the investment tax credit ($10 billion) and capital gains treatment ($8 billion), both of which are widely held to have an important beneficial effect on investment and hence on future GNP and tax revenue levels.

The elimination of other major tax preferences could, in practice, be accomplished only by increasing budget outlays to achieve the same social or economic goals. Although outlays might not rise by as much as the revenues gained, these revenues would not be fully available for the kinds

"Other folks have to pay taxes, too, Mr. Herndon, so would you please spare us the dramatics!"

of programs that advocates of tax reform often favor. For example, past congressional debates on the tax exemption for interest on state and municipal bonds ($5 billion) indicate that it could not be eliminated without a new, compensating subsidy to the governmental units issuing those bonds. Similarly, the tax exclusion for income security transfer programs, such as social security and unemployment insurance ($7 billion), could not be eliminated without a drastic increase in such payments. These transfer payments are so popular that the political process of converting them to taxable status might actually result in additional benefit payments beyond the revenue gains.

Despite the popularity of tax reform as a political slogan, the elimination of many large tax preferences would be so unpopular that it is almost inconceivable that congressional enactment would follow any presidential proposal. Elimination of the homeowner deduction, the tax-free status of income security payments, and the charitable deduction would be highly unpopular with a wide spectrum of voters. Only slightly less invulnerable are the medical deduction ($3 billion) and the double exemption for the aged ($1 billion). In some instances—perhaps charitable contributions and medical expenses—the deduction might be reduced, but their elimination seems politically improbable. The only hope, we believe, for major progress in eliminating tax preferences is as part of a massive package granting large tax-rate reductions to all taxpayers. In short, we are skeptical that sufficient revenue can be gained through tax reform to finance a new generation of social programs, as some proponents of further income redistribution hope. If effective tax reform is to be realized, it must be part of a thorough revamping of the entire tax system, and the Treasury will be lucky to break even.

In addition to the elimination of tax preferences, a wide variety of other approaches to tax reform have been advocated, some of which have become part of the tax code. For example, the minimum tax, embodied in the 1969 and 1976 tax acts, permits tax preferences to remain on the statute books while assuring that wealthy individual taxpayers do not make such lavish use of them that they pay an extremely low overall rate of tax or no taxes at all. Among the other ideas advocated under the banner of tax reform are such economically contradictory proposals as those by social reformers seeking a more progressive rate structure and those by economic reformers seeking to eliminate economic "disincentives" engendered by the tax system—for example, by integrating the corporate and individual tax systems to eliminate double taxation of income from corporate investment.

Even if executive branch policymakers can agree on the objectives of tax reform, they must be sensitive to certain implications. One is that in the process of congressional consideration, tax reform will simply become tax reduction; another is that some types of tax reform will further complicate rather than simplify the tax laws. A new overlay of rules, or a new exception to an existing rule, not only lengthens the tax code but usually lengthens tax returns. Complication is a cost to all concerned.

Yet sensible reforms do exist that would enhance the fairness of the tax system without compromising economic or social goals and without unduly compounding the complexity of the tax law. One such reform was the administration's 1973 proposal for a limitation on artificial accounting losses. The proposal addressed itself to the widely perceived unfairness of a system that permits some taxpayers to use existing tax preferences to escape taxation of much of their income while other taxpayers, with less income, pay a much higher average rate.

This anomaly results from the creation of so-called tax shelters which involve the use of rules permitting exclusions and deductions in the early years of an investment. The artificial losses thereby created reduce or eliminate taxes on the taxpayer's other income. Although in theory these losses might result in corresponding profits from the same investment (and hence larger taxes) in future years, many taxpayers have been able to arrange their affairs so that taxes are indefinitely deferred or so that future income from the investment can be converted from ordinary income into capital gains. A doctor or lawyer with a high income might, for example, reduce his taxes by buying an apartment building. In the first years of the investment, interest and depreciation deductions would more than offset rental income, permitting him to shelter some professional income as well. After a few years, when deductions fell off and he would otherwise have to begin paying taxes on the rental income, he would simply sell the building and use the proceeds to buy another building, sheltering income from professional fees once again. The dilemma for the policymaker is that the underlying rules that made the tax shelter possible were enacted, as we have described, in pursuit of particular economic or social goals. No doubt real estate tax shelters, for example, result in an increased rate of production of apartment and office buildings and thereby create (or preserve) jobs in the construction industry. But at the same time their notoriety causes the average taxpayer to view them simply as ways for the wealthy to escape taxes on nonrealty income.

The solution proposed in the 1973 administration plan was to disqualify artificial losses (such as real estate losses attributable to accelerated depreciation) from being offset against income other than that from the investment creating the loss. To the extent that income from the investment itself was sheltered, the full incentive sought by Congress through the tax preference would still operate, but the taxpayer could not shelter nonrealty income, such as medical or legal fees. This proposal thus attempted to reach a principled compromise between maintaining taxpayer confidence in the fairness of the tax system and achieving the goals implicit in the statutory preference. However, it was not acted upon by Congress.

Taxation and Self-Assessment

The U.S. income tax system is essentially a self-assessment system. In his tax return the taxpayer declares his income and calculates the tax due. Self-assessment, supported by withholding and by information returns by employers and others, is fundamentally different from the government-assessment approach used in most other countries. In those countries an administrative agency usually computes the tax payable in consultation with the taxpayer. A variation of government assessment is found in most states' property tax procedures, in which a local government agency estimates the tax, subject to challenge by the taxpayer, and sends the taxpayer a bill.

Self-assessment has great advantages. It would require a massive expansion of the IRS and cost hundreds of millions of dollars to switch to government assessment; such a switch might undermine the confidence of the taxpayer in the fairness and integrity of the income tax system itself. But the self-assessment system is fragile. It depends upon a level of tax morality not found in many countries. Tax morality, already on the decline in the United States, can be maintained only so long as taxpayers believe that the income tax system as a whole is fair and that other taxpayers are, by and large, fully reporting their income and paying their taxes.

Self-assessment is threatened from several sides. Aside from tax shelters, an insidious enemy is the growing complexity of the tax system as a whole. The amount of time and money that taxpayers as a class spend in filling out tax returns is staggering. Not only must this time and expense be considered a cost of self-assessment, but it lowers many taxpayers' respect for the tax system. Some taxpayers simply give up on trying to fill out their returns with precision and turn to hunches and guesses in place of records. Others turn to commercial tax return services to prepare their returns. One of the best measures of the complexity of the present law is the extent to which the average taxpayer is turning to these commercial preparers. According to 1976 IRS testimony, 44 percent of all individual returns were completed by someone other than the taxpayer. A single firm prepared over nine million returns.

The use of commercial tax return preparers has an important economic justification. It permits taxpayers to devote their time to pursuit of their own livelihoods and hence contributes to the efficiency of the economy. Moreover, many taxpayers believe that they receive more helpful advice from commercial preparers than they would at their local IRS office. But increasingly taxpayers appear to be turning to commercial preparers as a way of transferring moral responsibility for the accuracy of their tax returns. If the commercial preparer makes a guesstimate, some taxpayers feel personally absolved of responsibility.

Tax Simplification

Every tax policy decision that complicates the code thus threatens self-assessment. This is a critical defect in the endless proposals for promoting new objectives through the tax system. We worked hard in the Treasury Department to develop a proposal to simplify tax return preparation. Our first approach was directed toward simplification of the tax code itself. Yet despite a good deal of work within the Treasury, in cooperation with the staff of the Joint Committee on Internal Revenue Taxation, the results were disappointing.

The reasons for the failure of this effort tell us something about the dimensions of the problem. In addition to the complicating effects of tax preferences and the many technical rules governing the timing of income and deductions, the tax code suffers from the legislative efforts over many years to treat equitably taxpayers who, in an economy of extraordinary complexity, find themselves in countless special situations that would make equal application of broad general rules inequitable.

Tax laws are drafted by lawyers. Unlike economists, who try to see unifying principles underlying a welter of differing circumstances, lawyers are by training and disposition more inclined to concentrate on the distinctions between these differing situations. The history of the tax code reflects a consistent movement from broad rules to highly detailed rules addressed to the manifold differences among taxpayers. To attempt to simplify the code itself would run counter to the effort to achieve equity among taxpayers and would require reopening thousands of decisions and compromises made over many years by the code's draftsmen.

When the Treasury's initial attempt to simplify the tax code failed to produce results, we took an entirely new tack. With leadership from IRS counsel Leo Henkel, the effort to simplify was directed at the tax return rather than the code itself. The idea was to create a return that would permit the taxpayer with few sources of income and few financial transactions to use a tax form requiring relatively few entries.

In order to accomplish this goal it would be necessary to do something about itemized deductions. Although homeowner deductions produce few complications for most taxpayers, the process of itemizing the rest of the great variety of possible deductions often submerges even a low-income taxpayer in a sea of canceled checks, receipts, and hazy recollections. The only politically feasible way to deal with this problem is to substitute some kind of fixed-sum or fixed-percentage overall deduction for the many specific deductions authorized by the code. To a certain extent this kind of simplification has already been accomplished by the standard deduction; nonetheless, millions of taxpayers still itemize deductions.

The apparently simple solution of increasing the standard deduction would create a dilemma for tax policy. In order to make it profitable for a majority of itemizing taxpayers to switch to the standard deduction, the standard deduction would have to be increased for all taxpayers to the point where the revenue loss would create a major budget problem. Meanwhile, those who continued to itemize would conclude, quite correctly, that they were being asked to carry an increased share of the tax burden even though the absolute level of their tax obligations did not rise. If tax rates were increased to offset the revenue losses from the expanded standard deduction, taxpayers who continued to itemize would be paying more dollars in tax, and among those taxpayers claiming the standard deduction, some would lose and some would gain. Thus, expanding the standard deduction sufficiently to achieve major simplification would either result in an unacceptably high loss of revenues or would shift the tax burden and engender political opposition to simplification.

The key to resolving this dilemma is the recognition that a great proportion of taxpayers who itemize deductions do so because they are homeowners and that their homeowner deductions alone exceed their standard deduction. The essence of the administration's 1973 tax simplification proposal was to permit such taxpayers to continue to itemize their homeowner deductions (as well as charitable deductions) while creating a new miscellaneous deduction of $500 for all taxpayers to replace the numerous relatively small deductions that create a disproportionate share of documentation and calculations problems. At the same time, we proposed that some other extremely complicated deductions taken by relatively few taxpayers be eliminated entirely. These changes would make possible a new simplified form that could be used by millions of taxpayers who would otherwise itemize deductions. The revenue loss from the simplification would have been about $400 million a year, a small fraction of the revenue loss that would arise from an increase in the standard deduction sufficient to move an equal number of taxpayers from the present long form to the present short form.

Not only was the 1973 proposal not adopted but, if anything, the 1976 tax reform act actually complicated returns. Tax simplification, unfortunately, is more talk than action; this is especially disappointing because a practical method—embodied in the 1973 proposal just discussed—is available to simplify the returns of many taxpayers. If American taxpayers become exasperated with the tax system and adopt the level of tax morality that now plagues many other countries, our income tax system will become an increasingly less robust source of revenue and even less flexible as an instrument of fiscal policy than it is today.

Audits

Another enemy of the self-assessment system is the difficulty of maintaining an optimum level of audits of taxpayers' returns. As they say in the IRS, "Conscience is that small voice saying, 'Someone may be watching.'" Audits deter not only fraud but also petty underreporting of income and overdeducting of expenses. Studies have repeatedly shown that the additional revenues derived from audited taxpayers repay the expense of audits manyfold, quite aside from the deterrent effect of audits on taxpayers who escape auditing. Even accepting that it would be undesirable (either from the viewpoint of the requisite massive growth of the IRS bureaucracy or the public relations of the IRS) to increase the number of auditors to the point where audit expense equaled revenue gained, one may nonetheless ask why the present level of audits is not higher.

One answer is that because the IRS has the best mass bureaucracy in the federal government, it is constantly asked to lend its assistance to other government programs. The most dramatic, but far from the only example was the use of the IRS in the enforcement of wage and price controls in the early 1970s. Another answer is that, with the increasing complexity of the tax code, a large number of auditors must be used for such specialized and time-consuming tasks as auditing returns of foundations and trusts. Those auditors are not available for auditing individual and corporate returns.

Finally, the budget system treats IRS outlays like any other outlays even though an increase in the IRS budget can be expected to generate sufficient revenues to more than pay for the IRS budget increase (though not in the first year). Moreover, the normal OMB review tends to focus on an outlay target dictated by the President's fiscal policy and the realities of budgetary politics. It is the job of OMB budget examiners to shave outlays of the various agencies so that the overall target is met. A failure to meet the target is a failure for OMB. Yet in that process a dollar budgeted for IRS audits tends to be treated like any other expenditure. In this respect, as in so many others, the one-year horizon that necessarily conditions so much of the budget has important long-term consequences.

The Treasury and Tax Policy

The Treasury Department is predominant within the executive branch on matters of tax policy, just as the OMB is on budget policy: OMB puts

*"Maybe we do bungle the spending of your tax dollar, but you'll
have to admit we do a bang-up job of collecting it."*

together the budget under the President's direction, and the Treasury
formulates the President's tax proposals. Just as the President's budget
seeks to establish parameters for debate in Congress, so too tax hearings
often revolve around administration proposals (though, since there is no
annual tax cycle like the annual budget cycle, Congress has much more
freedom of action in ignoring executive branch tax proposals).

Nonetheless, in one sense the Treasury plays an even more crucial role in congressional tax deliberations than does the OMB in congressional budget deliberations. After the President's budget is sent to Congress, the director of OMB appears before the House Ways and Means Committee, the Senate Finance Committee, the House and Senate budget and appropriations committees, and the Joint Economic Committee, but thereafter he seldom testifies. It is up to the individual department and agency heads to defend their part of the President's budget.

In contrast, most of the executive branch testimony on taxation, particularly on the detailed technical aspects of tax proposals, will come from the Treasury. Testimony by other administration officials will normally be limited to broad policy questions—a relationship between broad policy and technical detail that is almost the inverse of the respective roles of OMB and the departments in congressional consideration of budget matters. And when congressional committees considering tax matters go into executive session, a Treasury official will almost always be present, usually sitting at the table and taking part in the discussions. This right to sit at the table, a right of unparalleled importance in shaping legislative details, is one rarely enjoyed by OMB officials in budget matters.

The central role of the Treasury Department rests on expertise. Common sense and economic insight are an insufficient basis for specific amendments to the tax code. The executive branch's tax expertise is overwhelmingly concentrated in the Treasury. When the time comes for the executive branch to make a tax proposal, only the Treasury will have the mastery of detail necessary to put it together. This is particularly true when the proposal is a complex package of disparate amendments, as is usually the case. Whether or not the Treasury's dominant position is "good" in the abstract, the Treasury does enjoy an important blocking position on tax legislation that prevents the advocacy process—working through executive branch agencies representing particular constituencies in society—from running away with tax policy.

This dominant role of the Treasury is illustrated by the outcome of the extensive discussions on the introduction of a value-added tax within the Executive Office of the President in 1972. Such a tax, which was popular with the President's White House advisers, had little support in the Treasury. The Treasury opposition had less to do with technical tax considerations than with the fear that the enormous revenue collection possibilities opened by a broad-based value-added tax would inevitably lead to a much higher level of outlays and hence to a growth of the power of government over society and the economy. Without Treasury support, the White House staff lacked the competence to put together a legislative proposal, a task of great technical complexity. The issue was eventually shunted off to the Advisory Commission on Intergovernmental Relations and disappeared from the policy scene when the Advisory Commission made a negative recommendation.

At the congressional end of Pennsylvania Avenue, organization for tax policy is shaped by the constitutional requirement that revenue bills originate in the House of Representatives. This requirement strengthens the hand of the House Ways and Means Committee, which usually establishes the framework for tax legislation, with the Senate Finance Committee somewhat in the position of amending the parts rather than changing the overall significance of the House bill. The central position of Ways and Means has largely precluded the fractionalization of tax policy that has characterized budget policy, where, until the enactment of the 1974 congressional budget reform act, the growth of back-door spending techniques stood in the way of congressional judgment on overall budget totals.

The coincidence of several superficially minor circumstances has reinforced the central position of the Ways and Means Committee. One has been the use, until recently, of a closed rule for tax legislation. Under the closed rule no floor amendments were permitted to a Ways and Means bill, and consequently—except as might be agreed between the Ways and Means chairman and the House Rules Committee—the Ways and Means bill, in its entirety and without amendment, had to be voted up or down by the House membership. This closed rule protected not only the structure of major Ways and Means amendments but also minor tactical concessions to crucial interest groups.

Another circumstance that long shaped the tax legislative process was the dominance of Wilbur Mills, the Ways and Means chairman until 1975. By dint of hard work and attention to detail, as well as long years in the chairmanship, Mills had an influence on the shape of the tax code and on the administration of the tax system that would be difficult to exaggerate. He simply knew more about the history of the tax system than other members of his committee and than most of the witnesses who appeared before him. His role over the years shows that an individual can have an important, even a decisive, impact on public policy if he has talent, energy, and a long government career.

Mills also organized his committee in a way that helped to diffuse any tendency toward fractionalization of tax policy. He did not permit subcommittees; consequently all tax legislation had to be considered by the committee as a whole. If the various aspects of tax policy had been divided among subcommittees, it is likely that a self-selection process would have begun to operate in the manning of the subcommittees and that the advocacy process would have gained the scope for operation that it has in budget matters. There, the specialized authorizing committees and appropriations subcommittees are able to push budget policy—at least in its details—in parochial directions. It is still too early to tell whether the restructured Ways and Means Committee, even with the talented leadership of Al Ullman and Barber Conable, as chairman and ranking Republican member, will be able to avoid centrifugal tendencies associated with varied interests.

The existence of the Joint Committee on Internal Revenue Taxation has also played an important role in resisting advocacy influences on tax legislation. The most important by-product of the existence of the Joint Committee has been its staff. The Joint Committee staff has maintained over the years a level of institutionalized expertise that, though analogous to the Treasury within the executive branch, is quite unusual within Congress. The Joint Committee staff provides the technical underpinning essential to competent tax legislation. It also brings to bear a degree of analytical ability and bureaucratic know-how that, even if sometimes not a match for the pressures of the advocacy process, nevertheless assures that the potential impact of interest-group proposals on the tax system as a whole will at least be sensed by the House Ways and Means Committee and Senate Finance Committee members. Having made that observation, however, one should not underestimate how convoluted tax legislation can be and usually is. As Russell Long, chairman of the Senate Finance Committee, remarked in frustration during questioning from senators about the 1976 tax reform act, "If the members insist on knowing what's in this bill, we'll never get it passed!"

The tax system is overloaded with special provisions on a bewildering variety of subjects, too burdensome on those who pay the high marginal rates and hence too conducive to tax shelters, and insufficiently focused on the essential function of revenue collection. A drastic and comprehensive overhaul would be far better than however many well-intentioned attempts to plug loopholes. We should return to the concept of the tax system as a necessary tool for raising revenue and abandon attempts to achieve social and microeconomic goals of the moment.

It may be true that Congress—in order to achieve a broad-based, low-rate tax—would not be willing to take on the multitude of interests that have been nurtured by a vast array of special exemptions, credits, and deductions in the present code. But the continued shrinking of the tax base, the rise in taxpayer frustration with the complexity of tax returns, and the decline of tax morality threaten a collapse in the present tax system. Perhaps we shall have to await that collapse to rebuild, but it would be far better to undertake a comprehensive restructuring while we still have the degree of taxpayer cooperation and tax morality necessary to continue on a self-assessment basis.

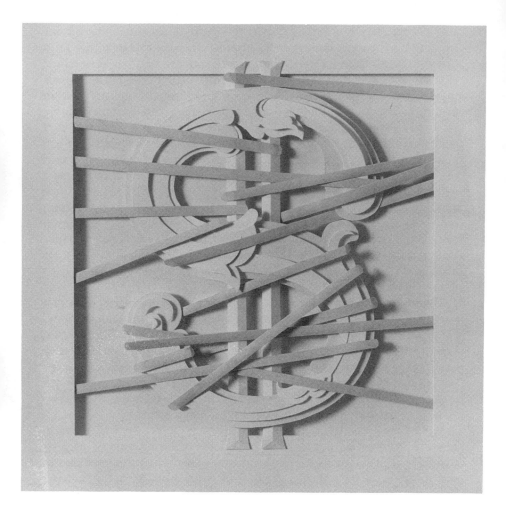

CHAPTER FOUR

The Life Cycle of
Wage and Price Controls

PRESIDENT NIXON STATED before his election and on a number of occasions thereafter his opposition to government intervention in wage and price decisions. But by late 1970 conflicting views on this subject emerged within the administration, and by August 1971 a freeze was imposed on wage and price movements, to be followed by an elaborate system of controls. Both of us were at Camp David with the President and others during that fateful weekend when his decision was made final to impose a freeze, along with other actions of great and lasting significance. And we both participated in the continuing struggle to administer the controls, once instituted. The controls experience reveals much about all dimensions of economic policy; the subject—unfortunately, in our view—is destined to have continuing practical importance.

Important segments of our society may at any time be found at almost any point on the spectrum of views about wage and price controls. Some people oppose their use in any form, whether as a formal system, a set of guidelines used informally, or any variation in between. Others think that some formal or informal incomes policy should be a permanent instrument of economic policy. Still others believe such intervention in individual wage and price decisions can occasionally be useful, even though it may not be desirable as a permanent fixture. Whatever the state of advocacy at a particular time, it will almost surely change. Even if incomes policies are not used, intense debate about their desirability will periodically become prominent in public discussion of economic policy, and the discussion itself may have an impact on the decisions of both private and public economic institutions.

In reflecting on the 1971-74 experience with wage and price controls, we shall not attempt a comprehensive discussion, either chronological or analytical. Nor shall we attempt to evaluate the costs and benefits of controls. There have already been a plethora of such efforts. Rather we shall concentrate on the dynamics of an incomes policy, a central problem in any future attempt to institute a formal or informal controls program. The problem may take the form of a question: Why is it not possible through careful advance planning to design a simple controls program that can be put in place, once and for all, to control wages and prices for the indefinite future?

Whatever one thinks of direct regulation of particular industries by the independent regulatory agencies or of indirect regulation, say, through the tax system, these kinds of regulatory programs have been much less volatile and sporadic than controls programs have been in this and other countries. Adjustments have necessarily been made in these other regulatory programs from time to time because of changes in technology and other underlying conditions, but the adjustments have usually been infrequent and have seldom altered the programs' basic operation. In contrast, a short life and frequent changes in method (called phases in the 1971-74 experience) have been a peculiar, and we believe inherent, characteristic of controls programs.

In puzzling over this central question, we have come to the conclusion that wage and price controls programs have a "life cycle" of their own. This phenomenon occurs to some extent in other regulatory areas, but controls programs appear unique in both the inevitability and the remarkable shortness of their life cycles. The controls life cycle is quite unlike cycles in the physical universe where, for example, one spring is much like another and leads inexorably through high summer to autumn and winter and then back to spring again. A controls program does not leave the economy where it was at the outset, much less at the point intended when the program was instituted. Rather, the loop itself spirals and winds to a new level, so that the cycle of controls produces a new and usually unforeseen situation. One important residue of a controls cycle, for example, is a set of fears, expectations, and conjectures about the possibility of a new cycle.

Before turning to a study of the controls life cycle, it is useful to consider four themes that come through "loud and clear" in wage and price controls. These themes help to explain the existence of the life-cycle phenomenon.

Some Prominent Themes

The first is the problem of dealing with anticipations and expectations. Although this problem is most visible prior to the start of any formal controls program, it remains a concern throughout. People always speculate about whether and when changes will be made in the rules and regulations—let alone the coverage—of the controls, and anticipations themselves have an effect on private-sector behavior in a way not always consonant with the goals of the program.

Second, it is a gross oversimplification to believe that the private sector of the economy can be subjected to a new government action or regulation and remain reasonably passive. The administration of controls must take into account at all times that the tableau to which the controls are applied is itself changed by them. Controls illustrate the continually interactive relationship between public and private actions.

Third, any new and important program, especially one so pervasive as wage and price controls, brings a new element into the advocacy system in which government policy is made. Issues formerly submerged in a specialized bureaucracy dedicated to a particular interest are thrown into a more general governmental policymaking framework and into public discussion. Interconnections that were once obscured thus emerge into public view. New considerations are brought to bear, and old ones are reweighted, often with severe political repercussions which may even bring down the whole program. In any event, the advocacy element in the making of public policy is brought into sharp relief during the administration of wage and price controls.

Fourth, the controls life cycle demonstrates the dynamic nature of most public programs. One step leads to the next—often a misstep—until those in charge eventually find themselves nowhere near the intended destination. Thus, a sense of strategy is imperative if the momentum of tactical evolution is to be turned in a desired direction.

The 1971 Freeze

The life cycle of the 1971-74 controls program had its beginning in earlier actions and discussions. The jawboning and arm-twisting of the Johnson administration had been consciously put aside in the early days of the Nixon administration. The game plan was for a continuation of the bipartisan effort to cool the economy, an effort begun in mid-1968 with a tax increase and attempts to hold down spending, thereby reducing the large full-employment deficits of the fiscal 1967 and 1968 budgets. This fiscal effort to stabilize the economy—initially opposed by the expansionary policies of the Federal Reserve in the latter half of 1968 but then buttressed by the extraordinarily tight money policy throughout almost all of 1969—brought on the mild recession of 1970. The general price level was slow to respond, perhaps because of that mildness; real GNP declined only in the quarter of 1970 in which there was a protracted General Motors-United Automobile Workers strike. But the rate of increase in consumer prices did fall from a little over 6 percent in 1969 to about 5.5 percent in 1970 to 3.7 percent in the eight months of 1971 preceding wage and price controls.

That rate of inflation and the progress in bringing it down were not, however, satisfactory to the American public. The unease and impatience of the public and the increasing insistence that the government step in and "do something" were reflected in the attitudes and demands of labor and management. To be sure, the business community wanted some government leverage on the rate of increase in wages, whereas labor was concerned primarily with prices. Nevertheless, both labor and management were at least talking about—and in a great many instances clearly pushing for—some form of intervention in wage and price decisions.

Congress had earlier, as a political dare, granted the President sweeping authority to impose controls on the American economy. But as 1971 wore on, the drumbeat in Congress for a formal incomes policy became more insistent, and many within the administration privately joined Federal Reserve Board Chairman Arthur Burns, who called publicly for the President to change his course. An anticipatory response was clearly gaining momentum, with many industrial prices raised in order to beat any possible change in policy.

To grasp the political dimension of such an important economic policy decision, the reader might ask himself what he would have done if he had been the President, facing this insistent demand for direct action and possessing a broad grant of authority, especially if he had decided that politically he had no choice but to respond in some way. Widespread public discussion and congressional hearings about the form, structure, and timing of formal restraints would only add to the momentum of price increases instituted in anticipation of possible controls.

Under these circumstances, any President would be sorely tempted to impose a freeze on wages and prices. However arbitrary a freeze might be, it would readily gain public support and it would provide him with an essential breathing space—a respite from anticipatory behavior—during which a more elaborate incomes policy or controls mechanism could be designed.

A freeze would also command attention. As it happened, the debate over an incomes policy coincided with a growing realization among U.S. trading partners that the dollar was overvalued and a growing unease about the large and persistent negative balance in our international payments. By mid-July 1971, the President and his economic advisers knew that the dollar could not continue to be tied to gold at the fixed price of $35 per ounce and would have to be, in effect, devalued. However much sense this might make from the standpoint of healthy trading relationships, we also knew that it was bound to have an inflationary impact. Furthermore, the idea of "devaluation" would probably have adverse political overtones unless surrounded by other major decisions. And so, on August 15, 1971, the "New Economic Policy" was born: stimulate the economy toward faster growth, close the "gold window," impose a surcharge on imports to force a fairer deal for American products on world markets, and impose a freeze on wages and prices to deal with potential inflationary consequences.

Any such freeze, it is clear at the outset, cannot last very long. It is inherently arbitrary. In view of the complexities and the dynamism of the American economy, wages and prices cannot be frozen for any length of time without creating serious distortions. At the same time, a freeze presents an administrative nightmare. A freeze is beautifully simple, or perhaps a better word is simplistic, but it does tend to have an immediate and clear effect. People love it. As soon as discussion turns to the possible alternatives to follow the freeze, the general reaction may very well be, and certainly was in 1971, why change it?

Early in the game, therefore, it is necessary to take one's heart in one's hands and state unequivocally and irrevocably that the freeze will end within a very short, prescribed period of time. Ninety days was the period selected. That was the minimum time judged necessary to develop a wage and price control structure with some staffing, at least at the top. After 90 days the freeze, known as Phase I, would end and Phase II, a system of bureaucratically administered controls, would begin.

The Effort to Gain and Maintain Support

For the subsequent controls program—let alone the original freeze—to be at all effective, it must have wide support, not only from the public generally but also more specifically from the principal parties immediately involved, especially labor, management, and farmers. A broad acceptance of the rules and a willingness to live by them, at least for the time being, must be developed. Apart from the need to design a program that is inherently fair, understandable, and workable, this point suggests the importance of certain procedural considerations.

Wide and visible consultation before the controls program itself is decided upon is essential. Once the regulation-writing process is rolling, the publication of draft regulations with opportunity for comment, coupled with a genuine willingness to change in the face of justified criticism, will help. The composition of administering boards must be arranged so that the parties can feel that their arguments will be heard attentively and, at the same time, the public will retain confidence in the integrity of the process.

The wage side of such institutional arrangements has always received special treatment. The historic pattern of developing a tripartite wage board reflects the importance of involving both labor and management in the program; such involvement is needed to obtain their input into the wage control policies and their administration and to generate acceptance of the program. Under a tripartite board, though all members are presumably acting in the public interest, the labor and management members are also expected to bring, and do bring, the point of view of their respective constituencies.

The proper and expected role of the public members on a tripartite wage board is not so clear. To some degree, they must mediate between opposing views of labor and management, which has been their typical role in the past. However, in a period of buoyant labor markets it is not at all clear that labor and management interests will diverge. It is all too typical that labor and management make joint applications in particular cases for settlements that exceed whatever standards have been set out. A strong case can therefore be made that the public members should be thought of as a genuine "third force" in the situation, not oblivious to their role of mediator, but certainly not limited to that conception of their duties. We had this "third force" idea very much in mind as appointments were made to the Pay Board in 1971. Some of the abrasiveness in the early days of the Pay Board may well have stemmed from that decision.

The activities of those to whom controls will be applied—labor and management—will also be affected by their perception of how long their freedoms will be curtailed. If they think that the controls are to last indefinitely, their natural reaction will be to dig in administratively and learn how to live within the rules while still attaining as many of their private objectives as possible. Labor will seek the maximum wage package possible under the rules. Management will seek the maximum immediate profit possible under the rules or at least a use of permissible costs that will buttress a firm's long-range position.

On the other hand, if a program is viewed as temporary, designed to solve an immediate and short-term problem, then the reaction may be more one of living within the spirit of the program and refraining from extensive sharpshooting at the rules. With this point in mind, we placed considerable emphasis on the transitory nature of the controls program, partly because that was what the President and his close advisers felt was proper, but also because a permanent system seemed likely to call forth a pattern of behavior sharply and undesirably different from what a temporary effort would evoke. In short, anticipations about the system have important consequences for behavior under the system, illustrating the interactive process of public policy and private reactions.

In any case, the life cycle of controls will be heavily influenced by a set of early decisions not only about what is to be done but also about how it is to be done. A primary objective in these decisions will be to develop support for the program. Without at least tacit support from the principal parties involved, controls will certainly not last long.

Reactions to Controls

However the post-freeze controls mechanism may be designed, experience with it over a period of time, say, six to eight months, leads to several developments. Distortions of various kinds emerge. With all of the goodwill and intelligence and hard work in the world, the controllers cannot possibly master the vast and complicated economy with which they must deal. The application of a set of rules to a dynamic economy and a changing business environment renders some necessary goods relatively unprofitable. People stop making them. This process leads to artificial scarcities, artificial in the sense that they represent a misallocation of resources induced by the controls themselves. But since these artificial scarcities are nonetheless real, they tend to slow production and projects and can gradually have a debilitating impact on economic growth.

Distortions arise not only in product markets but also in the collective bargaining process itself. Although the wage board may have a role to play in settling a dispute between a particular union and management, the more likely event, as labor markets tighten, will be that the board's wage-increase guidelines will be below what both labor and management would prefer. Sometimes management may find the path of least resistance to be no resistance, and will join the union in an application to the board, fully expecting that the board will do management's job for it by cutting the union's demands down to size. Wage controls may thus generate a decline in the vigor of collective bargaining.

At the same time, it is almost inevitable that people soon start questioning whether this so-called transitory program is not taking on a rather permanent appearance. Once the suspicion of permanence sets in, gamesmanship develops between the private and the public sectors. It becomes apparent that the controls process is not a one-way street in which the government does something to the private sector; rather, it is a two-way street, with the government taking an action, the private sector reacting to it, the government reacting in turn, and so forth. It is a continual process of interplay and interrelation through which those "controlled" develop ways of doing whatever they really want to do, but within the rules of the controls system. It is an impressive tribute to the ingenuity of private enterprise and collective bargaining how quickly and skillfully people find loopholes in any set of rules.

For a while the controllers engage in a process of plugging loopholes, changing a regulation here and there, and trying to keep things more or less in balance, but eventually these emerging problems in product markets and in collective bargaining will lead those in charge of the controls program to conclude that it is time to change the model. They say to themselves, "We have set out some rules and developed governmental bodies to administer them and these have all worked reasonably well for a while, but now the sharpshooters are getting to them, distortions of various kinds are arising, and so we had best do something different." In the meanwhile, one important result (perhaps achievement) of the program has been delay of the inevitable price increases. A delay of a few months in the rise of any particular price means that the average rate of increase in the price indices is reduced, at least for a time.

Changing the Model

By the time the controls program has progressed to this point, it has undoubtedly developed a strong and loyal bureaucracy. When the controls agency is new, many employees find the work exciting and interesting, they find satisfaction in working long hours, and their work is heavily covered by the press. Such a bureaucracy can quickly develop aspirations for permanence. As it acquires a life of its own, the bureaucracy seeks to perpetuate that life. Those in charge of the program may thus conclude that if a new model is to be brought out, it should encompass a change in the institutions running the controls program, as well as a change in the substance of the program itself.

This analysis contains some of the rationale for the shift in January 1973 from Phase II to Phase III in the recent controls experience. Institutional rearrangements were made: The new system of administration was designed to emphasize the continued concept that controls were a transitory matter, and a renewed effort was made to enlist the support of labor, management, and other groups for the new version of the system.

Disengagement

As the controls system proceeds in its life cycle, the realization grows that the system is a wasting asset—if it can be called an asset at all. The system may work for a while, or at least appear to. Presidents have certainly found it good politics, again for a while. But it grows more and more apparent that the system's useful life is limited. Having grabbed this tiger by the tail, those in charge must inevitably start thinking about how they are going to let go. This need to disengage has engulfed every controls program, even when those in charge were not so set on limiting the period of controls as they were in the most recent experience.

The classic means of disengagement for a controls program has been a blowup. The system puts out an edict of some kind, the private sector defies it, and the whole thing just blows up. In the past, labor has usually said, in effect, "We believe in free collective bargaining, we don't accept the decision of the wage board, we withdraw from the board, and we will strike against any effort to impose its will on us." As a matter of strategy, those in charge might view a labor boycott of the program as a tenable way out and decide to let it happen. On the other hand, the effort to administer the program in a responsible and orderly manner leads to a desire for more orderly disengagement.

The process of orderly disengagement can propel a controls program in a number of directions. One such direction is to cut down on the scope of the controls system itself by eliminating small firms from coverage and by exempting sectors of the economy where the burden of controls could lead to disaster. Letting go of rent control at the start of Phase III, for example, was both extraordinarily difficult and critically important to the health of the housing industry.

During Phase III, self-administration accompanied reduced coverage. The central idea behind this approach was to relieve companies and unions of the bureaucratic entanglements of the controls system. The rules, the duties, and the possibility of fines and rollbacks in the event of violation would all remain the same as in Phase II. But instead of administering the rules by the Phase II process of application and administrative review, followed by disapproval or approval in whole or in part, companies and unions would self-administer.

The guiding principle was that once the rules were published, it was up to those to whom they applied to self-administer them properly. It was, as was said at the time, "as voluntary as your income tax." The taxpayer fills out his own form and sends it in to the IRS at his peril. The IRS judges whether or not he has complied with the rules and, if not, the taxpayer is punishable, subject to the possibility of judicial review. For the most part, taxpayers self-administer honestly and the system works.

One important effect of the self-administration strategy of disengagement is that the tactic of delaying wage and price increases drops out of the system: The parties decide for themselves whether to raise a wage or a price, and if the increase is permissible under the rules, they simply act. Consequently, when the gears are shifted from bureaucratic review to self-administration, a bulge in wage and price increases is almost inevitable—simply because all of the increases in the bureaucratic pipeline are released at the moment of the shift.

Other Tactics of Disengagement

The Phase III effort to disengage through self-administration was abandoned because it was blamed for a development with which it actually had little connection. The composition of the price increases during the first half of 1973 shows clearly that price increases outside the scope of the program led to an escalating rate of overall price increases, which in turn undermined confidence in the program. During Phase III, food and energy prices—essentially internationally traded commodities not subject to controls—increased by 20 percent and 19 percent, respectively. In contrast, nonfood commodities and services, which were largely subject to self-administered controls, increased by 4.8 percent and 4.3 percent, respectively. If the country again has the misfortune to be saddled with controls, the facts concerning self-administration should not be overlooked.

The experience with disengagement under Phase III strongly suggests that, regardless of the reasons for a bulge in prices, political tolerance limits the size of an "acceptable" price bulge. The 1973 bulge was politically unacceptable, and the reaction was apparent in press and congressional criticism and in a move toward a congressionally imposed freeze. In response, the President imposed his own freeze in June 1973, followed by a severe form of bureaucratically administered wage and price controls, known as Phase IV. The President's economic advisers vigorously opposed this second freeze and, in fact, his Labor-Management Advisory Committee met in special session and expressed its opposition to even a tightening of controls, let alone a freeze. Perhaps we should have seen the handwriting on the wall when, in response to Chairman of the Council of Economic Advisers Herb Stein's remark, "You know, Mr. President, you can't walk on water twice," the President replied, "Maybe you can if it's frozen."

The second freeze came at a bad time in the economic cycle, compared with the timing of the first one. In 1971, seasonal factors worked in its favor in the food area, international prices were relatively stable, and the general tide of inflation was already receding. In 1973, by contrast, all these forces were working strongly in the reverse direction, and U.S. price levels were also feeling the full effects of two devaluations. Whatever political justifications may be offered for this decision to impose a second freeze, only one thing can be said for it on the substantive side: The results were so bad that everyone could see the inherent limitations of controls.

After reimposing a mandatory set of controls, complete with

notification periods and other means of reinstituting delay in wage and price changes, a different disengagement strategy was necessary. A sector-by-sector approach evolved. Decontrol by sectors is at best a very tricky process. Because the American economy is such a closely interrelated and interdependent system, if something is done to one part of it, other parts will be affected, often quite rapidly. The interrelationships that exist between products are often surprising. Fertilizer and explosives, for example, both use the same raw material, ammonium nitrate. If fertilizer is decontrolled, allowing that use of the raw material to become relatively profitable, the raw material will be drained away from explosives. If keeping coal mines going is a good thing, then decontrol of fertilizer without decontrol of explosives (of vital use in mining) is not a wise idea.

The director and staff of the Cost of Living Council closely monitored such interconnections, and on the whole the sector-by-sector approach succeeded moderately well. The controllers bargained with the private sector, price by price and, to a degree, wage by wage, since wages and prices in an industry were almost always decontrolled at the same time. Those who wanted to be decontrolled were asked for a variety of guarantees: about average price behavior over some period into the future, investment plans and commitments, limitations of export of critical materials, and the development of improved structures of collective bargaining.

Whenever any price was decontrolled, a slight bulge in overall price indices resulted. The sector-by-sector strategy of decontrol is based on the premise that only so much of a bulge is politically tolerable; any greater bulge will lead the political process to throw the program back into a tight bureaucratic system. The goal is to disengage as rapidly as possible without incurring a politically intolerable bulge at any one time.

In the end, Congress provided the final act of disengagement by refusing to extend the life of the Economic Stabilization Act beyond April 30, 1974. By that time, labor and management were thoroughly fed up with the whole thing, and the President's Labor-Management Advisory Committee had some time earlier publicly recorded its view that controls should end.

Unfortunately, however, total disengagement is not the end of the life cycle of controls. The fact that controls were used remains very much in the public mind and has created a set of attitudes that complicates the problem of dealing with inflation. Although the 1971-74 episode provided some public education about the limitations of controls, there nevertheless seems to be an undying willingness to believe that, somehow or other, with enthusiastic administration, controls will work.

Controls have the political appeal of action: A legislator who wants to "do something" about inflation can always espouse controls, and a President who wants to be seen as a man of action can impose them. Public discussion by highly placed people can in turn easily lead to the kind of anticipatory price increases that tend to force a government to reinstitute controls. In a sense the problem then becomes, assuming one wants to stay out of the wage and price control business, how to keep the barn door open long enough to allow the stolen horses to be returned.

Limitations of the "Large-Unit" Approach

Controls or almost any other type of incomes policy will almost inevitably be directed primarily at the large units—unions as well as companies—of the economy. They are the ones that can be dealt with directly, that have public visibility, and that, particularly on the company side, fear public criticism.

This large-unit approach conforms to one popular and continuously propagated theory of how the economy operates. According to this "administered-price" school of thought, the big units in our economy administer prices and wages to a considerable degree at their own discretion, and their decisions in turn tend to dominate the economy. From this point of departure, those favoring controls but desiring (for whatever reason) to exempt small firms from the controls argue that if the big units decide to follow a moderate course, then smaller firms will follow suit. They will follow, so the argument goes, in part because as competitors they must do so in order to sell their products, in part because as suppliers they feel pressure from the buying power of large units, and in part because a tone is set creating an environment to which everyone must conform.

The administered-price view—the intellectual foundation for the large-unit approach to controls—is widely held among politicians and is supported by a substantial number of economists. The popularity of this view is attributable primarily to the brilliant polemics of a few members of the economics profession. But the weight of the evidence is against the idea that firms in relatively concentrated industries (e.g., steel, autos, rubber) have higher-than-average price increases during a period of inflation and are, therefore, in part "responsible" for the inflation. Consequently, there is little analytical support for the proposition that if their prices were moderated somewhat, a broad beneficial impact would be enjoyed. As Albert Rees, at the time executive director of the President's Council on Wage and Price Stability, commented in testimony before the House Committee on Banking, Currency, and Housing (June 17, 1975):

> Although it is probably true that concentrated industries charge higher prices than they would charge if they were more competitive, it does not appear to be true that prices in these industries rise more rapidly than other prices. This last hypothesis would

require not only that concentration confer a price advantage, but also that this advantage be continuously increasing.

Any attempt to use controlled prices of large firms to discipline prices charged by smaller ones breaks down in a period when the commodity is in short supply. Then, control of large firms' prices would simply result in a flow of the commodity to smaller firms that could buy it and subsequently sell it at the higher price. Over a long enough period, we would have large firms with low prices and nothing to sell.

Whatever the merits of the arguments for and against the administered-price view, the facts of life during most of the recent controls period differed from assumptions of the large-unit theory. Prices and wages rose most rapidly in the sectors of the economy that were (1) competitive (composed of small units), (2) characterized by special problems on the wage side, (3) dominated by government, or (4) heavily involved in international markets, either on the importing or exporting side. It was the increase in these prices that caused the overall price indices to rise so rapidly and that generated the political demands for further government action.

In the health sector, for example, there was a rapid escalation of prices to the consumer in an industry populated by local hospitals and many individual entrepreneurs, most importantly doctors, who are organized into what may be viewed as a union, the American Medical Association. The steady escalation of costs was largely a direct result of the vast and increasing flow of federal funds to this area. A tremendous effort was made to adapt the idea of controls to this situation, and some success was achieved in concept, if not indeed in actual effect on health service prices: A labor-management panel and health advisory committee were formed to generate ideas from knowledgeable people and transmit information and decisions to those affected, and direct limits were placed on increases in the prices of many health services. The rate of increase in these costs did slow for a time (and for the first time in a long while). The basic problem, however, was one of grappling with government-induced cost increases, a far cry from the stereotyped problem of dealing with price increases imposed by large companies.

Food was another sector of the economy that plagued the controls program. The rapid increases in consumer food prices were basically caused by price increases in highly competitive markets for raw food materials. These markets were in turn strongly affected by worldwide crop failures and resulting scarcities in international markets, on the one hand, and by government policies tending to restrict supply in domestic markets, on the other. The fruitful ways of dealing with scarcity-induced price increases surely do not include lowering price below cost in the markets where the problem originates.

An example is useful. Although raw agricultural products were exempt from controls on the solid justification that to cover them would discourage supply and therefore be self-defeating in the long run, broilers were covered. The problem was that, whether one starts with the chicken or the egg, by the time the product emerges at its first point of sale, it is no longer "raw." It has been plucked and prepared for use. At the same time, the underlying raw material—feed grain—was, as a raw agricultural product, free of all controls. The resulting interaction between rising prices for feed grains and controlled prices for broilers was disastrous for profit margins in the broiler industry. Yet the Price Commission was loath to permit much of an increase in broiler prices because of consumer sensitivity. The predictable consequence of holding price below cost was a drying up of supply as broiler producers literally could no longer afford to stay in business. In the end broilers were declared a raw agricultural product, and their price, automatically released from controls, shot up by over 50 percent. Supply responded rapidly, however, in this short-production-cycle industry and within a matter of months the price had fallen to near its original level.

The theory that controlling prices charged by large units in the economy would strike at the essence of the inflation problem thus simply had no application to the sectors of the economy where prices were rising most rapidly. The relevance of the large-unit theory to the inflation problem is paralleled by the old story of the drunk who was looking for a key under a lamp post. When asked by a passerby what he was doing, he replied that he was looking for a lost key. When the passerby asked where he lost the key, the drunk replied that he had lost it down the street. "Well, then," he was asked, "why are you looking here?"—"Because the light is so much better."

To continue the analogy, the drunk is like the politician who knows the political mileage to be gained by pushing around the big boys in the economy, whether or not it makes any economic sense. Attention in any controls program will thus inevitably be directed at the large units because they are what the controllers can most readily get their hands on, and the administered-price school of thought provides a ready justification. But as we have seen, concentrated industries often are not where the problem lies. The focusing of controls on large units is thus a distinct and inherent limitation on their potential usefulness and may contribute in turn to public dissatisfaction with their performance and to their eventual collapse.

Interactions with Other Policies

A wage and price controls system interacts not only with the private sector which it seeks to regulate but also with a host of government policies

"It says here the full impact won't be felt till next month."

that bear directly or indirectly on the general price level and on particular prices. One of the most powerful and important of these interactions is the potential impact of controls on fiscal and monetary policy. The proclaimed existence of controls almost inevitably creates the feeling that the controls policy is contending, at least in some fashion, with the problems of inflation. It follows from this feeling that the government can be more aggressive in stimulating the economy. Those who find tough monetary or fiscal policies inconvenient or contrary to their interest conclude that easier monetary and fiscal policies have become feasible.

This line of thinking was at least implicit in the August 1971 package, which included some fiscal stimulants to the economy. The same view can be discerned in the plea from the Federal Reserve for an incomes policy, a plea frequently heard when the rate of inflation calls for a tight monetary policy. The argument is that monetary policy has carried too much of the burden of controlling inflation and cannot do the job alone, and therefore some help from an incomes policy is needed. Certainly the implication is that if an incomes policy is adopted, then monetary policy can be easier. This tendency toward self-deception is a central problem with controls. It is the explanation for the otherwise puzzling fact that countries using controls the least tend to have the best record in fighting inflation. The outstanding example, of course, is West Germany, which has enjoyed a consistently superior performance in fighting inflation.

This point deserves particular emphasis for those inclined toward econometric studies of the effects of controls. The studies typically start with a given fiscal and monetary policy and then compare price and wage performance under controls with what might have been expected without controls. Such studies have the fatal weakness that they leave out of account what is perhaps the most important variable—the impact of the existence of controls on changes in fiscal and monetary policy.

A second important interaction is the interplay between controls and international economic policy. In the case of the United States, the 1971 and 1973 devaluations and the institution of a flexible system of exchange rates undoubtedly aggravated the inflation problem. A correction in the exchange value of the dollar was long overdue. Moreover, the more flexible system now in place enables individual countries to maintain a more independent fiscal and monetary policy, if they choose to do so. Be that as it may, these results were achieved only with considerable pain. The first effect of a devaluation is to raise the price of imports and, by adding to the capacity of the international community to buy domestic products, to bid up domestic prices. An upward movement of the price indices inevitably results. In addition, in 1971 the refusal of some major countries to accept what the United States regarded as an adequate devaluation resulted—through their purchase of dollars in foreign exchange markets in order to maintain exchange rates favorable to their export industries—in a great increase in their foreign exchange reserves. This increase in the world money supply was a major contributor to the worldwide inflation in the 1972-75 period.

A third interaction is between a domestic price controls policy and developments in international markets for particular commodities. In any discussion of the design of a controls program it is almost instantly and universally agreed that costs of internationally traded goods must be passed through in the product price if the country is not to be cut off from access to those supplies. Articles produced and used in the United States but also exported present a more difficult and potentially more dangerous dilemma. Agricultural commodities are leading examples. If the controlled price of a domestically produced good is below the world market price, exports will surely rise. The obvious alternatives must be to put up with the scarcity, to allow the price of food to rise to the world price, or to impose controls on exports.

The attempt in 1973 to deal with this latter problem through export controls demonstrates how a controls program tends to spread from one area to others. Fortunately, the United States was not drawn very far into export controls. Although the pressure for widespread export controls on food was great, they were imposed—and then but briefly—only on soybeans. The experience with soybean export controls, though short and perhaps justifiable as a short-term measure, provides a lesson in what *not* to do. These controls tended to undermine the confidence of other countries in the United States as a secure source of supply. Soybean export controls were also a blow to farmers who depend on exports of that crop for their livelihood. In addition, some of the demand for soybeans spilled over into markets for other feed grains, illustrating the inherent indivisibility of the economy.

Here, also, the existence of authority to impose controls on exports and the fact that this authority was used on at least one occasion produced a problem in anticipations that aggravated an already difficult situation. Intentions to export were artificially pumped up (as noted in Chapter One) as exporters guarded against a possible program of export controls that would allow them to export some fixed percentage of their "intended" amount. Since this possibility created an incentive to inflate intentions, it became more difficult to judge true export demand—a difficulty that occurred not only in soybeans but in many other agricultural commodities as well.

Any comprehensive controls system must eventually face up to the dilemma produced by attempts to control the domestic price of an internationally traded commodity. It is worth noting also that commodity agreements worked out internationally can very well spread into the domestic area, a point U.S. negotiators must keep in mind as they deal with insistent demands to stabilize prices through international agreements. Foreign and domestic markets are intimately intertwined; over any period of time it is impossible to control one market without affecting the other.

Government Policies Toward Supply

If one area of genuinely constructive experience were to be singled out from the 1971-74 controls period, it would be the impact of the controls system on government actions affecting supply. In the economic package announced in August 1971, President Nixon coupled the imposition of wage and price controls with a request to Congress for reinstitution of the investment tax credit. Congress approved both the credit and a previously announced administrative liberalization of the depreciation provisions of the federal income tax code. Both were actions taken to increase supply. Another was the sustained and partially successful effort to limit price increases of certain commodities by selling out of government stockpiles articles no longer considered "strategic." Similarly, in the process of disengagement from controls, strenuous efforts were made to obtain a commitment to greater capacity in bottlenecked industries of the economy, such as fertilizer.

Perhaps the most interesting development was the emergence of a new center of advocacy within the government. With economic policies for the most part in the hands of departmental bureaus and congressional committees representing special interests, governmentally imposed restrictions on supply, designed to gain a higher price for those interests, are commonplace. In an advocacy system of government, there has been little organized resistance to these raids by special interests.

The controls system created a new group within the executive branch devoted to keeping prices down and, therefore, to expanding rather than restricting supplies of almost everything. The Cost of Living Council and its staff and the more recent Council on Wage and Price Stability were the institutional base for this new advocacy group to represent the general public interest. With a staff large enough and expert enough to develop independent information and analysis, this group was able to challenge departmental views and, with presidential backing, to change many decisions. Excessive set-asides in planting, compulsory empty backhauls by trucks, restricted carloading of certain commodities, size standards for produce, and a myriad of other such restrictions were brought into question. In many cases important changes were made that relaxed government restrictions on supply. For example, marketing orders (under which restrictions were placed on the permissible volume of shipments of certain commodities) were discovered by people outside the Department of Agriculture, and a system was set up to review them.

It would, of course, be naive to believe that all or even most of these battles could be won, because the political forces that produced the restrictive measures in the first place are usually alert and powerful. Nevertheless, some battles were won, and the fact that a confrontation might develop undoubtedly has a healthy restraining influence on new measures to restrict supply. This function, which yielded important results during the 1971-74 controls period, holds the prospect for positive contributions to public policy with or without an economic stabilization program. It would be highly worthwhile for this effort, now the responsibility of the Council on Wage and Price Stability, to be made a permanent feature of the government.

Some Administrative Insights

Any formal system of controls will require an administrative apparatus to interpret the rules and regulations, to police compliance with them, and to provide service throughout the country. Particularly when the program is conceived of as temporary, it will be advantageous from the standpoint of the program to use an existing bureaucracy. Immediately, then, the Internal Revenue Service springs to mind. The IRS is large, has offices all over the country, and is a respected and to a certain extent feared organization (nobody likes to have a visit from the IRS). The Service's employees are also competent in the process of writing and interpreting regulations. The temptation is thus strong to give the IRS the duty of day-to-day administration, knowing that other tasks will easily absorb its manpower when this temporary program disappears.

Despite its appeal, such a choice presents an interesting dilemma for government organization. The IRS has an important job to do—collecting taxes. Manpower and budget support for that job are scarce and should not be unnecessarily diluted. Furthermore, one of the attractions of using the IRS is that its tax-enforcement role gives it special clout. But that fact itself raises serious questions about the propriety of attempting to harness the taxpayer's fear of tax enforcement for the achievement of an unrelated end, such as controlling prices.

Over the decades the practice has grown up of using IRS records and personnel in the effort to control organized crime, to deal with the problem of drug abuse, and so on. To its everlasting credit, the IRS is one bureaucracy that is not disposed to seek an enlargement of its jurisdiction. The attitude within the IRS is that the job of collecting taxes is important and should not be diluted by sharing the IRS stage with other responsibilities.

There is much to be said for this view. In the event of another outbreak of the wage and price control disease, some other means of administration should be found.

As in other experiments with controls in the United States, in the most recent episode a tripartite wage agency (the Pay Board) was adopted. The Pay Board hammered out the broad policies pursued throughout the entire 1971-74 stabilization period. Nevertheless, the Pay Board's discussions of administrative as well as policy matters were marked by considerable acrimony, and the situation gradually deteriorated. Most of the labor members eventually decided to walk off the board near the end of Phase II, an action that under some circumstances would have brought the whole program to an end. In this case, however, one labor member stayed and he was paired, so to speak, with one management member. The other management members chose to resign in order to maintain labor-management parity and to give a majority to the public members. All five public members stayed on the board, and it thereby became an essentially public body.

This structural change made the administrative processes of the board, which were then the predominant activity, much more efficient and workmanlike. The labor staff members continued to work with the Pay Board and the board's activities were more or less accepted, no doubt in large part because labor had participated in the formulation of the policies being pursued. The design of the wage side of the Phase III program took a lesson from this experience. A Labor-Management Advisory Board was formed, and it operated quite successfully on the policy level. Its views on the desirability of ending the controls were instrumental in creating a climate in which that could be done. At the same time, the administrative effort during Phase III and Phase IV was lodged with the Cost of Living Council, whose director, John Dunlop, was responsible for the administration of both wage and price controls.

This experience underscores an important distinction between policy formulation and administrative action, particularly where wages are concerned. The participation of labor in the formulation of policy during the early months of controls was not only more important than its participation in administration but was a vital condition of labor's willingness to cooperate with those administering wage controls.

The Politics of Controls

One of the most difficult problems in the administration of controls is how to insulate the process from political pressures exerted by special interests. Although the advocacy process is present in both the executive and legislative branches, it is more pronounced in the latter. One can predict, for example, that a running battle will ensue with certain congressmen and senators whenever a marketing order emanating from the Department of Agriculture is challenged by executive branch officials concerned with expanding supply. The politics of special interests in controls is dramatized by the experience of President Truman, who advocated a wage and price controls system after World War II but had to veto the bill that Congress ultimately passed. His grounds for the veto were that the bill was so loaded with debilitating amendments that it could not possibly work. The executive branch officials in charge of controls must somehow contend with a kind of political guerrilla warfare, in which particular members of Congress strongly advocate controls, on the one hand, and, on the other, continually slip into bills riders that would exempt from controls an industry or group very important to their own constituency.

A controls program must have administrative integrity if it is to survive. The administrators of the controls program must be in contact with Congress if the program is to be understood at all sympathetically. They must reconcile themselves to being denounced for the record and on the record and be satisfied with a wink and a nod that is supposed to tell them not to take the denunciation either personally or too seriously. It is up to the President, his cabinet officers, and the President's political assistants to provide a buffer shielding the administrators of the program from the most intense political heat. If ground must be given to special interests, those providing this political buffer must be prepared to take the responsibility for making that decision.

In short, the 1971-74 experience with wage and price controls shows how tempting it is to adopt controls and how difficult it is to get rid of them. They virtually assure easier and more inflationary fiscal and monetary policies. To yield to these temptations is to give bad medicine at a bad time. Once having put the economy on a regime of controls, policymakers will find that they have to change the dosage and the method of administration constantly. Even as the life cycle of controls seems to have run its course, its legacy remains: fear that another dose may well be in the offing.

CHAPTER FIVE

Income Security: The Vital Trade-on

WHAT CONTRIBUTION CAN income security policy make to the fight against inflation and unemployment? For most people the only relationship is that income transfer programs help the poor and the unemployed to maintain their command over goods and services *whatever* the economic situation. Income security programs are usually treated purely as issues of social policy. Yet so long as fiscal policy works imperfectly and then only slowly, economic policymakers must pay attention to the design of these programs. Within the income security sphere may lie the answer to the most baffling problem in economic policy: the universally recognized and deplored tendency of inflation-fighting programs to lead to unemployment.

This problem is often referred to as the trade-off between inflation and unemployment. Some economists express this relationship in terms of the so-called Phillips curve, in which a particular level of unemployment is associated with each rate of inflation, with higher levels of inflation leading to lower unemployment. However, the Phillips curve has proved most unstable, and each year a higher and higher level of inflation has been associated with a reasonable level of unemployment. In terms of policy, rising rates of inflation have accompanied the larger budget deficits and larger rates of increase in the money supply that have been created, in part, to deal with unemployment (an oversimplification in that, to a considerable extent, the budget deficits and money supply increases were often unintended outcomes of other policies).

The stark fact remains, however, that a willingness to accept rising levels of inflation has not produced falling levels of unemployment. On the contrary, inflation itself led inexorably to a burst in the 1973-74 speculative bubble—in real estate, commodities, inventories—and to a fall in consumers' willingness to spend, thereby contributing to the 1974-75 recession. To the frustration of economic policymakers, the fear that anti-inflation measures would further exacerbate unemployment thwarted attempts to deal with the inflation problem, even after it was generally recognized that inflation itself could lead to further unemployment.

The habit of thinking of a trade-off between inflation and unemployment has thus led into a blind alley. What is needed is some way of combining policies toward these two great economic problems so that the policies *reinforce* each other. What is needed, in short, is a trade-*on* rather than a trade-*off* approach. Income security can provide the vital new dimension for taking the measure of both inflation and unemployment. If unemployment can be made relatively painless for the unemployed so that anti-inflation policies can be given enough time to work, then the objective of stable prices with low unemployment may once again be brought within reach. Income security programs, if well designed, can play that role. Today's crazy quilt of poorly designed overlapping programs is not equal to the task.

Designing such an income security program and making it politically acceptable to the wide variety of advocacy groups represented in the legislative process is a major challenge. Here economic policy enters the picture again. Although a wide variety of professions and scholarly disciplines are necessarily involved in dealing with social programs like income security, such programs at root operate like other economic programs. Through budget expenditures and, as we shall see, through taxation (in this case implicit taxation), government attempts to increase the effective command of the poor or the unemployed over goods and services, to stimulate the supply of goods and services going to the poor, or to influence the rewards from work. Hence, the tools and experience of economists and economic policymakers have a large role to play in the design of social programs.

Even if these connections between income security issues and the central issues of economic policy did *not* exist, the macroeconomic significance of income security programs would command the attention of economic policymakers. Income security expenditures are such a large portion of the federal budget that decisions on them can make or break any budget objective. Moreover, total expenditures by all levels of government on income security constitute a large and growing portion of the GNP.

More than $138 billion of fiscal 1977 outlays of $414 billion was devoted to income security. Even if social security and federal employee retirement payments are excluded as somehow different from the rest of government income security spending, more than $40 billion would still be in the income security category. The magnitude of this income security spending represents a dramatic change in priorities. As late as fiscal 1971 income security came to only 26.2 percent of the budget and was surpassed by national defense outlays constituting 36.3 percent of the budget. Today this relationship has been reversed. Income security in the President's budget for fiscal 1977 reached 34.8 percent, while the defense category fell to 25.6 percent.

These figures actually underestimate the amount of federal spending designed to maintain standards of living. Veterans, for example, were expected to receive a further $9.1 billion in income security payments in fiscal 1977. Moreover, all of these figures refer only to the federal share of income security payments; states pay out many additional billions. These figures also do not include a number of major government programs—in health and agriculture, for instance—that are often justified as meeting income security needs. Federal Medicare and Medicaid outlays alone were estimated to exceed $30 billion in fiscal 1977.

Income security programs are growing rapidly, both absolutely and proportionately. In 1975 the Office of Management and Budget estimated that if transfer programs (of which income security programs constitute the major portion) kept growing at the present rate, they would reach more than one-half the federal budget in 20 years.

The size of income security programs poses more than just a budget question. When all income security expenditures—federal, state, and local—are included, the percentage of the GNP thereby transferred from producers of goods and services to consumers is highly significant. In 1976 transfers reached $184 billion, some 10.9 percent of the GNP, up from 5.5 percent of the GNP a decade earlier. These transfers loom even larger when one asks where the population receives its income: In 1975, a recession year, some 13 percent of personal disposable income came by way of income security transfers from some level of government. Such transfers exceeded total federal government purchases of goods and services for the first time in 1973.

The escalating level of welfare programs is only one factor that has contributed to the widespread feeling that these programs are out of control. Another is their sheer complexity. When leading economic policymakers and independent economic analysts cannot grasp the workings of these programs without lengthy study, it is difficult to judge their probable economic significance or to attempt to control their growth. Welfare outlays are at the very minimum uncontrollable in the budgetary sense, as Congress has learned in its attempts to implement the 1974 budget reform legislation. With income security payments constituting over 40 percent of all uncontrollable outlays in the federal budget and with benefits paid on an entitlements basis, neither the OMB nor congressional budget committees are able to budget accurately. As estimates of income security outlays increase, all budgeteers can do is add to their global budget figures or apply the scalpel to controllable programs whose proportionate importance in the budget is dwindling.

Income Security Today

To say that the federal government has an income security policy would be wishful thinking. Existing income security policies are a hodgepodge of inconsistent, overlapping, sometimes mutually frustrating programs, each designed for a particular category of recipients. These categorical programs are too often the repatched and mended versions of outcomes of nearly forgotten legislative compromises. Before investigating their deficiencies, it is useful to review briefly the major programs.

Placing social security to one side, the most important income security program is probably Aid to Families with Dependent Children (AFDC). It is the program that most people think about when welfare is mentioned. AFDC is administered by the states and localities and, within bounds established by broad federal policies, states set the benefit levels. The federal government pays a substantial share of the total cost of AFDC; this federal component amounts to some $6 billion in fiscal 1977. The state component of AFDC, often described as "state supplementation," costs the states nearly as much as the federal share. The AFDC program grew sevenfold between 1960 and 1973.

A relatively new federal program was passed in 1971, to be effective in 1974: the supplemental security income program (SSI). This federally administered and financed program replaced the so-called "adult categories" programs (welfare programs for the aged, the blind, and the disabled) formerly administered and financed by the states. State supplementation is permitted, however, and in some cases required. Federal payments under the supplemental security income program were estimated at over $5 billion in fiscal 1977.

The two programs just discussed are cash transfer programs. They are designed to transfer cash that—with important qualifications in the case of AFDC—the recipients may spend as they like. A different kind of program transfers the equivalent of cash but attempts to control the use to which the benefits are put, an end accomplished by selling a voucher, usable for a specific purpose, for less than its cash value. The leading example is the food stamp program. Under this program, run jointly by the states and the federal government, eligible individuals are entitled to purchase food stamps worth a specified amount by paying a portion of their value, the portion paid to be determined by the purchaser's income. The difference between the cost to the purchaser and the value of the stamps—the so-called "bonus value"—constitutes the income transfer. This program's primary purpose is to increase food consumption by the needy. A secondary purpose, not in the forefront of public rhetoric but no doubt politically important, is to increase farm income by increasing demand for food products.

The food stamp program has expanded faster than any other income security program, growing from $35 million in 1965 to about $5.6 billion in fiscal 1976, with participation growing from 400,000 to more than 17 million people in roughly the same period (though participation fluctuates with the unemployment rate). Particularly in the light of administrative flaws and abuses, it is hard to escape the conclusion that this program is not under control.

These various programs can be compared from other perspectives. One is the effect of payments on incentives to work. Because supplemental security income recipients—the aged, the blind, and the disabled—are usually unable to work, the design of the program has not created serious questions of work incentives. The vast majority of adult AFDC and food stamp recipients, on the other hand, are physically able to work; hence, grave issues for public policy are created by the effect of welfare payments on their incentive to work.

Another perspective involves the cost and manner of administration. Supplemental security income recipients receive cash benefits with no strings attached. Food stamps must be spent on food, but by substituting food stamps for what would otherwise be spent on food, most recipients can spend the "bonus value" on whatever they choose. Moreover, administration is limited to verifying eligibility and handling the mechanics of the system; there is no attempt to look over the food stamp recipients' shoulders to regulate their cash expenditures. In the case of AFDC, on the other hand, social workers and other middle-class professionals play an important role in supervising the recipients' lives, verifying not only eligibility but also the need for particular types of expenditures. This raises the cost of AFDC administration significantly and creates the potential for a paternal relationship between government and recipient not present in the supplemental security income and food stamp programs.

Still another kind of federal program transfers goods and services in kind. Rather than relying on cash transfers in order to permit the beneficiaries to make their own choices, in-kind programs transfer the goods or services themselves. Perhaps the best-known example is public housing ($1.5 billion in 1975), but there are other examples, including the school lunch program ($1.7 billion in 1975). Although the financing mechanism is somewhat different, the massive Medicare and Medicaid programs can also be classified within the in-kind category.

Unemployment insurance is quite different. Unlike the others, it is not a welfare program, although a large portion of benefits do go to the poor. In the first place, unemployment insurance payments are not "needs tested" benefits. A worker otherwise eligible does not become ineligible simply because family income remains high due, for example, to the earnings of a still-employed spouse. Moreover, the theory of unemployment insurance is that an unemployed worker should be able, for a time, to withhold his labor from the market while he seeks a line of work and rate of pay comparable to what he previously enjoyed. Benefits cease after a specified period, at which time the worker must presumably look for lower-grade employment (although recent practice has been to extend the duration of benefits).

As the period of coverage grows longer, unemployment insurance is thus becoming more and more like welfare. In the 1974-75 recession, benefits were extended to give up to 65 weeks of coverage. Extended benefits beyond the initial 26 weeks came directly from general revenues of the federal government, unlike the basic benefits financed by state payroll taxes on employers. The states determine the amount of the basic benefits and to a certain extent their eligibility conditions and duration. Thus, the adequacy of unemployment insurance varies from state to state. The amount spent on the program is obviously a function of the number of unemployed. But it also is highly sensitive to the everchanging federal legislative provisions on extended benefits. As a result of the 1974-75 recession, outlays escalated from $6.1 billion in fiscal 1974 to $19.5 billion in fiscal 1976.

The Present System Evaluated

The existing income security programs suffer from a number of weaknesses and perverse effects, particularly when their combined effects are considered. One of the greatest weaknesses, despite the plethora of programs, is that some people fall between the cracks. Although federal AFDC legislation gives the states the option of including so-called intact families, in about half the states AFDC remains a program for only female-headed households. The "working poor"—a euphemism for a broad group that includes male-headed households, single persons, and childless couples whose income from work is less than the AFDC recipient's income from welfare payments—often receive no welfare benefits. Unemployment insurance cannot fill this gap for the working poor, who by definition are employed; nor can it do much for the unemployed father who has never been employed or who has been unemployed for a substantial period and therefore has exhausted his benefits.

Even those who are not totally excluded from the present system sometimes receive payments that are derisively low. In large part these low payments result from the absence of a national floor on state-determined payments. For example, in 1976 the largest AFDC monthly payment for a family of four was only $60 in Mississippi, $117 in South Carolina, and $148 in Georgia, compared to $379 in California, $403 in Michigan, and $422 in New York. This is not to say that payments should be the same throughout the country. Differing costs of living and differing wage levels make varying payment levels appropriate. But a national minimum, even if only related to local wage levels, is appropriate in a national program.

Aside from whatever questions of human compassion are raised by uneven coverage and inadequate payment levels, these weaknesses undermine the contribution that income security payments can make to stabilization policy. Failure to cover adequately the male-headed family against the income loss from unemployment is failure to deal with the most explosive political consequences of unemployment. It is precisely the unemployed father whose need is greatest and who commands the most media coverage and the most public empathy in times of recession.

An equally serious problem is the disincentive to work created by the design of many existing programs. Nearly everyone understands that a program that induces recipients not to work is bad for the recipients and bad for the economy. But the way in which existing programs actually create these disincentives to work is little understood. To analyze this aspect of the programs it is necessary to move from broad considerations of compassion and fiscal integrity to the technical level of program design.

Program Design

One of the most important technical aspects of any program is the *benefit-reduction rate*—the rate at which a recipient's benefit payments are reduced as income from work rises. A revealing way to describe the benefit-reduction rate is as an implicit marginal tax rate. Although most people think of a marginal tax rate as the amount of income tax paid to the government for each additional dollar of income and therefore find it anomalous to speak of taxation in the context of welfare or unemployment insurance payments, the reduction in payments resulting from going to work is precisely a tax. An unemployed person returning to work will gain earnings but will lose benefits. The disincentive effect of a high rate of benefit losses in relation to added earnings is similar to the disincentive effect on upper-income workers of a high marginal income tax rate on a second job or on overtime work.

Prior to 1969, the benefit-reduction rate on income for AFDC recipients was 100 percent; for every dollar they earned by work, they gave up one dollar of AFDC payments. To those considering a part-time job, the disincentive effect was extremely powerful. Even a full-time job could hardly appear attractive unless the after-tax wages substantially exceeded the AFDC benefit level.

The 1969 reduction of the AFDC benefit-reduction rate to 67 percent did not eliminate the disincentive effect. In fact, the disincentive effect is compounded for those receiving benefits from a number of programs. Take the case of a New York City intact family of four (that is, a family including a father, mother, and two children) participating in AFDC, food stamps, school lunch, and Medicaid programs. If the unemployed father were to take a job paying $7,000 a year, the family's disposable income would increase by only $213. Working under such conditions hardly pays. The implicit marginal tax rate is 97 percent!

Even more destructive to the incentive to work than high marginal tax rates are the numerous "notches" built into some programs or resulting from the combination of programs. A notch refers to a situation where a small increase in earned income leads to a large reduction in benefits. A notch amounts to a marginal tax rate of more than 100 percent, and normally it is an unintentional but nonetheless real by-product of some arbitrary rule. Under the AFDC program in states where families with fathers may receive benefits, for example, a father may work up to 100 hours per month without any reduction in benefits. But let him work 101 hours in a month, and he and his family lose all benefits. Thus, an increase of a few dollars in income, at the 100-hour point, leads to a loss of hundreds of dollars in benefits.

Although notches can be found within particular income security programs, they are even more likely to arise from the interaction of separate programs. The New York City intact family described above would actually lose $1,231 in benefits if the family head worked longer hours in order to increase income from $3,000 to $4,000.

In addition to the disincentive to return to full-time employment, high marginal tax rates and notches have other perverse effects. For example, they encourage recipients to seek odd jobs that give rise to the kind of income that can be concealed. Income from part-time jobs in factories, offices, or stores would be reported by employers; hence, the high marginal tax rates lead welfare and unemployment insurance recipients to avoid such jobs, even though the concealed income jobs are often economically inferior.

The parallel to the behavior of high-income taxpayers faced by high marginal tax rates is striking. High-income earners respond with tax shelters, the poor and the unemployed with concealable-income jobs. In both instances, high marginal rates divert economic activity from activities that are superior from the standpoint of society to activities that are pursued only because high marginal rates render them more remunerative to the individual.

High marginal rates and notches produce not merely disincentives to work and distortions of labor markets. More tragically, they lead to a greater social problem—dependency. The person induced not to work develops a dependency, both psychological and economic, on government. Someone who does not work over an extended period may find it difficult to find work at all; by not working, a welfare recipient fails to make an adequate investment in his own skills. Welfare begets welfare.

Many of the procedural requirements for establishing eligibility and for receiving benefits also contribute to dependency. Consider a mother who passes up a short-term job because of the time and red tape that would be necessary to requalify for AFDC after the job terminates. The social problem goes well beyond dependency. The AFDC program, by placing the female-headed household in a favorable position, contributes to family dissolution. No one knows how many fathers have left home to assure their wives and children a decent standard of living.

Programs providing goods and services (such as the public housing and school lunch programs) cause other types of problems. The advantages of cash transfers over in-kind transfers are considerable. Cash payments are less paternalistic than in-kind benefits and they give the recipient a greater degree of personal freedom. Moreover, the government is often inefficient in providing in-kind benefits. Certainly the record of public housing shows that it is considerably more difficult for government to provide goods and services than the architects of the program thought. The social disorganization and physical decay in much public housing suggest that the attitude of welfare recipients toward what they buy with their own money (though the money comes from the government) is different from their attitude toward what is "given" to them in kind. Too often, yesterday's public housing project becomes tomorrow's slum.

Even vouchers, such as food stamps, have characteristics that are inferior to straightforward cash payments. Having to buy food stamps once a month takes time (plus the cost of transportation) and it creates cash flow problems for impoverished families. When cash is given directly, welfare programs may still interfere with family independence, for example, when a program requires that a social worker prepare a family budget in order to determine the amount the family will receive. Indeed, one of the great

Carpenters Building Wall by Ben Shahn.

advantages of no-strings-attached cash transfers is that a maximum amount of the budgeted funds go directly to the poor or unemployed; a minimum goes to middle-income professionals such as social workers.

A pure cash-payment strategy, whatever its merits, is unpopular precisely with the middle-income professionals who have a vested interest in their intermediary position—providers who furnish the housing for public housing and the food for school lunch programs, congressional committees that are responsible for in-kind programs and bureaucracies that administer them, not to mention millions of voters who believe they know better than welfare families how those families should allocate their all-too-scarce resources. Thus, the advantages of cash programs do not necessarily extend to the political arena.

A Labyrinth of Social Programs

A further series of problems arises from the labyrinth of categorical social programs. The problems here extend well beyond the income security area and include many educational, health, and housing programs. Most social programs are originally *categorical*: A rather narrow class of recipients or activities is authorized and a small amount of money, often modest enough to escape serious budgetary attention, is appropriated to finance the program. The money initially involved is usually far too small to satisfy the perceived need; where a particular category of recipients is involved, the money is often inadequate to reach more than a minute fraction of those nominally entitled.

Out of this situation a dynamic process develops that has plagued dozens of government programs during the last decade. The legislation creates an expectations gap. The problem defined in the legislation is so much larger than the means addressed to it that the government effort, rather than being welcomed, is viewed as pitifully inadequate. Second, amounts authorized by legislative committees grow more rapidly than do appropriations. As economists Lawrence Lynn and John Seidl (two informed and close students of categorical programs) have calculated, the gap between congressional authorizations and appropriations for Department of Health, Education and Welfare programs grew from 10 percent in 1961 to almost 150 percent in fiscal 1973 and nearly 200 percent in fiscal 1974. Filling that gap, they estimated, would have required an additional $250 billion per year in federal spending—in short, nearly a doubling of the federal budget.

For those who stand to gain from a particular program, this expectations gap represents a measure of the failure of the program and the stinginess of the public authorities. So long as anyone "deserving" is unserved, the pressure to increase appropriations is inexorable. For some programs the pressure to enlarge the recipient group also increases. For example, the school lunch program grew in a few years from a program for poor inner-city and rural children to become a program for suburban middle-class children as well. In programs where entitlements are involved, the courts have sustained legal actions by those entitled and have set aside regulations and upset other fiscal measures designed to hold down outlays. Meanwhile, the growth of each new categorical program creates a new set of interest groups—the recipients, the federal and state bureaucracies administering the program, and the providers of the goods and services for in-kind programs.

In areas such as education, health, housing, and manpower training, the Nixon and Ford administrations attempted to group categorical programs together and substitute block cash grants to states for them, but political resistance has prevented this "decategorization" from proceeding very far. In the income security area, the response of the Nixon administration to this "categorical" maze and to the other problems listed above was the Family Assistance Plan (which would have substituted cash payments for AFDC and food stamps and extended assistance to the working poor not qualifying for AFDC). The debate on this plan brought out many of the anomalies in the present set of programs, but in the end the reform proposal was defeated in Congress in 1970 and again in 1971—caught between those who found the proposed benefits too small and those who found the proposal too far-reaching. In 1974, a variation of the Family Assistance Plan was presented to President Ford, but the new proposal fell victim to a broader presidential decision to refrain from any new spending initiatives at a time when inflation was escalating. The costs of the present nonsystem, in terms of constraints on stabilization policy and the creation of social dependency, are so great that the question of reform must inevitably arise again.

Constructing a Comprehensive Program

No serious work can be done on constructing a comprehensive cash transfer program to replace the present crazy quilt of programs without recognizing the inevitability of a three-cornered trade-off. Any cash transfer program will have three key ingredients: (1) the basic benefit level, (2) the benefit-reduction rate, and (3) the break-even point. The basic benefit level is simply the amount to which any recipient will be entitled if the recipient has no other income. The benefit-reduction rate, which as described earlier is an implicit marginal tax rate, is the rate at which benefits are reduced as income rises. And the break-even point is that point at which, given the basic benefit level and the benefit-reduction rate, the recipient will no longer receive any income transfer. The way in which these three ingredients are mixed determines the adequacy, the cost, and the work-incentive effect of the plan. A three-way trade-off results because one cannot simultaneously maximize adequacy, minimize cost, and maximize the incentive to work.

The adequacy of the plan, from the standpoint of recipients, will turn on the level of the basic benefit and perhaps to a lesser extent on the benefit-reduction rate. But the greater the adequacy, the greater the cost. As a determinant of the cost of the program, the benefit-reduction rate is in one sense even more important than the basic benefit. This point is crucial, though often not fully appreciated, because the effect of the program on the incentive to work hinges on the benefit-reduction rate. The benefit-reduction rate bears heavily on cost because a low rate can cause the break-even point to rise to the level where relatively high-income families will be receiving some benefits. If, for example, the basic family benefit were $4,000 per year and if, to increase the incentive to work, the benefit-reduction rate were a modest 25 percent, the break-even point would be $16,000. A family with, say $12,000 of income would still receive a $1,000 cash transfer ($4,000 less 25 percent of $12,000). Such a plan would be impossibly costly because a majority of the population would receive some benefits. Not only would the cost be excessive, but a high break-even program would make tens of millions more Americans dependent on the government for a portion of their cash income.

This example is not extreme: The present food stamp program is so designed that, according to the Brookings Institution's 1976 budget study, about 10 percent of those people receiving food stamps have incomes above the national median. The eligible population has been estimated as high as 40 million people—the result of allowing various deductions from income before applying the benefit-reduction rate. Thus, high levels of income and consumption are compatible with eligibility, which shows that hidden within the three main concepts are a host of technical issues that require close analysis in constructing any new program. The benefit-reduction rate, for example, may be varied as income rises. There are strong reasons for preferring a benefit-reduction rate of zero for low amounts of income. Such a "disregard" of small amounts of income has a proportionately great work-incentive effect and can be compensated for by higher benefit-reduction rates near the break-even point.

A disregard of, say, $30 per month will tend to compensate for the fact that working costs money. Thus, assuming that the $30 just covers work expenses such as transportation, the cost of working does not unduly discourage work. Allowing a deduction for actual work expenses accomplishes the same result with greater precision, but it increases administrative costs dramatically and leads to more intervention in the recipient's life because of the inevitable political and administrative pressure to verify those expenses. Similarly, a disregard of small amounts of income encourages part-time work, which, in the absence of sufficient full-time jobs, is surely good for the economy and the individual. The unskilled worker, whose wages roughly equal the basic benefit and who is therefore the most likely recipient to be discouraged by benefit-reduction provisions, gains proportionately more from a disregard than from a uniform benefit-reduction rate costing the taxpayer the same amount.

The Family Assistance Plan set only a floor under benefits and looked to the states to supplement the federal benefit. The principal reason for this shared responsibility was that it paralleled the shared cost of AFDC. The cost of any new plan would be too great to accommodate within the federal budget if state AFDC supplementation were to be taken over by the federal government. Such state supplementation also allowed federal benefits to be uniform across the country while the state's share varied, providing higher total benefits in some parts of the country than others. Budgetary reality in any new plan is likely to lead to a basic benefit level that, though high enough in some states, will in fact be supplemented in others.

Therefore, it is necessary to consider the impact of state supplementation on the plan and particularly on the benefit-reduction rate. Unless the benefit-reduction rate used in the state supplementation scheme is subjected to federal regulation, it may not be possible to assure that the overall effect will be to provide an incentive to work. If, for example, the state supplementation were to be reduced by $1.00 for every $1.00 of income, then there would be no work incentive, whatever the federal benefit-reduction rate might be.

One of the most important questions about any new plan is how comprehensive it should be. Politically, interest groups have large stakes in existing programs. Conceptually, if one agrees that cash grants are superior to existing categorical programs, there is no policy reason not to substitute a comprehensive cash plan for all existing programs (other than unemployment insurance, which is already a cash plan that protects even high-income workers against income loss from temporary unemployment). This substitution of a comprehensive plan involving untied cash payments for categorical programs is usually called "cashing out."

The advantages of a comprehensive cash program are plain. The primary technical advantage is that many benefit-reduction rate and notch problems arising from the interaction of existing programs would disappear. Greater national uniformity would also be possible. A comprehensive cash plan would save money in the long run, if only because its existence would make it easier to resist new categorical programs in the future. Even voucher plans have the disadvantage that they tend to proliferate, with each new program piled on the one before, without adjustment in levels or attention to combined benefit-reduction rates. Although a proliferation of voucher programs has not yet occurred, housing stamps may well be just around the corner and fuel and transportation stamps have been proposed. Meanwhile, multiple participation in welfare programs has become the rule rather than the exception. Even as early as 1971, according to a Brookings Institution study, nearly all AFDC families were eligible for Medicaid, 68 percent received food stamps or surplus food, 59 percent participated in the school lunch program, and 13 percent lived in public housing.

Political realism dictates that no comprehensive cash plan would be accepted that substantially reduced welfare benefits. But the political barriers to cashing out go well beyond the political impossibility of reducing existing total benefits. Nineteen congressional committees now deal with income security matters. Aside from the logistical difficulties of multiple committee referral, few congressmen like to be cut out of the action by losing control over a program. Each program generates its own set of interest groups which, even if they cannot expand their program, may nevertheless be able to block its absorption into a broader program over which they would have less influence. These considerations have led some critics of the present system to oppose a comprehensive cash payments strategy, because they believe that at the end of the congressional day the various interest groups will have retained the existing programs and the comprehensive cash grants will simply be added on top. Or, they argue, even if a program is cashed out once, that does not guarantee that it will stay cashed out.

As thinking evolved within the executive branch after the legislative failure of the Family Assistance Plan, the advantages of tying any new cash plan more explicitly to the tax system became clearer. Conceptually, some economists have always thought of any comprehensive cash program as a negative income tax. After all, a system that pays more as income falls is to that extent the mirror image of the positive tax system; hence, the earliest proponents of comprehensive cash reform, such as Milton Friedman, have called their proposals a negative income tax.

More than a change in vocabulary was involved, however, in the executive branch rethinking. A negative income tax would be conceptually clearer than cashing out because the relationship between income and benefits would be more apparent. With a negative income tax, it would be more likely that the Internal Revenue Service would administer the scheme. The IRS is the best mass bureaucracy in Washington, it has demonstrated its ability to handle a complicated nationwide program, and its reputation for rectitude and persistence might lead to a reduction in the amount of welfare fraud. Yet, with some inevitable fraud involved in any welfare program, the IRS's reputation for efficiency might be clouded.

The greatest advantage of a negative income tax approach would not lie in the locus of administration, however, but rather in the fact that it could be integrated, at least in part, with the positive income tax. The break-even point for the negative income tax system would be the point at which taxes begin in the positive tax system. Integration of the positive and negative tax systems is not just conceptually satisfying; it would present an important advantage whenever expansion of welfare benefits is examined. Since outlays and taxes are not closely linked in the congressional mind, welfare benefits tend to be expanded without sufficient thought about where the revenues will come from to pay the benefits.

Just as a separate payroll tax has provided a counterweight to the tendency of social security benefits to grow, so too proponents of greater negative income tax benefits would have to accept that, unless they were prepared to break the link provided by the common break-even point, an increase in benefits would reduce the rate of taxation on positive income (by eliminating taxes on those taxpayers just above the break-even point and by increasing the amount exempt from taxation—either by increasing personal exemptions or by increasing the minimum standard deduction). Most likely, benefits would rise in a period of inflation and the consequent impact on the break-even point and the positive tax schedule would have an additional and desirable result: The tendency of inflation to increase the real burden of taxation on the taxpayer would be muted.

In addition to the greater conceptual clarity of a negative income tax, there are also lessons to be learned from the vast body of experience derived from positive tax legislation and administration. Many questions about the design of a comprehensive negative income tax plan have their counterparts in the positive tax system. Since income will determine the level of actual benefits for a recipient under any comprehensive plan, such a plan requires a definition of income, a definition of the recipient unit (family versus individual filing, etc.), and a definition of the period over which income is to be measured. Although these definitions under a negative income tax system would have to be different from those under a positive system, the experience under the positive system nonetheless helps to frame the technical issues. The Internal Revenue Code provides, in fact, a checklist of the issues to be resolved under any comprehensive negative income tax plan.

Take, for example, the definition of income. Although social security payments are excludable from income under the positive tax system, they would doubtless count against benefits in a negative income tax system.

Gifts are excludable from income in the positive system, but it may be desirable to treat various kinds of gifts differently under the negative system (such as parental gifts to college students). On the deduction side, should political contributions now deductible on the positive side also be deductible for measuring income for the purpose of determining benefits? To fail to do so might be thought to constitute political discrimination against the poor. Should capital gains be treated as fully taxable or should the special treatment in the positive tax system be accorded? What about municipal bond income? The questions go on and on. Many welfare systems fail to deal adequately with these questions, and as a result there is a great deal of administrative discretion built into benefit determination—a situation that may be one of the root causes of the present dissatisfaction with welfare administration.

Not all of the questions to be resolved are related to the positive tax issues. For example, under a negative tax system it may be desirable, or at least politically necessary, to consider assets as well as income. It is difficult to see why a person with a low income but with large holdings of non-dividend-paying common stock should receive full benefits. But an "assets test" creates many technical problems. For example, how should owner-occupied residences be treated? The equity in such residences is often large, particularly for homeowners who have been paying down their mortgages for decades, but to deny benefits to homeowners may require many low-income workers to sell their homes. And how is the value of a home to be measured? How should one treat an automobile? Does it make any difference whether the automobile is used to commute to work? Or that the particular benefit recipient has access to public transportation?

One can see the great technical complexity of any comprehensive cash payments plan. However, all of these issues arise in existing programs and are either poorly analyzed or committed in practice to the administrative discretion of a social worker or a low-paid functionary. We believe, not solely on the basis of personal conviction but more specifically as a result of studies that have been made within the executive branch, that these technical problems can be surmounted.

With the technical problems mastered, the advantages of a comprehensive negative income tax system would extend well beyond the welfare field. An income security program in this form would then provide a trade-on with fiscal and monetary policy by tempering the human tragedy resulting from the unemployment that is the unwanted by-product of anti-inflationary fiscal and monetary policies. Thus, an adequate and comprehensive negative income tax program could reduce the instinctive and understandable opposition to these key elements of economic policy.

So we are back to our starting point: the juxtaposition of the economic imperative of efficiency and the political imperative of equity. One of the arguments against a comprehensive negative income tax proposal is that it works against the discipline of the marketplace, in this case the discipline of the labor market on the tendency of wage rates to rise. This line of argument harks back to Karl Marx's notion of the "reserve army of the unemployed" as the disciplinary force of capitalism or, in a more modern version, to the Phillips curve relating rates of inflation and rates of unemployment, with a consequent emphasis on the trade-off.

What about that? First of all, the United States already has a gigantic income maintenance program. It is a patchwork and it is expensive. We can reasonably argue then that in the changeover to the type of program suggested here, the country need not spend much, if any, additional money. We are not proposing something brand-new; we are advocating doing much better something already attempted, with a greater incentive to work built into the system.

But beyond that we argue that the trade-off idea has been greatly oversold. Unemployment is not the primary discipline on the system. Certainly, labor markets do exert a discipline through unemployment, but the real discipline and the more powerful one comes from the effect of stringent monetary and fiscal policies on the product market. It is the difficulty in selling the product and maintaining a reasonable profit margin that causes the manager to try to save on his costs. He looks at his labor costs, but he looks at all the other costs as well. It is astounding, for example, what American industry has saved in response to the rising cost of energy. Conservation of 10 to 20 percent is common, and many cases can be cited of much larger percentage savings. Discipline operates across the board in all markets, not just labor markets. It is extremely difficult to believe that when there are 19 out of 20 in the labor force employed, the movement from 5 percent to 7 percent unemployed is what is disciplining the whole economic system.

A sweeping change in the existing income security system would thus be a most constructive step. Establishing a comprehensive cash system of income maintenance through a negative income tax would help to solve many problems energy, housing, inflation by making it more possible to let the market do its work. It would help to make the tax system more rational and would be easier to administer than the present labyrinth of programs. Yet a comprehensive cash income maintenance system is not merely a matter of fiscal prudence. If we fail to undertake such reform, the spiraling growth of existing categorical programs for the poor will, in the end, break the federal budget without ever achieving effective delivery of resources to the poor.

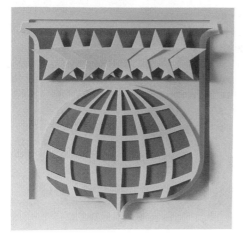

International Economic Policy

THE MOVEMENTS FOR MONETARY and trade reform that began in 1971 and are still, to an important degree, under way take place in separate international organizations peopled by different individuals. In most governments, international monetary policy lies within the domain of the finance ministry (such as the U.S. Treasury Department) whereas international trade policy is generally handled by an industry ministry (such as the U.S. Commerce Department). A similar division of responsibility prevails in international organizations. Monetary matters are primarily the province of the International Monetary Fund (IMF). Trade, particularly trade negotiations, is largely the responsibility of an organization that bears the name of the agreement it administers, the General Agreement on Tariffs and Trade (GATT). The line between these two organizations is sharply drawn. One is seldom in doubt as to whether a particular issue is a General Agreement matter or an International Monetary Fund matter.

When, at one point in the work of international monetary reform, we in the U.S. Treasury thought about a merger between the two organizations, the general reaction within the government was that although the idea made theoretical sense, such a merger was unthinkable in practice. Not only would both international organizations resist the merger, it was argued, but, because such a merger would adversely affect the fortunes of one of the ministries having responsibility for money and trade, so would every foreign government. Here one sees the interdependence between international organization and the division of authority within national governments.

Yet the distinction between trade and money makes little economic sense. Barter being rare, every sale of goods is simultaneously a trade matter and a money matter. An export (or import) involves a payment. Money and trade are closely linked in policy, not just in actual transactions. An import surcharge is in effect a currency devaluation: It alters the rate of exchange for goods subject to the surcharge. Unlike a devaluation, of course, it leaves the exchange rate untouched for services and capital transactions. A surcharge affects only imports, but an export subsidy can have the same effect on exports that a surcharge has on imports. Thus, surcharges and subsidies may be, for policymakers, short-term substitutes for exchange rate changes. A government might seek to reduce imports, for example, either by a surcharge or by exchange rate depreciation.

Trade measures often support exchange rate policies. In 1970 and 1971 many in the U.S. government believed that some countries with persistent balance-of-trade surpluses (particularly Japan) were protecting their surplus position for the benefit of their exporters through trade measures restraining imports. Against this background U.S. officials frequently emphasized the importance of trade matters in international monetary discussions. Perhaps the most significant result of this emphasis was the 1974 Declaration on Trade Measures, in which each member of the International Monetary Fund subscribing to the Declaration undertook not to introduce or intensify trade measures without a prior finding by the IMF that there was a balance-of-payments justification for such measures.

We place international monetary policy and international trade policy in separate chapters since each does have an institutional life of its own. Still, it is important to recognize that at the apex of government economic decision making, they often become a single issue, as was the case in the early 1970s when the overvaluation of the dollar had the effect of unnaturally stimulating imports and discouraging U.S. exports at the expense of U.S. industry and labor.

CHAPTER SIX

International Monetary Policy

INTERNATIONAL MONETARY AFFAIRS provide an uncommonly difficult terrain for the policymaker. The subject is preeminently the specialist's. The intelligent citizen knows little of exchange rates, gold, and capital flows. Even businessmen and economists in government defer to international monetary specialists in a way they would never defer on issues of fiscal policy or domestic monetary policy. Yet international monetary policy can be just as important as domestic fiscal or monetary policy. The exchange rate—the price of one currency in relation to other currencies—is the most important price in an economy. Under a fixed exchange rate system, for instance, the domestic money supply is clearly related to foreign money supplies; domestic monetary authorities consequently have less control over their own money supplies than is commonly assumed.

In fact, the most important economic events in the U.S. during the early 1970s may not have been the imposition of wage or price controls, nor the large budget deficits, nor the Federal Reserve's money supply policies. At least as important were the closing of the "gold window" in August 1971 (ending U.S. willingness to exchange gold for dollars at a set price) coupled with the twin devaluations of the dollar in December 1971 and February 1973 and the emergence of a system of market-determined (floating) exchange rates.

The complexity and transcendent importance of international monetary policy have led to the creation of special decision-making institutions to direct it. The Treasury and the Federal Reserve Board have always considered this field their special preserve and have seldom welcomed advice from other parts of the executive branch. (The Secretary and chairman are now, respectively, governor and alternate governor of the International Monetary Fund [IMF], which has a large staff of its own and brings together leading officials from 129 countries.) Yet the political significance of international monetary negotiations and of changes in exchange rates are profound. Although foreign policy officials, for example the redoubtable Henry Kissinger, more or less ignored monetary matters so long as the fixed rate system was in effect, they quickly learned after August 1971 that they could not afford to leave the question to the experts. Similarly, although it would be an exceptional President who concerned himself with international monetary matters on a continuing basis, no major change in international monetary policy could be carried through without the President's concurrence and support.

The Path to Camp David

Because the early 1970s were marked by such far-reaching changes in the international monetary system, it is difficult to analyze the recurring questions of decision making in this area without an understanding of the events of that period and the institutional arrangements then in place.

The President's Camp David decision on the weekend of August 15, 1971, made with the full support of his economic advisers, marked a turning point in U.S. policies toward the international monetary system. The U.S. commitment to buy and sell gold at the fixed price of $35 per ounce had long been the keystone of the fixed exchange rate system that had evolved from agreements made among nations in the international trading community at Bretton Woods, New Hampshire, in 1944. The President's August 15 decision to end that commitment came as a surprise, if not a shock, to the international financial community. Yet in an important sense it was inevitable. Not only was that decision inescapable, but it had been delayed for so many years that in the end it could be postponed no longer, perhaps not even for another day. By then, dollars in the hands of foreign governments exceeded by three times the dollar value of gold at Fort Knox. A British demand for conversion of dollars into gold (or its equivalent in guarantees) was made in the course of the preceding week and forced final decisions to be made by the weekend. If the British demand had been honored, it would surely have started a "run" on the Fort.

How did the United States get into such a predicament? After World War II the world had suffered from a shortage of dollars: The war-ravaged economies of Europe and Japan had a great demand and need for U.S. goods, but lacked the dollars to pay for them. The United States provided those dollars through loans and foreign aid, thereby incurring a persistent balance-of-payments deficit. By the time this dollar shortage disappeared in the 1950s and the U.S. began persistently losing gold, U.S. officials and politicians had become so accustomed to the dollar-shortage world that for some years they failed to notice that a new and, for the United States, more troubling world had emerged. When the deficits continued, despite the recovery of the European and Japanese economies, the official reaction was to treat the condition as temporary. The U.S. trade account was showing a surplus, and the payments deficit was "caused" by outflows of dollars in the forms of foreign aid, foreign costs of U.S. military programs, and investment by U.S. firms in other countries. A series of palliatives followed, one upon another, throughout the 1960s as the government tried to deal with the consequences of what by then had become an overvalued dollar, held at a value above its free market price by the U.S. commitment to exchange the dollar for gold at $35 per ounce.

In 1964 Congress authorized and the Treasury Department imposed an *interest equalization tax* on the acquisition of foreign securities, thereby slowing their acquisition by making them more expensive. This tax may have succeeded for a few years in reducing foreign borrowing in the United States, with its consequent outflow of dollars, but it also led inexorably to the displacement of New York as the world's leading capital market center. In 1965 the Commerce Department adopted a voluntary program restricting the growth of private investment by U.S. corporations outside the country, particularly in Europe. (When this voluntary program failed to achieve the desired results, the Commerce Department made the *foreign direct investment program* mandatory in 1968.) Also in 1965 the Federal Reserve introduced a parallel voluntary *foreign credit restraint program* to reduce bank lending to foreigners. Because the Fed's influence over banks far exceeded the Commerce Department's influence over manufacturing corporations, it was never necessary to make mandatory these restraints on the freedom of U.S. banks to extend credits outside the U.S.

All three of these programs—the Treasury Department's interest equalization tax, the Commerce Department's foreign direct investment program, and the Federal Reserve's foreign credit restraint guidelines—were merely disguised forms of exchange controls. The U.S. government was attempting to control directly an outflow of dollars that it could not stem, or at least was unwilling to try to stem, either by taking stringent anti-inflationary fiscal and monetary measures or by devaluing the dollar in an attempt to establish a new rate at which, presumably, the outflow would have ceased.

As it became clearer that these direct controls were not working, the U.S. devoted more and more attention to alternatives. On the international front, U.S. negotiators sought, and eventually obtained, an expansion of international liquidity through the creation of Special Drawing Rights (SDRs), under which member nations of the International Monetary Fund short on hard currencies could obtain them without using gold (SDRs were therefore labeled "paper gold"). This action postponed the day when the United States would have to face up to the weakness of the dollar. Meanwhile, great emphasis was placed on reducing U.S. government expenditures abroad, sometimes at the cost of increasing expenditures at home by more than an equal amount. For example, troops stationed abroad were supplied with items purchased in the U.S. at prices above those charged locally. (The excess spending became known as the Defense Department's "gold budget.")

Throughout the 1960s and well into the Nixon administration, more and more emphasis was placed on increasing U.S. exports as a way of achieving payments balance. The Export-Import Bank, a government financing agency dating from the Depression, was rapidly expanded as a way of financing the greater volume of exports. Although the Bank theoretically was supposed to provide government financing when private financing was unavailable, in reality it increasingly provided financing at interest rates well under those available in the private market. It thereby subsidized the effective price (the price including the cost of financing) of U.S. exports in world markets and provided a selective devaluation of the dollar on the export side.

In 1971 the administration proposed and Congress enacted a further subsidy to exports, this time through the tax system. By creating a direct investment sales corporation, a U.S. enterprise could postpone taxation and thereby enjoy a lower rate of taxation on income from exports than on domestic sales.

The interest in subsidizing exports, whether by low-rate loans or through the tax system, is partly economic and partly political. The economic interest, as we have seen, is merely one of avoiding more fundamental economic measures. The political incentive stems from the fact that greater exports mean more jobs, at least in the short run. Few people realize that exporting is costly to an economy in the sense that it consumes real goods and services. Export subsidies are justifiable from a policy perspective as a means of paying for imports or serving other national objectives, such as providing foreign aid or conducting military or diplomatic activities abroad. The subsidies through the Export-Import Bank and the tax system are often viewed as essentially costless because they make possible new exports and, in periods of unemployment, jobs that would not otherwise exist. It is even argued that the new jobs and greater corporate profits generate extra tax revenues that exceed the cost of the subsidy. For these reasons export subsidies and other export promotion activities inevitably have a wide political constituency.

The political concern with exports and jobs took on exceptional urgency when the progressive overvaluation of the dollar coincided with the 1970 recession. The United States was said to be, in the phrase of the time, "pricing itself out of world markets." At the same time, imports were threatening the viability of certain basic industries, such as autos and steel. Some observers thought that the United States was becoming a "service economy" and worried about the social and international implications of an economy without basic industries. A few stopgap attempts to protect special industries had already been made, notably the 1962 Long-Term Arrangement in Cotton Textiles and the 1968 voluntary steel quotas under which various foreign producer associations agreed to restrict their shipments into the U.S. market.

By 1971 the domestic political effects of increasing imports could not be overlooked. Japanese automobiles were "flooding" the market in California. The labor movement, a proponent of reducing tariffs and freeing trade during the two decades following World War II, had returned to its protectionist tradition and was actively pushing the Burke-Hartke bill, which would have imposed import quotas on a wide variety of goods. Here one sees not only the interconnections between international monetary and trade policies and between international monetary policy and domestic employment policies, but also the domestic political significance of international monetary policies.

Overvaluation of the U.S. dollar had important international political effects as well. On the one hand, the governments of our major trading partners, also aware of the importance of exports to jobs and hence to domestic political support, were quite content with the converse of our overvaluation—namely the undervaluation of their own currencies, which facilitated exports to the United States and made their exports more competitive with U.S. exports in third-country markets. But these governments did not like the side effects of the dollar's overvaluation. As a result of our balance-of-payments deficits and the widespread intervention of foreign monetary authorities in the foreign exchange markets to prevent their own currencies from appreciating, official holdings of dollars by foreign central banks escalated. Their holdings grew from $14.9 billion at the end of 1966 to $23.8 billion at the end of 1970 and to $36.2 billion by July 30, 1971. These countries urged the United States to "adjust," meaning that we should pursue a stronger anti-inflationary policy. At the same time, they did not favor a policy so anti-inflationary as to produce a

U.S. recession, which would have reduced the demand for their exports in the U.S. market. In the meantime, the U.S. government, unwilling to let its domestic fiscal and monetary policies be controlled by balance-of-payments considerations, hoped that the exchange rate problem could be solved by appreciation of foreign currencies rather than by devaluation of the dollar.

Thus, the decision was made at Camp David on the weekend of August 15, 1971, to terminate the U.S. unilateral undertaking to convert dollars into gold at the fixed price of $35 per ounce. It was forced by the almost certain run on the bank that was expected when the foreign holders of dollars sought to convert those dollars into gold before the U.S. holdings disappeared. By August 15 foreign official holdings of dollars totaled about $40 billion, more than three times U.S. gold holdings of about $12 billion (valued at $35 per ounce). Although the U.S. government attached no great importance to the gold as such, a run on this gold would have been a sorry spectacle, almost surely weakening the U.S. government's capacity to negotiate a new exchange rate regime. A valuable claim on foreign goods and services would also have been dissipated since the dollar price of gold and therefore the purchasing power of our gold holdings would almost surely rise.

The more important and more positive purpose of the August 15 decision was to force a change in existing exchange rates. The United States wanted to bring about an appreciation of the currencies of its major trading partners or, what was largely the other side of the same coin, a devaluation of the dollar. Because of the impetus given to their exports by the current exchange rates, the major European governments and the Japanese government had been unwilling to agree to such a change, even in the face of tough talk from Secretary of the Treasury John Connally.

The international aspects of the Camp David decisions, then, had to do with more than simply the defensive act of closing the gold window. We recognized that the United States could not simply announce a devaluation, as Britain did in 1967 and as France had done repeatedly in the postwar period. Our trading partners had become accustomed to having the United States play the role of the passive center of a fixed exchange rate system. They would probably seek to maintain the relative values of their currencies to the U.S. dollar. Technically, a U.S. devaluation was an increase in the dollar price of gold. Other governments could have engaged in a competitive devaluation, leaving their export position untouched, by the simple device of declaring a similar increase in the value of their currency in terms of gold and buying dollars in exchange markets to preserve the existing rate. Since some of these governments, particularly France, hoped to see an increase in the price of gold in any event, such a competitive devaluation was thought likely.

We realized that foreign governments would have to agree to a change in exchange rates (which at that time U.S. officials hoped would take the form of appreciation of foreign currencies rather than of depreciation of the dollar). We wanted to get their attention, to make them realize how serious we were, and to equip our negotiator, Secretary Connally, with more tools for bargaining. A 10 percent import surcharge—an implicit devaluation on the import side, an attention-getter, and a bargaining chip—was therefore introduced in the August 15 package. Although we knew that economists could and would show that the import surcharge had a perverse market effect by reducing U.S. imports and thereby offsetting the tendency for the U.S. dollar to weaken on the exchange markets, we regarded the surcharge as a temporary part of our negotiating strategy. It was designed to be a signal that the United States was seeking a fundamental change not only in existing exchange rates but also in the monetary system itself.

Secretary Connally flashed the signal in true Texas style, with both guns blazing in the corridors of international finance. He did gain the attention of foreign governments at the highest level and used the surcharge effectively in negotiations. It was withdrawn when a new set of exchange relationships, resulting in a devaluation of the dollar in terms of gold of 7.9 percent, was agreed upon at the Smithsonian Institution in December 1971.

Although negotiations were important in arriving at the new rates, market forces had resulted in a de facto change in many of the rates well before December. When private holders of dollars became convinced that the United States intended to force a change in exchange rates and was capable of doing so, they began to convert their dollars into other currencies. To maintain existing exchange rates in the face of these private flows, foreign monetary authorities had to absorb immense amounts of dollars in the exchange markets. Even before the Smithsonian agreement in December, a new series of rates had emerged in the market. The German mark and Japanese yen had appreciated by the middle of December by over 12 percent and the Smithsonian agreement provided for a 13.58 percent and 16.88 percent change, respectively, in the new central exchange rates over the old official rates. In essence, U.S. officials had formed an alliance with the market itself to force a change in the behavior of foreign officials.

Connections Between Monetary and Foreign Policies

From a political point of view, the import surcharge and the alliance with market forces were strong medicine. Foreign governments began to react and took their grievances not merely to U.S. monetary officials but also to U.S. foreign policy officials. Henry Kissinger, who at that early point was not much involved with economic affairs, could readily see that economic developments were having an important impact on international diplomatic relationships. He therefore engineered a series of international conferences between the President and foreign leaders designed to calm troubled international waters and to force U.S. economic officials to come to terms with their counterparts in other countries. These meetings led directly to the Smithsonian.

In the most important of these meetings President Nixon met with President Pompidou of France in the Azores on December 13-14. The meeting was, in governmental jargon, an "action-forcing event" that led to an agreement between the two countries. The United States abandoned its insistence that foreign governments revalue their currencies without any U.S. devaluation, and in a partial reinstatement of the fixed exchange rate system, the two countries committed themselves to maintain market exchange rates at or near agreed central-rate levels. The joint statement negotiated at the meeting provided that France and the United States would "work toward a prompt realignment of exchange rates through a devaluation of the dollar and revaluation of some other currencies."

Without this bilateral agreement the Smithsonian multilateral agreement of December 18 would undoubtedly have come much later and might not have included any understanding on the nature of the exchange rate regime. Indeed, without the intervention of Kissinger the devaluation of the dollar would almost surely have been greater, thereby obviating any need for a further devaluation in February 1973, and the predominant role of market forces would have been more apparent. Moreover, that part of the Smithsonian agreement which partially reestablished the fixed exchange rate system might not have been settled upon, and the world might have moved more quickly to the managed floating regime that was adopted de facto in 1973.

Whatever might have happened if economic forces had been allowed free rein, events showed how difficult it is to separate international economic policy from foreign diplomatic policy. Although the intervention of Kissinger caused the accommodation between our economic and our political interests to be made earlier than would otherwise have been the case, some sort of accommodation was inevitable. U.S. monetary officials could not have continued indefinitely on a path that might have led to a rupture of our diplomatic relations with Europe, with all of the implications that such a rupture might have had for our national security interests and perhaps in the end for our military arrangements with the Europeans within NATO.

Domestic Aspects of the Camp David Decisions

Thus far we have discussed the decisions of August 15 and their aftermath solely from an international perspective. But the decision to seek an exchange rate change was of great domestic importance, both political and economic. Under a system of fixed exchange rates governments committed themselves firmly and visibly to the inviolability of existing rates. The determination of financial officials to "defend the currency" would discourage speculation forcing an undesired rate change. As a result, any government's decision to devalue was inevitably interpreted as a signal of defeat on the domestic political front. If devaluation was an admission of failure for most governments, how much more likely it would be that the U.S. public, unfamiliar with international monetary matters but accustomed so long to the almighty dollar as the invincible currency, would draw the same political conclusion. The fear that devaluation would have this kind of domestic political backlash shaped the August 15 decisions in several important ways.

First, wage and price controls were also introduced on August 15. Whether such controls would ever have been introduced if devaluation had not been necessary is one of the great "what ifs" of recent U.S. economic history, but the linking of devaluation with controls transformed this situation. Precisely because the pressure for controls had been so great—with the Democratic party, many of its allies in organized labor, and the bulk of the business community (which apparently read "wage and price controls" simply as "wage controls") actively advocating their introduction—the imposition of controls was an immensely popular political act. It dominated the news and was regarded as a sign of presidential strength, manifesting concrete action against inflation. It therefore diverted public attention from the mysterious act of "closing the gold window" and swamped any tendency to regard the devaluation aspect of the August 15 decisions as weakness.

Second, the decision to impose the "temporary" import surcharge and to push initially for revaluation of foreign currencies, as opposed to devaluation of the dollar, put the administration on the offensive. John Connally had the political prescience to realize that waving the red flag of the import surcharge in the face of foreigners (who were being blamed for the flooding of U.S. markets with "cheap" goods and thereby for a loss of U.S. jobs) would be immensely popular at home. His aggressive posture dominated attitudes toward these events and, remarkably, the devaluation came to be seen at home as a victory of U.S. foreign policy and hence a political asset for the President and for Connally.

Our objective in pushing for revaluation of foreign currencies, however, went far beyond domestic considerations. As discussed earlier, we wanted not only an exchange rate change but also a fundamental reform of the international monetary system. Under the old system of fixed exchange rates, the burden had typically been on countries with balance-of-payments deficits to devalue rather than on countries with payments surpluses to revalue. The U.S. demand for foreign appreciation was the opening shot in a battle to impose symmetrical responsibilities on countries with payments surpluses. Thus, domestic politics and international negotiating strategy converged behind the same approach.

Third, uncertainty as to the congressional reaction to a devaluation of the dollar was a further ground for the U.S. demand for revaluation of foreign currencies rather than devaluation of the dollar. Although as a pure exchange rate matter appreciation of an undervalued currency and depreciation of an overvalued currency were equivalent, they differed on the congressional front. Devaluation of the dollar required an increase in the official price of gold, and such an increase required legislation. Moreover, devaluation of the dollar required an increase in terms of dollars of U.S. contingent commitments to various international organizations (such as the World Bank) under the maintenance-of-value provisions of their charters. These additional funds might in fact never have to be paid, but the increase in these commitments might make devaluation look extremely expensive to a congressional committee. If our trading partners were to revalue their currencies, congressional action would not be required.

Unlike many situations where congressional action may be necessary to support a foreign policy initiative, there was little or no opportunity for consultation with Congress before August 15. Any suggestion that the United States was about to close the gold window would have precipitated the very run on the gold bank that U.S. officials blocked by closing that window.

However, through extensive consultation by Secretary Connally after August 15 with the principal members of Congress concerned with international monetary issues, notably Representatives Wilbur Mills and Henry Reuss and Senators Jacob Javits and Russell Long, and through their efforts in turn with their colleagues, a broad understanding was developed within Congress as to the need for devaluation. When major foreign governments flatly refused to revalue their currencies and when over the next few months the exchange markets forced a change in de facto exchange rates, these members of Congress were able to assure U.S. officials that congressional approval of the change in the dollar price of gold and the increase in terms of dollars of international organization commitments would be forthcoming. In effect, they persuaded their colleagues that at least under these extraordinary circumstances, international monetary policy could not be subjected to the usual political struggle in Congress. The Smithsonian agreement of December 1971 followed promptly, and Congress supported that agreement by passing the necessary legislation.

Toward Reform: Substance and Procedure

Once the realignment of exchange rates had been achieved, attention turned to the question of international monetary reform. From the U.S. viewpoint, the goal of reform was not simply to impose on countries with payments surpluses some of the burden of adjustment but also to gain for the United States some of the freedom of action for its own exchange rate that was available to all other countries, whether they had payments deficits or surpluses. Symmetrical freedom of action for the dollar seemed crucial to the pursuit of sensible fiscal and monetary policies at home. The Smithsonian rates could not be expected to be "right" forever, and if the dollar subsequently became overvalued or indeed if it proved to be still overvalued despite the Smithsonian realignment, U.S. officials did not want fiscal and monetary flexibility constrained by worries over balance-of-payments deficits or over unemployment created by imports of goods from countries with undervalued currencies.

But there were a number of questions to be answered within the U.S. government before reform of the monetary system could be achieved. There was no consensus within our government as to what specific reform objectives (beyond the general goals just stated) should be sought in the upcoming negotiations. To achieve the flexibility it desired, should the United States push for a system of floating exchange rates? Or should it be content to live with the modified fixed exchange rate system implicit in the Smithsonian formula of agreed central rates with somewhat widened bands for fluctuations of actual rates on the exchange markets? The Europeans clearly preferred a fixed exchange rate system.

Within the U.S. government, opinion was also divided over the role of gold in the reformed system. Should gold be completely phased out? Or should it be maintained as a reserve, with the United States perhaps one day to stand ready once more to buy and sell gold at a fixed price? The Europeans, particularly the French, were much more interested in preserving a central role for gold than were any key U.S. officials. In short, no agreement was at first in sight on the nature and degree of reform to be sought.

The executive branch agencies that dealt on the most intimate terms with foreign governments favored reestablishment of the fixed exchange rate system and maintenance of a major role for gold. The Federal Reserve was in constant contact with foreign central bankers and tended to share their views of the value of fixed parities and gold. Similarly, the State Department and the National Security Council staff were sensitive to the diplomatic problems any demand for fundamental change would undoubtedly generate. The Treasury Department, the Council of Economic Advisers, and the Office of Management and Budget, on the other hand,

STEVENSON

"O.K. *The forward rate for marks rose in March and April, combined with a sharp increase in German reserves and heavy borrowing in the Eurodollar market, while United States liquid reserves had dropped to fourteen billion dollars, causing speculation that the mark might rise and encouraging conversion on a large scale. Now do you understand?"*

tended to be more concerned with the constraints that a return to fixed parities and a U.S. gold commitment might have on domestic economic policy.

Even if it had been possible to agree internally on fundamental reform as an objective, it was not clear whether to move incrementally, changing a detail here and a detail there in the fixed exchange rate system, or whether to lay on the table a broad plan for monetary reform. The incremental approach was favored by most other countries, both because they did not favor major change and because they mistrusted rapid change in monetary matters. A related issue was whether additional flexibility for the United States was to be accomplished by a change in the rules or by ad hoc management. In other words, should the Articles of Agreement of the International Monetary Fund be changed to describe a new, fundamentally reformed system? Or could the flexibility desired by the United States be created through bilateral negotiations with countries with payments surpluses, various multilateral arrangements (such as those worked out in the 1960s within the Group of Ten), and short-term ad hoc agreements on exchange market intervention practices?

Finally, the choice of the forum for negotiation was itself an important matter to be resolved. Any new rules would most likely take the form of amendments to the Articles of Agreement of the International Monetary Fund, but that did not mean that the negotiations had to take place within the framework of the Fund. The IMF staff, with its attachment to a fixed exchange rate system, could hardly be completely objective and disinterested. Any move toward generalized floating might be expected to reduce the role of the Fund as a lender of reserves since official reserves would presumably have a more limited role under a floating system.

But the alternatives to the IMF as a forum had other drawbacks. Bilateral negotiations with major countries might be a first step toward agreement, but they could hardly accomplish a change in multilateral rules. The Group of Ten was another possibility, and indeed the Smithsonian agreement was reached at a ministerial meeting of this group. But to U.S. negotiators it seemed too much like a "nine against one club," to use Secretary Connally's phrase. Five of the ten countries were members of the European Economic Community (EEC), and those five—France, Italy, West Germany, the Netherlands, and Belgium—caucused before meetings. With the entry into the Community of Great Britain at the beginning of 1973, a majority of the Group of Ten would be EEC members. Normal protocol at meetings required that the EEC members each be able to repeat the Common Market view, while the United States could state its view only once. The other three members—Japan, Canada, and Sweden—had independent views, more often opposed to U.S. views than in accord with them. In short, the United States wanted a forum in which its inherent economic and financial power could not be offset by procedural conventions.

The Group of Ten had the further disadvantage that less-developed countries were not members. Not only would the developed countries have to come to terms with the demands of the developing nations for a "link" between international monetary reform and development assistance, but U.S. officials hoped—mistakenly as it turned out—that an alliance between the United States and the less-developed countries might be possible on at least some issues in the reform negotiations.

The forum question was resolved by creating a new committee within the framework of the International Monetary Fund. The effect of its creation was to move the negotiations out of the Fund proper, thereby reducing the influence of the Fund staff. The negotiations would not be handled by the IMF's executive directors who, although representatives of their governments, were nevertheless civil servants personally close to the Fund staff and in some cases may have had a stake in preservation of the pre-1971 role of the IMF. Rather, the negotiations would be handled at the ministerial and senior subcabinet level among governments. It was thought that this new forum would make possible a more far-reaching reform agreement and would make it difficult for the IMF staff to become an independent force in the negotiations.

The new group became known as the Committee of 20 (the C-20) in view of its membership of 20 countries or groups of countries. Each country with an executive director in the IMF (or constituency in the case of small countries that shared an executive director) was entitled to membership in the new committee. This membership was as broad as that of the Fund and thus permitted participation by less-developed countries, as well as by those developed countries that had not been members of the Group of Ten. At the same time, the organization of the smaller countries into constituencies represented by a single spokesman prevented the highly technical negotiations from taking on the town hall aspects of many large international conferences.

The C-20 was not to be the sole forum for negotiations. Aside from important bilateral consultations, the Group of Ten also continued to meet from time to time. Moreover, when crucial questions involving principally the largest countries arose or when progress in negotiations required a prior agreement among those countries, ad hoc meetings were held among the finance ministers (sometimes accompanied by heads of central banks) of the United States, West Germany, the United Kingdom, France, and Japan. Although described in the press as Group of Five meetings, the group had no staff or secretariat whatsoever. The meetings simply reflected the importance of the personal element in international negotiations. Finance ministers needed to understand each other well since, as the largest countries recognized, they had both the largest stake in, and the largest responsibility for, the outcome of the C-20 negotiations. It was important that the highest-level negotiators be able to come together under circumstances permitting them to share ideas and views, free from the protocol and paraphernalia of a large international conference. That these meetings were often referred to as the Group of Five was more a reflection of the desire of the press and the national bureaucracies to catagorize what was happening than of the creation of yet another international organization.

Control of Negotiations

Placing the negotiations within the C-20 also placed leadership of the U.S. negotiating team in the Treasury Department. The C-20 was an IMF committee and the Treasury traditionally handled Fund work within the government. Had some other forum been chosen or created, it would have been conceivable for the State Department to lead such negotiations. In fact, after the oil crisis erupted in late 1973, the State Department increasingly began to handle negotiations, often jointly with the Treasury, that had important financial aspects. Similarly, the Federal Reserve from time to time handles financial arrangements with other governments. Trade negotiations, which obviously are closely related to monetary negotiations, are run out of an office in the Executive Office of the President. A new White House office for monetary negotiations would have been a possibility.

Control of negotiations often affects the outcome because of the differing policy views of the various U.S. government agencies, especially their relative sensitivity to diplomatic as opposed to economic considerations. What then were the advantages to the U.S. of Treasury control of the international monetary negotiations? Reflection on this question may serve to shed some light on the impact of governmental organization on international negotiations and to indicate why governmental agencies sometimes struggle not merely over policy but also over leadership of negotiating teams. The importance of this question is underscored by the probability that if the State Department had been in control from the outset, some international forum other than the C-20 might have been chosen.

Two preliminary points must, however, be kept in mind. First, all interested U.S. government agencies were involved in defining the negotiating objectives of the Treasury negotiators. Second, the President was always ultimately in charge. Although no President could be expected to take a day-by-day interest in such a complex, technical subject, President

Nixon became personally involved at each fork of the negotiating road. Moreover, other agencies could and in the case of the Federal Reserve and the National Security Council staff under Kissinger frequently *did* raise issues for presidential decision.

The most important advantage of Treasury control of the U.S. negotiating team was that all of the delegations of the other major countries were headed by finance ministry officials. To have placed the negotiations in other hands in the United States would have created practical difficulties. When, after Kissinger became Secretary of State in 1973, some negotiating responsibilities (on energy, for example) were taken over by the State Department that were handled in other governments by finance ministries, various problems arose. Placing an issue in State Department channels virtually assured that in other countries the foreign ministries would have to take an active interest; this fact created confusion and sometimes bureaucratic struggles within other governments. Another difficulty was that although the staffs of financial ministries knew each other well across national boundaries, as did the staffs of foreign ministries, such a relationship did not exist between the U.S. State Department and foreign finance ministries. To have placed the responsibility for international monetary negotiations other than in the U.S. Treasury Department would almost surely have made the negotiations more difficult, certainly more formal, and might have led to misunderstandings.

Placing the negotiations in the hands of the Federal Reserve would also have led to these problems and to several others besides. In some countries the central bank is under the direct control of the finance ministry. To place the negotiations at the central bank level would have tended to downgrade the negotiations, making compromise more difficult where important national interests were at stake. Even in the United States, though the Federal Reserve is independent for most purposes, it is well understood that independence ends at the water's edge and that the Federal Reserve is to take policy direction from the Treasury.

The Treasury differs in several major respects from foreign finance ministries. In the first place, the budget function, which in most countries is one of the most important responsibilities of the finance ministry, was transferred to the Executive Office of the President under President Franklin Roosevelt and is now in the hands of the Office of Management and Budget. A second difference stems from the fundamental constitutional choice of a presidential rather than a cabinet form of government. In the United States the Secretary of the Treasury is often a nonpolitical figure. In a cabinet government, by contrast, the Finance Minister is usually a major political figure and often a leading candidate to succeed the Prime Minister. Because of the combination of budget and other financial func-

"Damn it! How <u>can</u> I relax, knowing that out there, somewhere, somehow, someone's attacking the dollar?"

tions, the Finance Minister is often the most powerful cabinet member below the Prime Minister. For these reasons the Finance Minister in most governments is recognized as being in charge of economic issues in a way that the U.S. Secretary of the Treasury often is not.

Placing negotiating responsibility in the Treasury in the United States assured that the negotiations in other governments would be kept in the hands of the finance ministry. Keeping the negotiations in finance ministry channels maximized the probability that decisions would be made on economic as well as more purely diplomatic grounds and that if the negotiations reached the stage of major compromises of national interests, the finance ministers would be likely to have the domestic political power to gain acceptance within their own government for whatever bargain they might negotiate internationally.

The U.S. Reform Initiative

After the Smithsonian agreement, for many months little progress was achieved toward any kind of international agreement on the future shape of the monetary system. The absence of any serious negotiations created an increasingly unpromising atmosphere in international monetary circles. At the very time that agreement on goals and negotiating strategies was becoming more elusive within the U.S. government, it was becoming clearer that only the United States was in a position to launch a major initiative for negotiations. No other country had both the financial prestige and the political will to do so. The alliance among the other major countries was negative in character—strong enough perhaps to oppose any U.S. effort but not strong enough to pull together a concrete proposal that could serve as a basis for negotiations.

In the summer of 1972 we developed in the Treasury Department a central idea for a plan for reform: a system in which exchange rates could move freely and could be based on an agreement to limit changes in reserves (whereas the Bretton Woods system had been based upon an international agreement not to change exchange rates, except in the case of what the Articles of Agreement of the Fund described as "fundamental disequilibrium"). Under a system of freely floating exchange rates, reserves would be fairly constant because they would not be used to intervene in exchange markets to maintain existing rates. Further, a system based on agreements as to reserve levels would have the advantage of symmetry: As much attention would be focused on countries with payments surpluses as on those with deficits, thereby generating pressure to induce surplus countries to allow their currencies to appreciate rather than to pile up reserves.

A full-scale U.S. reform proposal was developed from this simple core idea. The process of development insured wide support in the U.S. government, since the proposal emerged from many long meetings among the individuals principally concerned: Secretary of State William Rogers, Federal Reserve Board Chairman Arthur Burns, Chairman of the Council of Economic Advisers Herbert Stein, Chairman of the Council on International Economic Policy Peter Flanigan, and, from time to time, a representative from the staff of the National Security Council. As Secretary of the Treasury, I (Shultz) chaired the meetings, and Paul Volcker, Under Secretary of the Treasury, directed the necessary staff work. The existence of this working group was not generally known, so that "departmental" positions were avoided and discussions proceeded on the basis of continuing individual contributions. The U.S. proposal was launched in general terms in my speech at the International Monetary Fund meeting in September 1972. The international financial world heaved a sigh of relief, not so much out of agreement with the proposal but because there was one. The importance to international monetary reform of a constructive and positive initiative from the U.S. was widely recognized.

Negotiations and Events on the Road to Reform

The Committee of 20 held its first meeting before the IMF sessions of September 1972 were concluded. A staff director, Jeremy Morse from Great Britain, was elected and the process of negotiation started on an international scale. The force of events changed the course and character of these negotiations in the ensuing years (we did not, for example, foresee the gigantic increase in 1973-74 in the price of oil and its momentous impact on international financial markets). But from the outset we envisaged the road to reform as consisting of two lanes: the one of negotiations and the other of reality. A conclusion would be reached only when these two lanes merged and the formal system and the system in actual practice came together.

It is interesting to explore how events shaped, one might say overwhelmed, the international monetary negotiations. The year 1973 was one of rapidly rising inflation on a world scale. No country was immune. The worldwide inflation forced prices up more rapidly in some countries than in others, however, and hence led to pressures for devaluations and revaluations. As private firms sought to get funds out of weak currencies and into strong currencies, central banks intervened massively in exchange markets in a futile effort to maintain the Smithsonian rates. In doing so, central banks increased the world money supply greatly, which in turn fueled further inflation. Early in the year, the dollar weakened in exchange markets, perhaps also reflecting the fact that the Smithsonian changes had not been sufficiently bold. In February 1973 a second devaluation took place, this time in the form of a 10 percent increase in the dollar price of gold. But this realignment was itself overwhelmed by events. International monetary confusion was the order (or disorder) of the day as country after country decided to let its currency float.

Attention shifted rapidly from a preoccupation with particular exchange rates to questions about the timing, coordination, and amount of intervention and about the conditions under which intervention by governments in exchange markets was appropriate. Then, over two traumatic Paris weekends in March 1973 involving an expanded Group of Ten, it was agreed that intervention would be undertaken to maintain "orderly markets" but not in defense of any particular rate of exchange. Though no one would or could specify the distinction between "orderly" and "disorderly" markets, once a country decided that intervention in defense of a particular currency rate was not justified, markets rather than governments were explicitly in charge.

Negotiations in the C-20 continued. Tentative agreement was reached on the principles of a projected system of "fixed but adjustable" exchange rates. Although negotiations to put these principles into effect came to naught in the end, they did serve one function of special importance. The sense of community among finance ministers was greatly strengthened. Close personal relationships emerged; the finance ministers from the five largest trading countries, meeting with some frequency, developed a spirit of mutual trust that stood their countries well in the times of stress to come.

Inflation continued to accelerate but at widely different rates in different countries. And then, in a relatively short span of time at the end of 1973 and the beginning of 1974, the price of oil quadrupled. Since oil was the most significant import of most developed and developing countries, the payments balances of almost all but the petroleum-exporting countries were thrown into substantial deficit.

The C-20 meeting in Rome in January 1974 was confronted with world inflation, high and rising oil prices, present and prospective deficits in the balance of payments of most oil-consuming countries, and a sense that world economics had changed drastically. Nevertheless, the sense of community carried the meeting. Agreement was reached to resist evident pressures to solve individual problems by beggar-thy-neighbor trade or monetary actions. And it was accepted not only that fixed rates were clearly impracticable for the time being but also that we were fortunate to have in place a flexible market system. That was a bitter pill for some to swallow. To others, including the U.S., the emergence of a market-based system was seen as a great improvement over the inflexible gold-based system that preceded Camp David.

The C-20 decided to divide its reform exercise into two parts. The first

"Then it's agreed. Until the dollar firms up, we let the clamshell float."

would be a long-term outline of a reformed monetary system. Although the document ultimately agreed upon tended to follow the structure of the U.S. plan (particularly with respect to the use of the size of a country's reserve holdings as the chief indicator of whether adjustment was needed), many details were left unresolved. Moreover, even to the extent that agreement did exist, it was not concurrence upon a particular plan to be implemented in the future, but rather upon, in the committee's words, "the general direction in which the committee believes that the system could evolve in the future."

This emphasis on evolution reflected a basic shift in orientation for the governments of the major participants. Europeans who favored fixed rates had long believed that governments could control their economies in such a way as to make changes in exchange relationships unnecessary or at any rate infrequent. And the U.S. proposal, although creating a structure in which changes in rates were expected, nevertheless had reflected a constitution-building approach to the international monetary system. Governments now appreciated and acknowledged that, because events tended to overwhelm the best laid plans, it was necessary to think of changes in the international monetary system in evolutionary terms. The monetary system had a life of its own, just like domestic economies, and though governments could create a better climate for international economic activity, it would be self-deception for them to believe that they could foresee the future and force a rapidly evolving international economy into rigid categories of a comprehensive agreement.

The second portion of the program recommended by the Committee of 20 involved immediate measures. This program was agreed upon in general terms in June 1974 and in much more specific terms as amendments to the Articles of Agreement of the International Monetary Fund in Jamaica in January 1976. In large part, these agreements merely made reality "legitimate." The full agreement arising out of the Jamaica meetings is quite complicated, especially because the members of the Fund took the occasion to make many changes to bring the existing Articles of Agreement, drafted in 1944 at the Bretton Woods conference, into conformity with current needs and practice. But for present purposes, it is sufficient to focus on three major changes: (1) the legitimation of floating; (2) the recognition that domestic economic stability is a prerequisite to exchange rate stability; and (3) the reduction in the role of gold in the international monetary system.

First, the reality of floating was made legitimate by a formal change in the rules to bring them into conformity with the way the international monetary system had evolved since the beginning of 1973. While maintaining the view—especially favored by European governments and central bankers throughout the world—that IMF members might in the future agree by a qualified majority vote to make a fixed exchange rate system the dominant system, the voting arrangements were so designed that the United States could defeat a move to return to a fixed rate system. To underscore the right of the United States to remain on a floating system whatever other countries might choose to do, the Jamaica agreement specifically provided that any country might even after such a vote continue to float.

The Jamaica agreement, while recognizing the de facto reality of generalized floating among the major countries, did provide that countries could intervene when market conditions became unacceptably turbulent. Indeed, at Rambouillet in November 1975 six governments—the United States, France, West Germany, Britain, Italy, and Japan—had laid the groundwork for Jamaica and agreed that their monetary authorities would "act to counter disorderly market conditions and erratic fluctuations in exchange rates."

The second change at Jamaica was the recognition that stability of domestic economies was necessary for exchange rate stability. This change was an explicit reaction to the view that exchange rate stability can be achieved by international agreement coupled with central bank intervention in exchange markets. This view, although still held to some extent in some financial ministries and central banks, had proven demonstrably wrong so long as conditions were unsettled—as they had been during the period of inflation and oil crisis prior to the Jamaica agreement.

The third change involved gold. No longer was gold to be the common denominator in which the values of currencies would be expressed. Special Drawing Rights would henceforth play that bookkeeping role. As a corollary, there would be no official price for gold. Each country would be free to value gold at its price in the private market. And finally, to underscore the point that gold was to be phased out of the international monetary system, the IMF was to sell one-sixth of its gold holdings at auction and to return another one-sixth to member countries.

Of course, agreeing to phase gold out of the system is one thing, and causing it to become "just another industrial commodity" is another. Gold did not achieve its earlier central position by agreement. Rather, Bretton Woods merely reflected the position of gold in the international monetary system as it had evolved up to 1944. No doubt many countries, including the United States, will continue to hold gold in their reserves. But, at least insofar as officially agreed intentions of governments are concerned, the international monetary system will be based on something more economically fundamental than a golden metal.

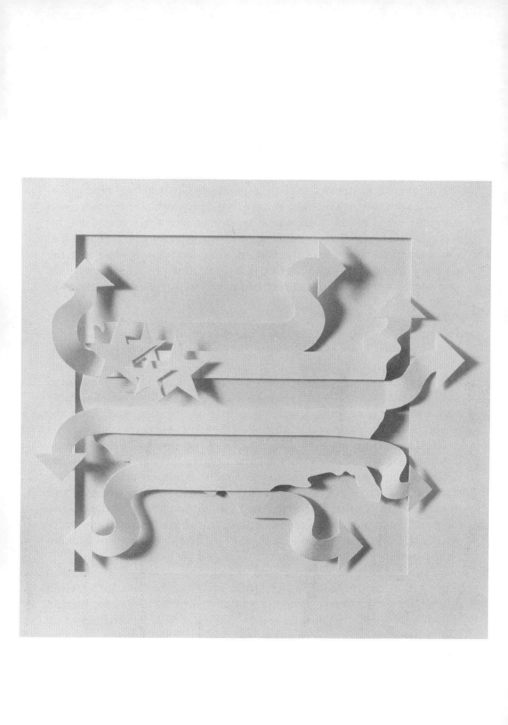

CHAPTER SEVEN

International Trade Policy: New Dimensions to Old Problems

NOTHING IS MORE DOMESTIC than international trade policy—or so it seems when one is working on the subject. In 1976, more than eight million people were employed in the United States in jobs related directly or indirectly to exports. U.S. consumers depend upon imports for some essential goods, the choice of products on our shelves is vastly enhanced by wide availability of imports, and the cost and price performance of many companies is sharpened by competition from abroad. At the same time, U.S. workers are employed and extensive capital is invested in industries threatened by imports. In the making of international trade policy, once again we see the interplay of efficiency and equity. The potential efficiency gains from free trade are great, but the political process tends to focus on the issues of equity. Who will bear the burden of the workers and indus tries displaced by increased imports?

The process of drafting and enacting the Trade Act of 1974 highlighted these and other pressures that surround the flows of international trade and their regulation. We were closely involved in this process and will use it as a vehicle for examining the new dimensions to what are in many respects perennial problems. The 1974 Trade Act authorized the new round of multilateral trade negotiations that has been in progress for several years in Geneva and that will likely continue for the full five years authorized. In the process of carrying on these negotiations, U.S. trade policy will no doubt evolve in its details, but—barring some unforeseeable revolution in international affairs—the main outlines for trade policy have been set in the process of drafting and enacting the statute. Meanwhile, the act sets the framework for any new trade policy initiatives that might be undertaken in Washington. Development of the Trade Act passed through two distinct stages: the preparation of the administration's trade bill and the year and three-quarters of congressional consideration from the submission of the trade bill in April 1973 to enactment in December 1974.

The Objectives of the Trade Bill

From a domestic economic perspective the most important considera- tion in deciding whether to go forward with a trade proposal was how best to hold at bay the protectionist forces that had been gathering strength since the conclusion of the Kennedy Round of trade negotiations in the late 1960s. The Kennedy Round had been the most ambitious and most far-reaching of the six rounds of negotiations held since World War II under the auspices of the General Agreement on Tariffs and Trade (GATT). In these negotiations the participating countries had bargained with one another for reciprocal reduction of tariffs and some other trade barriers. But despite the success of these negotiations, there was always the possi- bility of considerable backsliding as individual governments felt compelled to raise particular barriers to help troubled domestic industries. The issue facing the U.S. government since World War II had been how to fight this recurrent tendency toward protectionism. The conventional wisdom had been that the best defense was a good offense. According to this theory, new trade negotiations would keep protectionist forces under control because the executive branch could counter arguments for protecting particular industries by pointing to the obvious importance of avoiding action that would undermine U.S. negotiators abroad. Moreover, the vision of expanding world commerce implicit in a trade bill would, from this traditional perspective, capture the political stage and make protec- tionist arguments less appealing in Congress.

By the early 1970s, however, it was no longer so clear that this strategy, which underlay the drafting of the Trade Expansion Act of 1962 (the statute that had authorized U.S. participation in the Kennedy Round) fit the new situation. For one thing, the very success of the Kennedy Round in reducing tariff barriers to trade and the growing disillusionment with the commercial policies of Japan and the European Economic Community (EEC) made a new round of trade negotiations seem less appealing. In addition, many labor unions, most of which supported the 1962 act, had subsequently reverted to their traditional protectionist stance, and they were joined by many industry groups. The union view was expressed as strong support for the Burke-Hartke bill, which would have required extensive quotas on imports. The tactical question was whether a major administration trade proposal would provide impetus for congressional action on the Burke-Hartke bill. Or would such a trade-expanding proposal, following the reasoning of the 1960s, bury Burke-Hartke?

Experience with a presidential trade proposal in 1970 underscored the danger of protectionist action by Congress. The 1970 proposal had a relatively narrow scope, but it had been amended in the Ways and Means Committee and the House of Representatives with a provision for a formula requiring an import quota on a product when imports of that product were increasing. The effect of the amendment had been to turn a bill for more open trade into a protectionist weapon. When the 1970 bill eventually died in the Senate at the end of the session, administration trade officials were greatly relieved.

Experience with the 1974 Trade Act demonstrated that the traditional wisdom of using a pro-trade bill to offset protectionist legislative efforts still had some validity. The Burke-Hartke bill proved not to have the political support that some had feared and in the end was never strongly pushed by its proponents. But the arguments for protection had made their mark. The trade bill, even as proposed in 1973 and particularly as finally passed in 1974, had a much tougher—more protectionist—flavor than had the 1962 Trade Expansion Act.

Beyond economic objectives, proponents of the trade bill within the administration argued that its passage and the subsequent negotiations would support diplomatic initiatives, improving relations with Europe in the post-Vietnam period (1973 was to have been, one may recall, the Year of Europe) and helping to prevent the growth of trade blocs that could be a source of political tension. But here too there were skeptical voices expressing fear that trade negotiations would simply be a new source of diplomatic disagreement between Europe and the United States. In every trade negotiation, they argued, there is inevitably a crisis stage. No trade negotiation succeeds in accomplishing substantive trade results unless the negotiators are willing to countenance a breakdown of the negotiations if their minimum demands are not met. The general diplomatic fallout of such a breakdown in trade negotiations, or even the imminent threat of it, worried Henry Kissinger and some other foreign policy officials.

Another factor in the calculus was the President's promise to the Russians in the 1972 U.S.–Soviet trade agreement that the United States would end tariff discrimination against the U.S.S.R. To those concerned with diplomatic relations with the Russians, eliminating this discrimination—or at least honorably discharging the presidential commitment by attempting in good faith to induce Congress to do so—was a cornerstone of our détente policy. To the Russians, elimination of trade discrimination was important not only for the economic benefits of access to the U.S. market, but also for its political significance indicating our desire for more normal diplomatic relations.

As a result of U.S. retaliation against the Soviet Union during the Korean War, imports from the Soviet Union were subjected to the high duties of the infamous 1930 Smoot-Hawley Tariff and no longer enjoyed the sharp reductions in duties that other countries received as a result of the successive rounds of GATT trade negotiations. Although the Soviet Union had not participated in the GATT negotiations, until the Korean War the U.S.S.R. had nonetheless received the benefits in lower U.S. tariffs as a result of our most-favored-nation (MFN) policy, under which every country receives the benefit of tariff reductions accorded the "most-favored" nation. To eliminate this trade discrimination, that is, to accord the Soviet Union MFN treatment, would require specific authority from Congress. Within the administration, it was debated whether such authority would be easier to obtain as part of a general trade bill or as a separate bill. Tying the most-favored-nation issue to the trade bill, as it turned out, nearly resulted in legislative defeat for the trade bill.

Still another objective of a trade bill would be to provide authority for generalized tariff preferences to less-developed countries. Generalized preferences would award exporters from these countries access to the U.S. market under lower tariffs than those faced by exporters from developed countries. Such preferences had long been a basic demand of the less-developed countries, and President Nixon had made a commitment in 1969 to institute such a program. Not only are generalized tariff preferences important diplomatically, but many people argued that trade would be more effective than aid in promoting economic development within the developing world.

Although the EEC and Japan had already instituted generalized tariff preference programs, the expectations that Congress would resist lowering tariffs without a quid pro quo from the less-developed countries had led to a delay in seeking congressional authorization. The need to seek such authority weighed heavily among those in the State Department and elsewhere who had to deal with the less-developed countries in the diplomatic arena. Without the support of a broad-based trade bill, a generalized preferences proposal seemed doomed. Yet tying the two together might endanger the trade bill. In the end, the generalized preferences proposal was accepted by Congress without great opposition, in part perhaps because the proposal of most-favored-nation status for the Soviet Union became so controversial that generalized preferences captured little public attention.

More important than these diplomatic considerations in the decision to go ahead with a broad-based trade proposal were the economic policy objectives. Lower tariffs mean greater scope for competitive forces and hence a more efficient world economy. Prior rounds of trade negotiations had made tariffs much less significant, but nontariff barriers—quotas, discriminating taxes and administrative procedures, and restrictions on government procurement—had become increasingly important. One popular theory was that nontariff barriers had proliferated as a substitute for the reduced tariffs and that perhaps there was some kind of political law of trade at work under which protection could not be effectively reduced below some minimum level or more rapidly than at some maximum rate. When tariffs go down, it was argued, nontariff barriers go up. Whether or not this theory was correct—and surely there was something to it—the practical implication was that much more emphasis had to be placed on nontariff barriers.

Although exports were an economic cost in that they involved sending resources out of the country, they were necessary to pay for imports that U.S. consumers were increasingly demanding and they were important to particular domestic industries. The future of American agriculture, for example, was clearly dependent in part upon continued access to European markets. The Common Market was pursuing agricultural self-sufficiency policies that threatened traditional U.S. markets in Europe, even though the United States was for many agricultural products (soybeans and wheat, for example) a more efficient, lower-cost producer than its European competitors. In contrast to the conventional image of the United States as the world's leading industrial country, our comparative advantage in international trade in fact lay more often in agricultural products.

American industrial exports also were threatened by an increasing web of preferential tariff agreements that the EEC was entering into with African and Middle Eastern countries as well as with Spain, Sweden, and other nonmember European countries. Not only did exports from these countries enjoy access to the huge EEC market on tariff terms that discriminated against U.S. exports, but the Common Market had also succeeded in obtaining agreement from many of these same countries for reverse preferences permitting EEC exports to enter those countries on terms that likewise discriminated against U.S. exports. Since the growth of these preferential arrangements had not been arrested through diplomatic means, trade negotiations had the attractive quality of leading to a reduction in the degree of discrimination. If foreign tariffs were to be reduced by, say, 50 percent across the board, then the discrimination against U.S. exports would necessarily be reduced by 50 percent. A complete elimination of tariffs on a particular product would eliminate any preference entirely.

A new round of negotiations also provided an opportunity to support the administration's objectives in the international monetary realm. Trade negotiations could be used to attack the foreign nontariff barriers that contributed to the trade surpluses of some countries. Surplus countries that maintained undervalued exchange rates were able to outcompete U.S. exporters in third-country markets and to penetrate domestic U.S. markets to the detriment of domestic industries and workers. Finally, a trade bill would provide an opportunity to obtain specific congressional authority to impose a temporary surcharge on imports from countries with continuing trade surpluses. The 1971 import surcharge was challenged in the courts. Although it was eventually sustained, sufficient doubt had arisen as to its statutory basis to make more explicit authority desirable.

Although economic policy objectives weighed most heavily with the President's economic advisers, they were not decisive with President Nixon himself. Diplomatic questions were of great importance in his thinking. In February 1973, a critical moment in the executive branch debate on whether or not to propose a trade bill, British Prime Minister Edward Heath visited Washington. Most of an afternoon of discussion with President Nixon was devoted to diplomatic matters outside the economic sphere. The late afternoon was, however, to cover economic issues, and as Treasury Secretary, I (Shultz) was invited to join the discussions. When I arrived and the subject changed to economic matters, Henry Kissinger excused himself and I was the only American official left with the President and the Prime Minister.

The discussion turned to trade negotiations. Heath displayed enthusiasm for these negotiations as well as considerable knowledge of the issues. He felt it was essential that negotiations go forward, if for no other reason than to avoid losing ground in the battle to maintain open trade channels. We discussed various troublesome points in the draft trade bill then in preparation, with a generally satisfactory outcome. The discussion continued for more than an hour until the approach of the evening's state dinner forced an end to the meeting. When Heath left, the President reflected aloud on Heath's comments, clearly impressed with the importance that Heath attached to the economic dimension of relationships not only between the two countries but among all countries of the world. As we parted company, the President remarked that he now believed that the trade bill should indeed go forward.

Trade Reform

Every major legislative proposal, if it is to be successful, must be presented in policy terms. Congress, the people, and the executive branch itself must understand a proposal's central purposes. Unless the one or two central concepts underlying the legislation can be easily grasped, the proposal is likely to be lost in a fog of public confusion. Such a requirement was particularly important for a trade bill, which would cover many separate subjects ranging from trade negotiations, through most-favored-nation treatment for the Soviet Union, to generalized preferences for less-developed countries. Not only is a trade bill automatically attacked by narrow protectionist interests, but the gains from freer trade strike many well-informed people, including members of Congress, as highly abstract, if not illusory.

The central concept therefore became trade reform rather than simply freer trade. It was not to be just an authorization of trade negotiations. The objective would be to reform the world trading system, especially by eliminating the nontariff barriers and deliberately undervalued currencies that restricted U.S. exports. In a bow to the unions and other supporters of the Burke-Hartke bill, the trade reform bill would provide improved procedures for temporary "import relief" (a euphemism for tariffs and quotas) for industries that suffered serious injury from increased imports.

Unlike previous trade bills that had been limited in practical effect to dealings with the major developed-country trading nations, this bill was to have a global scope. It would authorize the end to trade discrimination against all countries including the Soviet Union that, because they were not parties to the General Agreement on Tariffs and Trade, were not benefiting from GATT's most-favored-nation clause. This trade bill would also address more directly the needs of the less-developed world by providing for generalized tariff preferences.

Finally, the trade reform bill would be linked to other domestic concerns. Separate proposals would be made at roughly the same time to deal with the insecurity faced by workers displaced by increased imports. It was therefore to be treated as a policy package with concurrent administration proposals on improved unemployment insurance and pensions. A separate and moderate proposal was also to be made on taxation of foreign income, a highly technical area of taxation (and a key part of the Burke-Hartke bill) that had great significance to the unions because of their fear that multinational corporations were shifting production facilities abroad.

Adjustment Assistance

The troublesome issues involved in adjustment assistance provide a striking illustration of the difficulties of dealing with complex connections between different policy areas. The concept underlying adjustment assistance, introduced into trade law in the Trade Expansion Act of 1962, was that those who lost from freer trade should be compensated by those who gained. Since the country as a whole gained from freer trade, special provision should be made, according to this line of thinking, to assist workers who lost jobs, firms that lost sales, and communities that suffered because of injury to local workers and firms.

We concentrate here on assistance to workers, although adjustment assistance to firms and communities did raise serious policy issues as well. Firms that cannot compete with imports may be propped up rather than led to shift to fields where they can compete. Moreover, since one can rarely tell whether the firms applying for assistance are suffering primarily from increased imports or from bad management, adjustment assistance for firms is difficult to administer sensibly. Community adjustment assistance, in turn, would duplicate the Commerce Department's economic development assistance program, a politically popular but economically inefficient program that the administration was attempting to phase out. The administration therefore opposed adjustment assistance to firms and communities, but both categories were included in the Trade Act by Congress.

Worker adjustment assistance is certainly defensible as a program, but it too raised important policy issues. In fact, the administration officials who most enthusiastically backed worker adjustment assistance were not those who would administer the program or even those who had had any experience with the design of job security or other social programs. Rather, the leading proponents were officials whose primary interest was in obtaining passage of the trade bill—most notably officials from the Office of the Special Trade Representative and from State Department trade offices whose raison d'être lay in conducting trade negotiations. These internationalists knew that without a trade bill there could be no trade negotiations. From their point of view, worker assistance was simply a price to be paid to obtain trade legislation. Even this legislative judgment could be challenged because the unions, the primary opponents of the trade bill, regarded worker assistance as "burial insurance." The unions preferred retention of jobs through greater tariff protection rather than government payments to workers rendered unemployed by lower tariffs.

The administration proposal included trade-related worker assistance only on a limited transitional basis. The internationalists' legislative judgment was vindicated, however, when Congress expanded worker assistance well beyond the administration proposal. Congressional voters who were torn between union arguments against the trade bill and economic arguments for it were apparently swayed by inclusion of worker assistance in the legislation. As a social program, generous trade-related worker assistance was, from the administration's viewpoint, poorly designed.

Moreover, worker assistance would stand in the way of a more comprehensive approach to income security for workers rendered unemployed whether because of foreign trade or purely domestic economic developments. Each of these points warrants more detailed explanation.

Worker assistance had not worked well under the Trade Expansion Act of 1962, since strict statutory standards for benefits severely limited its applicability. It was not used at all until 1969, when an administrative ruling was made providing benefits for workers at three steel plants. On the other hand, if the standards for obtaining worker assistance were to be made easier to satisfy and if the benefit levels were to be substantially increased, different complications would follow. In the first place, it is extremely difficult to determine why a worker is thrown out of work. Industries suffering from foreign trade would often be experiencing difficulties even if there were no foreign trade, for they are often simultaneously suffering from technological change or changes in consumer tastes at home. Management competence in some affected companies may be modest. If levels of assistance were to be much higher for workers rendered unemployed by imports rather than by other causes, determining the cause of unemployment would be a constant problem. But even more important, why should a worker displaced by imports receive better treatment than one displaced by a change in defense procurement or by some other government action or, for that matter, by purely economic causes such as technological change?

In addition, high assistance levels could create serious work incentive problems (discussed at greater length in Chapter Five). Just as welfare programs may discourage work, so too a worker receiving a tax-free payment under a worker assistance program equal to 70 percent of prior pre-tax earnings may have little incentive to go back to work. When the unemployed worker's spouse is employed, and hence the marginal rate of income tax for the couple is already substantial, worker assistance may yield the worker nearly as much in spendable income as would a job, particularly after deducting the costs of commuting.

Another weakness of any approach that concentrates on liberalizing worker assistance was that such assistance is concerned merely with income security. For most workers an even more important cost of losing a job is the loss of a pension. The pension frequently represents a worker's most important source of savings. To this problem, worker assistance provided no solution.

Because of the limitations of worker assistance as a social program, the administration felt that a more comprehensive approach would be desirable. Since all workers are concerned with income security, not merely those rendered unemployed through imports, and since the determination

Detail from *Lumber, Corn, Wheat* by Thomas Hart Benton.

of the cause of unemployment (imports or something else) is a difficult matter, we preferred to concentrate on improving the principal income security program covering workers, namely, unemployment insurance. If the levels of worker assistance needed to encourage passage of the trade bill were to be so liberal as to create work incentive problems, unemployment insurance levels were by contrast clearly inadequate in many states. Trade adjustment assistance would take some pressure off efforts to improve unemployment insurance generally and might spawn other categorical forms of assistance. For example, Congress was considering environmental adjustment assistance, under which special payments would be made to a worker displaced when a plant was closed because of new environmental regulations. How much better it would be to make unemployment insurance benefits adequate and available to all displaced workers, whatever the cause of displacement.

For these reasons, the administration proposed, concurrently with the trade bill, an amendment to the unemployment insurance laws that would set minimum federal standards for benefit levels. Each state, which had previously set its own levels, would have to meet the federal standard, stated as a percent of average earnings in that state. The federal minimum standard would be high enough to bring up the level of compensation in laggard states but not so high as to create serious work incentive problems. The administration proposal also provided for more comprehensive coverage and for improved methods for determining when unemployment insurance coverage should be extended beyond the initial period in instances where widespread local unemployment made reemployment unduly difficult.

The administration also proposed, again concurrently with the trade bill, pension reform to give workers security for the savings implicit in their pension. These proposals involved vesting of pensions for long-term workers so that loss of a job would not result in loss of the pension, funding of pensions so that adequate funds would have been segregated from the assets of the company in the event that the company was not able to pay a vested pension, and establishing a new system of tax-deferred individual retirement accounts for the two-thirds of all workers whose companies offered no pension plan at all.

The unemployment insurance and pension proposals constituted major administration initiatives and were important quite apart from any relation to the trade bill. The pension reform bill passed in 1974 with many congressional additions including pension termination insurance and other provisions adding greatly to the complexity of administering a pension plan. In contrast, the unemployment insurance proposal was not acted upon. The failure to act can be attributed to three sources of opposition: (1) the state unemployment insurance administrators who feared minimum standards as a precedent for future federal takeover of the unemployment insurance programs; (2) some members of the business community who opposed the higher taxes that would be needed in many states to bring their compensation levels up to the minimum standards; and (3) union concern with a provision in the administration proposal that would have denied benefits to strikers.

The administration was nevertheless disappointed that its trade, pension, and unemployment insurance proposals were not seen as a related package. Conceptually, they formed a unit. Procedurally, they would move in Congress through the same committees—Ways and Means in the House and Finance in the Senate. The failure of Congress to treat these related proposals as a legislative package can be attributed to the eagerness of the trade bill's proponents (in the administration, Congress, and industry) to use adjustment assistance as a tactical concession to make tough decisions denying protection to domestic industries more politically palatable. It proved more appealing politically to satisfy equity arguments within the immediate field where they arose, in this instance trade, rather than in a more general or fundamental arena—through income maintenance or unemployment insurance.

The Most-Favored-Nation Controversy

Whether or not the Soviet Union should receive most-favored-nation status became the most controversial question in the trade bill when Senator Henry Jackson used the bill as a vehicle to raise the question of Soviet limitations on Jewish emigration from the Soviet Union. In one stroke, the esoteric field of tariff discrimination became connected in the public mind with domestic politics and moral considerations. How could the United States give most-favored-nation treatment, Senator Jackson argued, to a country that denied its citizens such a fundamental human right as the freedom to emigrate? Although the Jackson argument ignored the fact that most-favored-nation treatment is a misnomer because such treatment would not favor the Soviet Union in any way, but rather would merely eliminate an outdated policy of trade discrimination, the controversy over the Jackson amendment showed that one cannot treat international economic policy as a field divorced from broader diplomatic, political, and moral questions.

The controversy also illustrates some of the practical problems of the separation of powers between the executive and legislative branches. Since a trade issue was involved, Congress had the power to legislate. Yet some of the supporters of the Jackson amendment sought to use it as a lever to counter indirectly the diplomatic initiatives of the President leading to détente with the Soviet Union. Congress would probably have been outside its constitutional jurisdiction in attempting to regulate the President's diplomatic initiatives directly. Thus, although Congress was acting within its constitutional power, the effect of congressional action was to compromise the President's constitutional authority over the conduct of foreign affairs. This controversy was only one of a number of instances in which Congress has sought to dictate not merely the long-term strategy of diplomacy but also the short-term tactics. Another example was the congressional cutoff of military assistance to Turkey in 1974 in an attempt to influence Turkish policy toward Cyprus.

As passed by Congress, the President's authority to grant most-favored-nation status was severely limited. Both the elimination of trade discrimination and the eligibility of non-market-economy countries for certain U.S. government credits and guarantees were to be conditioned on a presidential determination and report to Congress that the country in question did not deny its citizens the opportunity to emigrate, either directly or by a tax or some other charge. The elimination of trade discrimination would then become effective only upon congressional passage of a concurrent resolution of approval. Since it was probable that no non-market-economy country could meet these standards, the President was given the power to waive the foregoing requirements upon a report to Congress to the effect that he had received certain assurances from the country in question with regard to future emigration. Extension of the presidential waiver beyond 18 months was predicated, subject to some intricate qualifications, on passage of an annual congressional joint resolution. This elaborate compromise was supplemented by a highly unusual and unprecedented exchange of letters between Secretary of State Kissinger and Senator Jackson concerning Soviet representations about future emigration. In effect, Congress became involved, through Senator Jackson, in direct diplomatic negotiations with a foreign government.

The aftermath of the most-favored-nation experience was that less, not more, Jewish emigration was permitted by the Soviet government. Moreover, the Soviet government subsequently renounced the 1972 trade agreement negotiated by the President that had been the cornerstone of U.S.–Soviet economic relations. That Congress went beyond the largely symbolic most-favored-nation issue and imposed emigration conditions on the bread-and-butter issues of government credits and guarantees may account for the Soviet decision to renounce the trade agreement. However that may be, the Soviet decision underscores the limitations of international economic policy. Although economic policy and diplomacy can work hand in hand, as they did in bringing about some measure of détente with the Soviet Union, our economic policy cannot be expected to bring about a change in the internal political system of a major (or perhaps any) country. Whatever the stakes, political or moral, economic concessions are unlikely to be sufficiently important to a country such as the Soviet Union to be successfully used as a lever to accomplish such far-reaching objectives.

Nontariff Barrier Authority

Earlier we noted the growing importance of nontariff barriers in world trade. The nontariff issue in the passage of the trade bill had less to do with trade than with executive-congressional relations. The conflict created by this issue was inevitably exacerbated by congressional sensitivity to separation of power issues arising out of Watergate.

The conflict was in one sense inevitable. Congress wanted to control any commitments that U.S. negotiators might make and therefore wanted to be able to review each nontariff barrier agreement after it was negotiated. This congressional desire was consistent with its traditional power over trade, and since most U.S. nontariff barriers are an integral part of domestic legislation rather than of the tariff laws, the more general prerogatives of Congress were also at stake. The nontariff barrier issue also raised problems of congressional organization. Since a tariff is a tax, the House Ways and Means Committee and the Senate Finance Committee had jurisdiction over tariffs. But a nontariff barrier issue, depending upon its character, might involve a subject within the jurisdiction of some other committee. Health and environmental regulations might, for example, constitute significant barriers to imports. The other committees affected could be expected to be jealous of any attempt by the Ways and Means and Finance committees, in the drafting of the trade bill, to authorize commitments by U.S. negotiators to do away with laws or regulations that would normally fall within their committee jurisdiction.

If Congress was concerned with preserving its control, the executive branch was equally concerned with being able to negotiate effectively with foreign governments. Negotiators who cannot speak for their government can hardly be effective; they will have little credibility. The problem of dealing with other governments was complicated by the fact that few other governments are structured with such a far-reaching separation of powers. Under a cabinet system, for example, cabinet officials are members of the majority party in the legislature. Their decisions on trade concessions, even if legislation is necessary, will normally be implemented unless the issue precipitates a crisis leading to a new election and a new government.

The difficulties of effective negotiation had been exacerbated by the refusal of Congress to implement a nontariff barrier agreement that arose out of the Kennedy Round. This failure, involving a commitment to abolish the American Selling Price system (under which imports are valued at the American delivered price rather than at the lower price at the point of export), had created a feeling in some foreign governments that the U.S. government was not entirely to be trusted in trade negotiations. Although these foreign governments had known full well that subsequent congressional action was required to implement the agreement, they chose—in part no doubt for purely tactical reasons—to characterize the incident as one in which the United States had failed to live up to its international obligations.

One of the issues in drafting the trade bill was therefore whether or not to seek advance authorization from Congress to implement such nontariff barrier agreements as might be negotiated. Advance implementation authority is routinely granted to Presidents for tariff negotiation. But two crucial differences between tariffs and nontariff barriers made it improbable that Congress would be willing to grant such advance authorization, even if the barriers in question could be identified in advance. The first involved the problems of congressional organization mentioned above. Any resulting change in nontariff barriers would be likely to change a domestic law—involving, say, health or environmental matters—that would fall outside the jurisdiction of the Ways and Means and Finance committees.

The second difference was that even if one could identify the nontariff barriers in advance, the elimination of their trade-restricting effect would often merely involve harmonizing U.S. law with the law of other countries. (A wide variety of product standards and regulations may inhibit international trade if they are different in every country, but since they serve legitimate nontrade purposes making their abolition impossible, the goal of trade negotiations is to harmonize them to reduce their trade-inhibiting effect.) It would therefore be difficult to specify in advance of such negotiations precisely what standards or regulations U.S. negotiators would be permitted to negotiate. If domestic law had to be changed, the amendments might be quite complex. Tariff agreements, by contrast, are comparatively simple. It is possible to specify quite precisely the percentage by which the negotiators are empowered to reduce a tariff; all that is involved in implementation is a change in the percentage or amount stated in the customs books.

In the case of tariffs it would be difficult to obtain congressional authorization to lower a single tariff, considered in isolation, because the industry protected by the tariff could be expected to lobby vigorously to maintain its existing protection. The carrot of obtaining reduction of other countries' tariffs against U.S. exports makes it possible to balance the domestic industries that gain and those that lose in trade negotiations. This balancing theory was behind President Roosevelt's 1934 reciprocal trade agreements approach to tariffs. As demonstrated by the 1930 congressional Smoot-Hawley donnybrook that resulted in a massive increase in tariffs, a system in which Congress votes directly on the level of each tariff (as Congress did before 1934) is likely to be a system of increasing rather than decreasing tariffs.

Yet even a negotiated package does not assure congressional acceptance, as indicated by the congressional rejection of the American Selling Price package agreement at the end of the Kennedy Round. The benzenoid chemical industry, which would have lost protection if the package had been implemented, was able to defeat the implementation bill. This incident illustrates that industries threatened with loss of protection will find it easier to defeat an already negotiated package, in which it is clear to all concerned which industries will suffer, than to defeat congressional authorization of negotiations that may or may not affect them adversely. For this reason, advance authority to implement tariff reductions is both feasible and highly desirable if the overall goal is a lower level of tariffs. However desirable advance implementation authority for nontariff barrier agreements would have been, the committee jurisdictional conflicts and the political disadvantages of specifying in advance which industry's ox was to be gored led the administration to abandon the effort to obtain such authority. The only exceptions were for relatively uncontroversial agreements concerning customs procedures and marks of origin.

Despite the judgment that it was hopeless to seek broad advance authority, it was important to minimize the chances of congressional rejection of any nontariff barrier agreements that might be negotiated. Under the administration proposal the President was to give Congress 90 days' notice prior to entering into any such agreement, and congressional review was to be limited to a veto. Under a one-house veto provision the agreement would automatically be implemented if neither house exercised its veto. Amendment of the bill in the Senate Finance Committee placed such agreements in considerable jeopardy. In place of the one-house veto it substituted a requirement that both houses vote affirmatively to approve the agreement. It also watered down provisions inserted by the House of Representatives requiring prompt congressional consideration.

These changes are bound to reduce the ability of the executive branch to negotiate effectively and to obtain congressional approval of such agreements. Congressional concern with its separation-of-powers prerogatives limits the progress one can expect in the round of trade negotiations now under way. Since it is generally agreed that nontariff barriers are today a more serious impediment to economic efficiency and to U.S. exports than are tariffs, the economic policy implications of these procedural decisions by Congress are of major significance.

Countervailing Duties

In our discussion of the balkanization of government (in Chapter One) it may have seemed that balkanization is usually a tactic adopted by interests that have traditionally fared poorly in the executive branch policy process. The creation of the Environmental Protection Agency and proposals for a consumer protection agency certainly point in that direction. But balkanization tactics are also used by powerful groups in the business and labor communities, as the countervailing-duty issue demonstrates.

Under a statute dating from the nineteenth century, the Treasury is required to impose countervailing duties on imports that have received a "bounty or grant" (a subsidy, in today's language) from a foreign exporting government. Although the imposition of such duties raises prices to consumers, the duties have the effect of merely offsetting a foreign government subsidy and therefore are consistent with the efficiency notions underlying the movement toward freer trade that is implicit in trade negotiations. Moreover, simple considerations of equity to domestic producers who do not receive subsidies yet must compete with subsidized foreign producers generate a demand for offsetting action by our government.

At the same time, practical difficulties have led some Secretaries of the Treasury to delay or even to avoid imposing duties in particular cases. Imposing duties is a diplomatic act to which foreign exporting countries sometimes take violent exception. In some cases they simply disagree that what in U.S. law constitutes a bounty or grant should be considered an export subsidy. From their point of view, the bounty or grant may be simply an integral aspect of their tax system (such as the refund of the value-added tax on domestic sales when a good is exported) or some domestic program unrelated to exports (such as depressed-area assistance). Whatever the justification for the subsidy, a foreign government is likely to consider the matter one for international negotiation rather than unilateral action.

To impose duties without taking these views into account may provoke a trade war in which the foreign government retaliates against U.S. exports to its country or may even cause the breakdown of ongoing trade negotiations. Negotiation is therefore more likely to be successful in eliminating the foreign subsidy than is the unilateral imposition of duties. Nevertheless, the possibility of imposing duties is a powerful weapon in the armory of U.S. negotiators.

Yet domestic interests suffering from competition with subsidized imports have felt, in many cases justifiably, that the Treasury over the years has too often simply stalled in considering countervailing-duty cases while at the same time failing to remove the subsidies through negotiation. The remedy that these domestic interests succeeded in incorporating in the 1974 Trade Act was to turn the Secretary of the Treasury into an "independent agency" and to prohibit him from taking into account the diplomatic aspects of the international dispute that inevitably accompanies any countervailing-duty proceeding. The act also imposed a 12-month time limit within which the Treasury Secretary must act, a period which is none too liberal in view of the great factual complexity of some of the disputes. Moreover, the act subjects his decisions to judicial review, not just for cases in which he imposes duties, as had been the law in the past, but also decisions involving no bounty or grant. On the other hand, the act does recognize potential international consequences of balkanizing sensitive trade issues and subjecting them to judicial review. Imposition of countervailing duties may be delayed during the five-year period envisaged for trade negotiations if the imposition of the duties "would be likely to seriously jeopardize satisfactory completion of the negotiations."

An important question for the future is whether or not the drive of many foreign governments for "independence" through the development of high-cost industries whose surplus must be sold on the world market, perhaps through subsidy, will provoke demands for protective counteraction. If this development gains strength, countervailing-duty proceedings can be expected to multiply and exacerbate the drive to treat the resulting disputes unilaterally in a balkanized proceeding controlled by judicial review. Where this drive will lead the U.S. government in its diplomatic relations will be crucial for the fate of the pro-trade policy that has been pursued by every administration since that of Franklin Roosevelt. With the growing importance of nontariff barriers that restrict our exports and foreign subsidies that threaten our import-competing interests, this traditional U.S. policy—so vital to the health of our domestic economy and to standards of living throughout the world—can only be pursued if trade is treated as a matter for negotiators, not for lawyers.

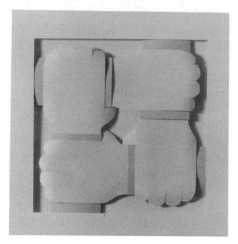

Organizing for Problem Solving

WHEN NEW PROBLEMS rear their heads in Washington, or when old problems take on new significance, organizational arrangements for solving them frequently tend to receive as much public attention as the analytical aspects of the problem itself. New administrations usually come to power with views at least as strong about how to organize to solve problems as about the solutions themselves. This fascination with government organization is understandable and healthy, so long as moving boxes around on organizational charts does not become an end in itself. Since the underlying substantive ideas are what ultimately count, organizational changes are most effective when they reflect a point of view about the substance of the problem the organization intends to tackle.

The starting point in considering organizational arrangements should be, though seldom is, the objective being sought. This objective may shift as time passes, and when it does, organizational changes may well help to achieve the new objective. Sound organization in government can therefore be expected to be considerably different from that in most private organizations. Contrary to typical public statements by advocates of government reorganization, efficiency as such is not usually the end being sought. The purpose of governmental arrangements, particularly at the policymaking level, is often not so much to do a batch of work efficiently as it is to have an impact on some other group, whether that target group includes other units of the federal government, state and local governments, or individuals and organizations in the private sector. A vast number of government programs, both economic and social, assume that governmental activity will influence the behavior of private groups.

We find it helpful, particularly where economic behavior is involved, to think of the group to be influenced as a moving target. Government cannot afford to lose sight of how the private sector will react to government action or even how it will anticipate such action. Indeed, any would-be government economic sharpshooter should bear in mind that these moving targets will also be taking aim at him, trying to anticipate government action in order to protect private interests. In the tax and regulatory areas, for example, an army of lawyers and accountants can be expected to find new loopholes as fast as—if not faster than—government can plug them.

The logic of organization suggests that activities of relevance to one another be grouped together, partly on grounds of efficiency but more subtly so that competing interests can be weighed and balanced against each other. We will examine a grand example of that kind of organizational effort in Chapter Eight. But a more common pattern is for interests to resist the balancing and weighing process by seeking organizational autonomy, thereby contributing to the further balkanization of government.

Organizations and Reorganizations

FEW IDEAS ABOUT the governmental process have greater staying power than the idea that improved organizational arrangements are critical to improved performance of government. Whatever the background of a new President, he sooner or later (usually sooner) chooses government reorganization as a policy instrument—investing time, energy, and sometimes considerable political capital in it. Hence, the rule of thumb, "When in doubt, reorganize." But to this cynical phrase must be added the observable fact that organizational change can, and sometimes does, improve performance.

In government perhaps more than in other parts of the society a reorganization may, however, be an end in itself. Both the American spirit and the American political system demand "action." Whenever a new problem hits the headlines, the instinctive demand is that somebody do something. Increasingly the demand is that that somebody be the government. Yet most problems important enough to become political issues are extremely complicated. Thoughtful people should recognize that solutions—let alone simple solutions—are hard to find and that government programs do not necessarily provide an optimum answer. "Doing something" about energy, for example, has meant interfering with the very market processes that could bring the problem under control. What may be bandied about in public discussion as the best and most direct way to solve a given problem may in fact be counterproductive, doing far more harm to other policy objectives than it contributes to a solution to the problem it attempts to tackle. Even when a solution is obvious, years may lie between the perception of the solution and its realization in practice. Still, the public demand for action—usually through government intervention, regulation, and spending—often remains unrelenting.

Is it any wonder that Presidents or department heads sometimes decide to quell the clamor for immediate action, or at least buy time for study and preparation, by reorganizing? The act of reorganizing departments and agencies and their constituent bureaus is a major public event, frequently accompanied by new appointments to the most visible offices and by intense media coverage. Often such reorganization, particularly if it quiets the cry for action, may become a substitute for developing a comprehensive policy. Yet it is doubtful that reorganizations are normally so Machiavellian in conception. More commonly, the substantive problem simply turns out to be more difficult than originally perceived, effective policies are not worked out, and, viewed in retrospect, the reorganization itself overshadows the policies actually implemented.

Although reorganizations are sometimes substitutes for policy, they may allow needed time for a policy to work. In the area of economic policy, for example, results take time. At the very period in mid-1970 when monetary and fiscal policies were slowing the rate of inflation, the public demand for direct action via wage and price controls was mounting steadily. It became apparent that the largely invisible processes by which monetary and fiscal policy can slow inflation would never have time to work unless the administration did something to satisfy public and congressional demands for more visible measures. Yet to take the most visible step—actually imposing wage and price controls—would be to abandon fundamental underlying "steady as you go" fiscal and monetary policies. The approach adopted in August 1970 to solve this dilemma was to create two new organizations, a National Commission on Productivity (a labor, management, academic, and government group of 24 members) and an interagency Regulations and Purchasing Review Board.

The concept behind the Productivity Commission was that with union and management leaders interacting with academic and government people, ideas could be generated about economic policy, methods of improving productivity could be identified, and a foundation could be laid for better wage and labor utilization practices. The Council of Economic Advisers was meanwhile instructed to issue periodic "inflation alerts," to be made public after circulation to members of the Productivity Commission, in order to focus attention on sectors of the economy where cost and price problems were most acute. The Regulations and Purchasing

Review Board, in turn, was to work toward elimination of government regulations and purchasing practices that imposed unneeded costs on the economy. The new groups addressed important issues and were worthwhile in and of themselves, although the actual results were certainly modest. More importantly, however, they allowed monetary and fiscal policies to work for an additional year before imposition of wage and price controls diverted attention from the need for emphasis on monetary and fiscal fundamentals. During that year the rate of inflation was reduced from 6.1 percent in 1969 to 3.7 percent in the first eight months of 1971. But that progress was still not sufficient to quell the demand for direct wage and price controls, to which the President finally succumbed in August 1971.

The Productivity Commission served an additional purpose not publicly perceived at the time it was established or even fully appreciated now: It identified a small group of top labor, business, and public leaders and gradually developed a forum for discussion among them. In 1971-72 the commission was most helpful in advising on the structure of the wage and price control system and changes in it, and several individual members agreed to serve on the Pay Board and the Price Commission. During 1973 and 1974, the President's Labor Management Advisory Committee was drawn from the members of the Productivity Commission, and this group played a key role in bringing wage and price controls to an end. President Ford sought advice on economic policy from the committee in 1974 and 1975. A sharp labor policy dispute over the President's veto in January 1976 of the common situs bill (which would have permitted unions to picket an entire construction site) ended this consultation with the President. The group reconstituted itself on a purely private basis, however, and meets periodically, seeking common positions on economic issues of general importance and sharing views on domestic and international economic developments. The individual members have changed over this period, largely so that all members are active heads of their organizations, but changes are not so frequent that continuity of discussion is at all impaired.

There are many ways that a reorganization can be used to support a new policy and thereby become part of the solution to a problem. Diverse bureaus and units, formerly scattered throughout the government, may be pulled together to function more effectively in a single agency. Sometimes, however, the support for a new policy afforded by reorganization is largely psychological. New agencies tend to have a much higher level of spirit and dedication than do old agencies. Agencies have a life cycle, and even considering time lost in the process of setting up and staffing, a new agency may far outperform the constituent parts separately housed in over-age agencies.

Reorganization can also support a new policy by dramatizing it. The decision to double spending on energy research and development from fiscal 1974 to 1976 was accompanied by the creation in 1975 of a new organization, the Energy Research and Development Agency. In addition to the advantages gained from merging formerly disassociated research funding programs and in-house research units from the Atomic Energy Commission and the Department of the Interior, the creation of the new agency was to symbolize a strong new thrust in energy policy.

Coordination of Policy

Viewing reorganization as a substitute for new policy or as an instrument to support or dramatize a new policy decision is outside the mainstream of most commentary on government organization. More commonly, reorganization is regarded as a means to coordinate better the formulation and implementation of policy. Since World War II, we have witnessed an almost continuous concern with organizational aspects of foreign policy. During the period from the inception of the Marshall Plan in 1947 until 1961, the government apparatus for foreign aid was reorganized about once every two years. More recently, organizational aspects of the triangular relationship of the State Department, the Defense Department, and the National Security Council have generated oceans of ink. The coordination issue is perennial. Whatever the sphere of government activity under discussion, the controlling question is always the same: How can issues transcending a particular department be handled? Inescapably, solutions tend to fall into one of four categories.

First, an interagency committee may be formed. Whatever its merits, this is hardly a solution. Although such committees may promote understanding and the flow of ideas across the bureaucratic gulf separating departments, decisions reached by an interagency committee tend to have all the least-common-denominator and splitting-the-difference weaknesses of all committee decisions arrived at by compromise. Too often interagency committees lead to an executive branch variation of legislative logrolling in which the committee gives each department what it wants, whether or not the decisions reached are internally consistent and even though they may compromise the more general interests of the executive branch and the public. Thus, far from providing a solution, an interagency committee may generate new problems.

Second, a single cabinet officer may be made preeminent on a particular issue and be asked to serve as the coordinator for executive branch policy. If that cabinet officer is seen by all to have the confidence of the President, this solution works rather well. But, as we shall discuss later in the chapter, this solution can create a variety of problems with Congress and with cabinet officers who find that they are in effect reporting to another cabinet officer.

Third, a policy coordinator can be chosen from within the Executive Office of the President. Sometimes the coordinator works through cabinet- and subcabinet-level officials of the contending departments, and to that extent, this mechanism is similar to the interagency committee except that a supposedly impartial chairman is imposed upon the committee. The budget bureau, first in the form of the Bureau of the Budget and since 1970 in the form of the Office of Management and Budget, has fulfilled this coordinating function for a wide variety of issues. The institution of legislative clearance, under which departments cannot propose new legislation or take an executive branch position on legislation pending in Congress without OMB approval, gives OMB a coordinating lever. Part of the growth in White House staff since World War II (and a stimulus for creation of the Domestic Council in 1970) stems from a desire to find alternatives to the budget bureau for policy coordination—a prime policy function, for which Presidents have often not fully trusted the bureau. The budget bureau inevitably has a bias against new and larger spending programs and most of its employees are career officials who, a President may fear, may not be politically responsive to him.

Fourth, it is sometimes possible, particularly in the early stages of formulating a new policy, for an Executive Office coordinator to work through a task force of departmental experts (rather than political-level generalists). The hope behind a task force approach is that departmental experts will, because of their greater knowledge of and respect for facts and data, find better ways to resolve differences than via logrolling or simple compromise. Task forces cannot, however, make policy decisions, much less implement them.

The exact organizational form of the coordination mechanism is usually far less important than is commonly supposed, especially when the interests of large departmental bureaucracies are at stake. For policy issues involving conceptual analysis, or for policy implementation where steadfastness of purpose and ability to compromise in the face of unforeseen obstacles are crucial, what counts more than the structure of the coordinating mechanism are the personal qualities of the key officials and their ability to work together. No substitute for individual ability can be found in organizational diagrams. Team spirit may be regarded by academics and pundits as a hackneyed concept, but nothing is more important for effective policymaking, especially in difficult periods.

Because policymaking is so vulnerable to delay and obfuscation in an advocacy system, particularly when departmental bureaucracies feel threatened, certain procedural mechanisms have grown up that provide "action-forcing events." The most important of these is the annual budget cycle (described in Chapter Two). Most policy decisions have budget implications, and as long as people believe that government spending is the best way to solve a problem, the budget cycle will sweep within its province a large proportion of major policy decisions.

Annual reports, such as the Report of the Council of Economic Advisers, provide another opportunity to create an action-forcing event, but perhaps because talk is cheaper than money, annual reports are not as effective as the budget cycle in forcing decisions. The President's State of the Union Message is especially effective in forcing action because once a President takes a strong position or makes a new proposal, it is hard for unhappy departments to reopen the issue.

In 1970 the concern for improved policy coordination brought about a major organizational change within the Executive Office of the President. The Bureau of the Budget was converted into the Office of Management and Budget (OMB) and the Domestic Council was created. The high aims and the less elevated results of this reorganization proffer several lessons.

By substituting the Office of Management and Budget for the Bureau of the Budget, the President hoped to change the primary focus of the organization from budget formulation and domestic policy coordination to the management of the government as a whole. Although the Bureau of the Budget had always had important management responsibilities, the change of name signified that management was now to be as important as the budget. Changes within the organization were made to correspond to this new dual focus, with various management activities grouped under Arnold Weber, the new and vigorous OMB associate director.

The Domestic Council, on the other hand, was an entirely new institution. It was not just another council (that is, a cabinet-level committee). A new office within the White House was created with a staff to engage in fundamental analysis of domestic policy rather than the day-to-day firefighting that had been the lot of most White House aides. Issues were to be fully analyzed, with departmental and other positions set forth in writing before being submitted to the President for written decision. The purpose of these formal procedures was to eliminate the "revolving-door" problem that had often plagued administrations, in which the last aide to come out of the Oval Office often claimed that he carried with him the definitive presidential (oral) decision.

The relationship between the Domestic Council and OMB was recognized to be crucial to the workings of the Executive Office. As envisaged by the planners of the reorganization and described by the President in his message to Congress on March 12, 1970, "The Domestic Council will be primarily concerned with *what* we do; OMB will be primarily concerned with *how* we do it, and *how well* we do it." This description implicitly reflected the view that the Bureau of the Budget, through its budget-making and legislative clearance activities, had become too powerful a voice in policymaking. The reorganizers' implicit goal was that the budget-making function of the OMB would become a more technical exercise in which the policy issues subsumed in major domestic budget decisions would be left to the Domestic Council.

Although the Domestic Council staff became an important and for a time a very large part of the White House establishment and although the OMB's management activities were more extensive and more visible than those of its predecessor, the reorganizers' blueprint was achieved in form only. The reasons for this failure are more interesting than the failure itself.

The first reason lay in the choice of members for the Domestic Council staff. The people selected, particularly in key positions, were young lawyers and politicians who, however talented, were inexperienced and in many instances uninterested in policy analysis. They were more attracted to day-to-day tactics than to the tedious, detailed analytical work required to improve social, transportation, and other domestic programs. As the Domestic Council staff turned to the departments and, increasingly, to the OMB staff to provide the facts and the underlying analysis, it fell into a role more congenial to its interests: brokering the various contending views, dealing with the press, and negotiating directly with Congress.

The second reason for the reorganization's failure is a corollary of the first. Budget making *is* policymaking, and OMB budgeteers remained participants in the White House policy process. The failure of the Domestic Council staff to fill the vacuum in White House policy analysis made it inevitable that the OMB staff would have to be consulted by the President and his closest aides if presidential decisions were to be made on the basis of facts and analysis rather than on advocacy views of the interested departments and on political judgments.

The Domestic Council and OMB staffs often worked together to provide the necessary policy analysis, but frequently they were rivals. The Domestic Council staff, oriented toward Congress and elections, favored new and larger social programs, while the OMB staff, inevitably oriented toward holding down spending in order to limit the repeated budget deficits, argued against new programs and against expansion of existing programs. Thus, the presence of the new Domestic Council staff, rather than contributing to White House policy analysis, all too often simply extended the advocacy process to the White House itself by providing departmental advocates with an Executive Office beachhead.

The third reason for the failure of the reorganization lay more in conception than in execution. Although OMB does play a greater role in the management of the federal government than did its predecessor, the budget will inevitably continue to dominate the attention of the OMB director and the bulk of OMB's most talented staff members. Not only does budget making carry with it the glamour of policymaking, but the drama and inexorable time pressure of the budget cycle provide a sharp contrast to the more mundane, and in many ways more demanding, task of improving departmental management at a distance.

Experience has shown, moreover, that OMB's major tool for applying pressure on a department to improve its management is the budget itself. The way in which this tool is used often reflects budget needs. For example, in order to hold down budget costs, it is relatively easy for OMB to impose personnel ceilings on departments and limits on the average grade of departmental employees. But it is arguable whether these controls induce greater productivity per dollar through better use of existing personnel or, on the contrary, bring about mediocrity and bureaucratic inertia by limiting promotions of talented employees and by making it difficult for departmental managers to hire new and expert people to handle new tasks. The OMB can improve government management, and it certainly has done so in a host of unglamorous but significant ways. Nevertheless, we must conclude that OMB will remain predominantly a budget-making and thereby a policy-oriented arm of the presidency.

Reorganization and the Advocacy System

Reorganization need not be an abstract exercise in improving the coordination of the policy process. On the contrary, proponents of a particular reorganization plan will often have rather precise substantive policy outcomes in mind. By changing the framework of policy formulation, they hope to tip the scales in favor of their preferred policies. Such a reorganization harnesses the advocacy principle by creating new actors in the policy process who will assure greater access and influence for particular groups. The creation of clientele departments, such as the Department of Agriculture, is the most obvious example.

In recent times not only private economic groups but also more broadly based social interests have sought to enhance their influence over policy outcomes by the creation of new agencies. The formation of the Environmental Protection Agency in 1970 is a particularly arresting example of a broadly based social group (here environmentalists) obtaining a voice in—perhaps even a lock on—the policy process via reorganization. This example is doubly interesting because it involves a successful attempt to balkanize the policy process: The favored environmental interest is pushed in splendid isolation without having to be weighed against competing economic interests.

Drawing by Reg Manning
The Arizona Republic

The Walled City

Sometimes agencies are created to introduce new perspectives into decision making rather than to represent any particular economic or social interest. The Council of Economic Advisers, created in 1946, has proved to be an important voice favoring economic rationality in executive branch decision making. The Council on Price and Wage Stability has also acted in part to offset the influence of special-interest advocates within the executive branch. Both of these councils are in no small measure intentional, explicit counterweights to the influence of clientele-oriented advocacy agencies.

Reorganization is sometimes proposed with the purpose of submerging advocates within more broadly oriented departments. Such a reorganization seeks to combat the advocacy process by forcing issues out of the Executive Office arena where the advocates would otherwise collide and into a lower level in the executive branch, thereby allowing the assessment of trade-offs between benefits and costs of competing policies to be made closer to the locus of operational responsibility. The Departmental Reorganization Plan of 1971 provides an ambitious example of such a proposal. Examination of the purposes of this proposal and the reasons for its rejection in Congress reveals a great deal about policy formation in Washington.

The Departmental Reorganization Plan envisaged the replacement of the most prominent advocacy departments and agencies by four new departments; only the Departments of State, Treasury, Defense, and Justice were to remain from the old departmental roster. The new departments would reflect a more functional perspective designed to force competing advocacy groups to resolve their differences at the departmental rather than the presidential level and to lead cabinet members rather than Executive Office assistants to make the crucial evaluations of the relative costs and benefits of competing policies. They were to be called the Departments of Community Development, Natural Resources, Human Resources, and Economic Affairs and were to replace existing departments whose names convey their advocacy perspective—Agriculture, Labor, and Commerce—as well as agencies such as the Office of Economic Opportunity and the Small Business Administration. Where existing departments were already conglomerates with advocacy more evident at the bureau level, the existing departments would form the core of a new department with additional pieces coming from other departments. The entire Department of the Interior, for example, was to be transferred to the new Department of Natural Resources.

In addition to these decentralizing and advocacy-dampening motivations, the proposal also sought to eliminate most of the duplication that had resulted from decades of departmental "imperialism." The President's message transmitting the Departmental Reorganization Plan asked Congress to "consider these facts":

> Nine different Federal departments and 20 independent agencies are now involved in education matters. Seven departments and eight independent agencies are involved in health. In many major cities, there are at least twenty or thirty separate manpower programs, funded by a variety of Federal offices. Three departments help develop our water resources and four agencies in two departments are involved in the management of public lands. Federal recreation areas are administered by six different agencies in three departments of the government. Seven agencies provide assistance for water and sewer systems.

The mechanics of the Departmental Reorganization Plan can be viewed from two perspectives: Where would the pieces of an existing department be transferred and from where would the constituent parts of an existing program come? From the first perspective, the Department of Agriculture, for example, would be split three ways. Construction-oriented bureaus such as the Rural Electrification Administration would be sent to the new Department of Community Development, resource-oriented bureaus such as the Forest Service would go to the new Department of Natural Resources, and people-oriented bureaus such as the Food and Nutrition Service would be transferred to the new Department of Human Resources. From the second perspective—looking at the constituent pieces of the new departments—the Department of Economic Affairs, for example, would be composed of relevant bureaus from the Commerce Department (such as the Bureau of Domestic Commerce), the Department of Transportation (such as the Federal Railroad Administration), and the Labor Department (such as the Bureau of Labor Statistics), as well as such nondepartmental agencies as the Small Business Administration.

In evaluating the fate of this proposal, it is important to recognize that this was *not* a partisan political issue. Consider, for example, the Senate testimony of Joseph A. Califano, Jr., chief counsel of the Democratic National Committee, President Johnson's principal assistant for domestic matters, and President Carter's Secretary of Health, Education and Welfare:

> Executive reform is not a partisan issue. . . . Democrats and Republicans will differ—sometimes sharply—over the people who should be placed in charge of the executive departments of the government. But they should not differ over the organization of these departments. As a Democrat, Mr. Chairman, I believe that any democratic presidential candidate, who might be successful in winning the White House in 1972 or thereafter, will be immeasurably helped in his ability to put into effect the policies upon which he is elected if President Nixon's reorganization proposals are adopted by the Congress.
> [Testimony of May 26, 1971, Senate Committee on Government Operations]

Califano revealed that a Johnson administration commission headed by Ben W. Heineman had recommended a "remarkably similar" reorganization in a proposal that President Johnson had not publicly disclosed. And John W. Gardner, Secretary of Health, Education and Welfare in the Johnson administration, and then chairman of Common Cause, testified that the proposed reorganization was "long overdue" because it was the best way to deal with the problems created by the advocacy system. Gardner also had the prescience to see how the advocacy system would itself defeat the program:

> It is a fact, unknown to the general public, that some elements in Congress and some special interest lobbies have never really wanted the departmental Secretaries to be strong. As everyone in this room knows but few people outside of Washington understand, questions of public policy nominally lodged with the

Secretary are often decided far beyond the Secretary's reach by a trinity . . . consisting of (1) representatives of an outside lobby, (2) middle-level bureaucrats, and (3) selected Members of Congress, particularly those concerned with appropriations.

In a given field these people may have collaborated for years. . . . They have traded innumerable favors. They have seen Secretaries come and go. . . . Often they couldn't care less about White House messages, or pronouncements from the top of the department. They have a durable alliance that cranks out legislation and appropriations in behalf of their special interest.

. . . If the departments are reorganized a stranger may appear on the bureaucratic leg of the triangle. The outside special interests are particularly resistant to such change. It took them years to dig their particular tunnel into the public vault, and they don't want the vault moved.

. . . When a reorganization plan comes up, the special interests move in like hornets, and most of our leaders tend to come down on the side of one or another of those special interests. And the reorganization fails to come off.

[Testimony of May 25, 1971, Senate Committee on Government Operations]

To understand why a reorganization of such unprecedented and comprehensive scope, with its strong overtones of "good government" and freedom from special-interest domination, should have been rejected by Congress, one must bear in mind the strong hold that the advocacy system has on the motivations of all concerned. Within the executive branch, for example, the President's own opposition to the advocacy system was not unqualified. This is not surprising because, as a professional politician, he well understood the role of the advocacy principle in politics. As the 1972 election approached, the President became increasingly concerned about the consequences of growing Farm Belt dissatisfaction. Although it stemmed initially from economic worries and policy disagreements, this dissatisfaction began to focus on the proposed elimination of the Department of Agriculture as an indication of a lack of administration interest in farm problems. In a political response, the President decided to have a separate Department of Agriculture after all: "not the old Department, but a new one." The presidential statement accompanying this move and the simultaneous appointment of a new Secretary of Agriculture emphasized that "this change will have a very, very significant effect not only in reassuring the farm community but perhaps just as important in getting the necessary support we need in the Congress to get action on our reorganization proposals."

One should not be too quick to criticize this decision because if the compromise on the Department of Agriculture had saved the overall proposal, the decision would have been a brilliant instance of half a loaf being better than none. But the compromise did not save the program and was cited by opponents as casting doubt on the degree of presidential support for the reorganization plan itself.

The congressional reaction to the reorganization program was cool from the start. Few legislators opposed the program in principle, but most opposed particular aspects of it. The program was nibbled to death. In addition to the opposition to particular bits and pieces by congressmen who chose to speak or at least to act quietly for interest groups whose effectiveness would be hampered by the new program, many congressmen had strong personal reasons for opposing specific aspects of the proposal. Departmental reorganization implied reorganization of the congressional committee system. If there was to be only one water and sewer program rather than seven, then there should be only one committee in each house passing on these programs that are so popular in the localities receiving the government grants.

The congressional committee system, perhaps even more than the existing executive branch organization, reflects a series of piecemeal decisions and forgotten compromises stretching back over decades. Power, prestige, and public visibility in Congress flow to the chairman and ranking minority members of committees and subcommittees. Reputations are made—particularly for representatives aiming at senatorial office and for senators aspiring to the presidency—through committee work. Even presidential aspirants find it difficult to make news on issues unrelated to the work of their committees. And the easiest way for legislators to enhance their visibility and reputation is through larger funding for the departmental bureaus overseen by their committees or subcommittees and greater protection for the interest groups involved.

For all the exceptions that one can think of in the national security and foreign policy domains, it is remarkable how broadly applicable this principle of self-protection is in the domestic arena, in such diverse areas as agriculture, public works, science, social welfare, and health. Any reorganization that threatens the existing committee structure, even indirectly, casts uncertainty on the power base and personal future of individual legislators. The Departmental Reorganization Plan thus threatened not merely the executive branch support for the clientele of particular departments and bureaus but the institutional base for their congressional support as well.

The very magnitude of the proposal created a procedural situation in Congress conducive to delay and the death-by-nibbling process. Reorganizations had previously passed through Congress under the Reorganization Act, originally passed in 1939, under which a presidential proposal becomes law if one house does not disapprove it within 60 days. The legislative procedure under this act was that the proposed reorganization was referred to the Government Operations Committee of each house rather than to the substantive committees most concerned with the programs of the affected executive agencies. But the Reorganization Act did not authorize reorganizations creating new executive departments or abolishing old ones. New legislation would therefore be required. The means were thus at hand for the advocacy system to defeat any attempt to modify the advocacy system itself. None of the four bills to create a new department ever reached a vote on the floor of either house.

The idea of thoroughgoing reorganization is not dead. Just as the need for reorganization also motivated the proposals of President Johnson's commission headed by Ben Heineman, it is not surprising that President Carter emphasized top-to-bottom reorganization in his election campaign.

After it became clear that the 1971 reorganization proposal would not be enacted, attention turned to the administrative steps that could be taken to achieve the proposal's goals. Since the President had no power to reorganize departments without legislation, attention would have to be focused on the cabinet officers themselves. How could cabinet officers be given a presidential perspective? Were there any means available to broaden the perspective of a cabinet officer who spends his days surrounded by bureaucrats and middle-level officials of his department, meeting with the private groups that form its clientele, and appearing before congressional committees and subcommittees whose perspective and interests are often even narrower than those of his department as a whole? It was hardly surprising that most cabinet members, new to Washington and unacquainted with the details of the work that lay before them, were quickly captured by their departments and took on the policy coloration of the departments' old-line bureaucrats.

In many other countries, tradition tends to offset departmental influence on a cabinet member's views and interests. For instance, in countries where cabinet members are politicians, unlike in the United States, a cabinet member may already have served in several departments and will usually harbor ambitions for appointment to a more important ministry or even to the prime ministry itself. In countries such as Great Britain where the full cabinet is a decision-making body, the discussion of extradepartmental issues in cabinet meetings develops a broad perspective. By contrast, in the United States most cabinet officers come to the job from the private sector. They often have no previous experience in government, and they soon find that a cabinet meeting is primarily a setting for the President to sell his program to them rather than an opportunity for them to advise the President.

Discussions about how to broaden the perspectives of cabinet officers led to the idea of giving all cabinet officers a part-time office near the President and away from their departments. Cabinet officers and their personal staffs might be given offices in, say, the Executive Office Building, across the alley (grandly called West Executive Avenue) from the White House. There they might be expected to spend their mornings, participating at least part of that time in discussions of matters that transcended the interests of their own department.

With that idea in mind, a somewhat more limited plan evolved. Four cabinet members were to receive White House appointments in addition to their department posts. These new White House positions corresponded to the supersecretaryships of the four grand departments envisaged by the 1971 proposal. In addition to the naming of myself (Shultz), then Treasury Secretary, as Assistant to the President for Economic Policy (a job whose range of substantive responsibility included that of the proposed Secretary of Economic Affairs), the President announced in January 1973 that Secretary of Health, Education and Welfare Caspar Weinberger was also to be Counsellor for Human Resources, Secretary of Housing and Urban Development James Lynn was to be Counsellor for Community Development, and Secretary of Agriculture Earl Butz was to be Counsellor for Natural Resources. Henry Kissinger eventually moved in the opposite direction, retaining his position as Assistant to the President for National Security Affairs and taking over as Secretary of State, though this appointment did not take effect until September 1973.

The three counsellorships were short-lived. For a time Weinberger, Lynn, and Butz maintained offices in the Executive Office Building and even built special supporting staffs. But the contradictions between their paper responsibilities and the underlying reality of departmental turf quickly became apparent. The counsellors were still only cabinet officials, and yet they were extending their authority over bureaus within other departments. In some instances, one counsellor had apparent responsibility over functions within the home department of another counsellor. Even if no jealousies and frustrated ambitions had been involved, the confusion was formidable. Who was to be called by congressional committees for testimony, the counsellor or the department head? In cases where two departments were competitors for a new function or for control over policy, would a cabinet officer who happened to be counsellor be entitled to resolve the issue in favor of his own department? Either the counsellors or the competing department heads would quickly lose credibility before Congress and within the bureaucracy. Only five months after the creation of the counsellorships, it was quietly announced that they no longer existed.

The dual positions of Kissinger and myself survived these difficulties for a while, although Kissinger was eventually relieved of his National Security Council position in 1975, and the formal White House role of the Secretary of the Treasury as Assistant for Economic Policy ended when I left the government in May 1974 (though the Treasury Secretary continues to take the lead on economic issues). Perhaps one of the reasons for the greater longevity of the dual foreign and economic policy coordinating positions was that there were major issues to be resolved that were not closely tied to the welfare of large departmental bureaucracies or of well-organized clientele groups. International trade issues and price controls, for example, were not so deeply enmeshed in the traditional departmental and congressional mechanisms of the advocacy system as were many of the subsidy, grant-in-aid, and regulatory issues faced by the counsellors.

The Balkanization of the Executive Branch

A key issue in the organization of the executive branch is the role of the President. The President, not the executive branch, is vested by the Constitution with executive power. Executive departments were foreseen in the Constitution, but their existence is the product of subsequent statutory law. The creation of most departments has been much more recent than many people realize. The Department of Justice, for example, did not exist until 1870. Although the Constitution grants the President formal executive power, it is by no means clear, across a wide range of issues, that the President does in fact possess that power. As a result of legislation, the growth of the executive branch in the twentieth century, the progressive intervention of the judicial branch in executive decisions, and the workings of the advocacy process, the President has increasingly lost the effective power to make executive decisions. Even when he does make the decisions, he cannot assume that they will be carried out at the working level.

Legislation has attenuated the President's power by creating independent decision-making centers within the government. The first wave of such legislation created a host of independent economic regulatory agencies, beginning with the Interstate Commerce Commission in 1887. In the twentieth century, regulation spread to other forms of transportation and to such diverse economic sectors as securities, banking, and broadcasting, usually by creating a new independent agency for each regulated industry (for example, the Securities and Exchange Commission and the Federal Communications Commission). The creation of alphabet agencies has accelerated as new, at least partially independent agencies have been created in recent years to deal with safety and environmental matters. The Environmental Protection Agency and the Consumer Products Safety Commission, for instance, are products of the 1970s.

In recent decades, legislation has given department heads the responsibility for making decisions that, through detailed statutory specifications of the criteria for the decisions and through the availability of judicial review, have become largely immune to presidential influence. To be sure, many of these decisions are said to be quasi-judicial, but the analogy to judicial proceedings merely underscores the determination of Congress to convert decisions that in virtually all other governments are executive prerogatives into decisions outside the reach of the Chief Executive.

In recent years there has even been a movement toward making certain executive branch departments independent of the Chief Executive. For example, presidential supervision of the Justice Department has in recent times been viewed by the media, the Congress, and the public as highly suspect. Although the Justice Department unquestionably makes economic policy in the antitrust field, the notion has gained ground that the President ought to have nothing to do with this crucial area because law enforcement is involved.

The judicial branch has collaborated actively with the legislative branch in this balkanization process. Court decisions have safeguarded the independence of administrative agencies. To the extent that Congress imposes decisions of a judicial character on cabinet and subcabinet officials, the courts have recently been prepared not only to review such decisions but to call the executive branch official to account for his decisions in court. There he has been interrogated to see whether he has based his decisions only on the statutory criteria themselves and not on broader considerations, such as the effect of the decision on consumer prices or the effect of resulting expenditures on fiscal policy.

When the executive branch official fails to act like a judge (by preparing a written opinion to justify his decision) and instead keeps his reasons to himself, he may have to give a deposition prior to trial or may be forced to testify at trial as to the considerations involved in his decision. For example, in the *Three Sisters Bridge* case, Secretary of Transportation John Volpe testified in court for over five hours to explain his decision to approve construction of a bridge over the Potomac River near Washington, D.C.

Perhaps the most important step taken by the courts in "judicializing" executive branch decisions is the vast expansion in the number and kinds of individuals who are permitted to bring actions. A line of Supreme Court decisions on what is justiciable vastly expanded the kinds of executive branch decisions that are subject to second-guessing in the courts and the kinds of people who may invoke the judicial power not merely to protect themselves but also to advance social and aesthetic values they hold dear. In the environmental area the expansion of those accorded "standing" in the courts to challenge executive branch action, coupled with a broad interpretation of the National Environmental Policy Act, has created a situation in which the delay and uncertainty created by judicial branch intervention has become one of the most important elements in a highly complex decision matrix. Whatever the legal merits of the actions filed, environmental litigation has become one of the principal barriers to expansion of domestic energy production and thus has had economic and diplomatic ramifications far transcending the bounds of what has traditionally been the judicial province.

The courts have imposed increasingly stringent requirements on the content of environmental impact statements that must be filed before many kinds of administrative decisions can be implemented by the executive departments. For example, prior to holding a lease sale of offshore oil and gas tracts, the Department of the Interior was required by one court decision to consider whether the same new energy resources could be obtained in some alternative manner, such as by an increase in the regulated maximum price of natural gas. The court held it to be irrelevant that the regulation of natural gas prices had been vested in an independent agency, the Federal Power Commission, and was thus completely outside the control and even the legitimate sphere of influence of both the Interior Department and the President. Some courts have even gone beyond the requirement that an environmental impact statement be issued and have undertaken to evaluate environmental effects themselves.

In the environmental area the courts may not have done much more than carry out the role Congress wanted them to have. The statutory requirement of a detailed environmental impact statement underwent a metamorphosis in the process of congressional consideration and judicial interpretation. What was initially an administrative device to assure that agencies took account of environmental considerations in making decisions became a judicially enforceable requirement, and finally a requirement judicially enforceable by anyone with a personal interest in the environment. The result was the creation of a litigation stage of indeterminate length in the planning of many important federal and private projects.

The judiciary has welcomed its new role in economic policymaking. In one of the first important cases *(Calvert Cliffs)*, which led to a delay in operation of five already constructed nuclear power plants and in the licensing of many more, Judge J. Skelly Wright exulted over the new activist role granted the judicial branch, commencing his opinion with a declaration that "at long last, the destructive engine of material progress" was to be controlled and that the courts would now be able to play a role in doing so:

> These cases are only the beginning of what promises to become a flood of new litigation—litigation seeking judicial assistance in protecting our natural environment. Several recently enacted statutes attest to the commitment of the government to control, at long last, the destructive engine of material "progress." But it remains to be seen whether the promise of this legislation will become a reality. Therein lies the judicial role.

The same interventionist judicial stance has been seen in the impoundment cases, where courts almost uniformly held that the executive branch could not refuse to spend what the legislature had appropriated. Whether the courts were right in reversing the longstanding understanding and practice that an appropriation is an authority, not an order, to spend is not a question that can be examined here. In discussing the organization of government, however, it is relevant to ask whether one can hope that fiscal policy can be used at all to steer the economy if control over the rate of spending is to be foreclosed by appropriations decisions made many months or even years before. Judicial intervention in the impoundment cases has meant that fiscal policy flexibility has been further limited. The impoundment decisions have technically been superseded by the 1974 congressional budget reform act, but the judicial attitude toward economic policy issues reflected in the impoundment cases has not changed.

In a balkanized executive branch, policymaking is necessarily a piecemeal affair; policymakers are under the constraint that they are not permitted to view problems whole. Although the trend toward balkanization seems almost irreversible, public discussions of economic and other policy issues are still carried on from the traditional classroom perspective that policymakers can deal with all aspects of a problem and can adjust outmoded policies instantly and costlessly. The reality is far different and the trend of events is toward greater fragmentation. One can only hope that common sense will be reasserted. The great (and even the small) issues of the day deserve balanced consideration. A government structure that forces broad policy decisions to be made in a legalistic framework will sooner or later be called to account by the people. From our perspective, the sooner the better.

Coordinating Economic Policy

Despite the increased balkanization of government, the executive branch retains the responsibility and, at least jointly with Congress, the tools for dealing with the larger issues of economic policy. The way in which executive branch economic policy decisions are made is therefore important. Since the end of World War II increasing attention has been paid, both in Congress and in the executive branch, to the organization of economic policymaking. The Employment Act of 1946 established the Council of Economic Advisers (CEA) to advise the President on the economic implications of decisions in support of the policy goal of "maximum employment, production, and purchasing power."

The creation of the CEA was a great step forward, though its internal government and public roles have varied considerably over the three decades of its existence. The first two chairmen represented extremes in the conception of the council's role: the detached professorial approach and the role of involved public advocate of the President's program. The public advocacy role made the council so political and controversial that the CEA was almost abolished by Congress in 1952. President Eisenhower's appointment of Arthur Burns as chairman and Burns' impressive performance saved the council. Burns was active in the policy process within the administration but would not engage at all in public advocacy, regarding himself exclusively as the President's economic adviser. Dignity and professional stature were restored. Subsequent chairmen, while working in varying degrees into a public role, have nevertheless been generally successful in maintaining a professional stance. Meanwhile, their influence on the process of policy formulation has been increasingly important, reflecting the high quality of the small council staff and the good working relationships of the chairmen with the President.

Even after the Council of Economic Advisers was established, economic policy tended to remain the by-product of other policies, some of which (for example, concerning the budget and taxes) were conceived in economic terms. But until the creation in 1962 of the Troika, which brought together the Secretary of the Treasury, the chairman of the Council of Economic Advisers, and the director of the Bureau of the Budget, there was no formal framework for considering fiscal policy as such. Because domestic monetary policy remained by statutory command within the province of the independent Federal Reserve Board, the chairman of the Federal Reserve sometimes met with the Troika. Such meetings were referred to as Quadriad meetings, but they did not necessarily result in any common view of desirable monetary policy.

Beyond domestic fiscal and monetary policy lay a vast realm of economic policy issues, which were handled in a wide variety of ways. Some, such as international monetary policy, tended to be within the control of a single agency, in this instance, the Treasury. Others were placed in balkanized compartments, often by command of Congress. A prime illustration is international trade policy, where trade negotiations were localized in a special part of the Executive Office of the President referred to as the Office of the Special Trade Representative, regulatory trade programs such as countervailing duties were localized in the Treasury (with further constraints from the International Trade Commission), export controls were in the Commerce Department, and a diverse assortment of trade matters such as international commodity agreements were handled by the State Department. Still other issues, such as oil imports before the 1973 oil crisis, were not regarded as matters for economic policy officials but rather were treated as part of general domestic or foreign policy, appropriate for coordination by noneconomic officials.

The Council on International Economic Policy

Well into the Nixon administration there was still no economic policymaking machinery beyond the Troika, which was perceived by those outside its membership (all of the executive branch departments other than the Treasury) as an exclusive club. Under pressure from some excluded cabinet officers, the President created a Cabinet Committee on Economic Policy in 1969. But it was used on only a few issues, in part because it suffered from the natural weaknesses of any committee that lacks both an accepted leader and an identifiable separate staff whose loyalty is to the committee and its leader rather than to the constituent departments.

The most pressing need for new policy machinery was in the international economic sphere. Responsibility was widely divided, as exemplified by the balkanization of international trade responsibilities. The National Security Council staff, with its necessary preoccupation with the political and military aspects of foreign policy, was not a promising locus for dealing with international monetary, trade, and natural resource issues.

The solution adopted in 1971 was to form a Council on International Economic Policy (CIEP). The council itself was composed of cabinet-level officials. Its nominal chairman at the outset was the President, but responsibility for supervising the CIEP staff was in the hands of its executive director. The CIEP staff became an important unit in the Executive Office of the President, and the executive director was an important White House official.

Despite its White House connection, the council had some difficulty in establishing itself. The Treasury Department under John Connally resisted any CIEP influence over international monetary policy, and only the energy and perseverence of Peter Peterson, the first executive director, and his successor, Peter Flanigan, permitted the CIEP to win a place in the international economic policy machinery. The CIEP's role in international trade matters remained problematical because of the statutory role of the

Special Trade Representative, whose staff viewed itself as a rival to the CIEP staff. Attempts to merge these two Executive Office units failed, and even attempts to rationalize their separate roles never fully succeeded. Although both groups might agree in principle that the CIEP staff was to deal with trade policy and the Special Trade Representative's staff was to handle trade negotiations, this distinction foundered on day-to-day realities and personal rivalries.

The Council on Economic Policy

The question of the role of CIEP was settled as a practical matter when the President, shortly after the 1972 election, created the Council on Economic Policy, vested with the responsibility to coordinate all economic policy, both domestic and international. Then Treasury Secretary, I (Shultz) also became Assistant to the President for Economic Policy and simultaneously was made chairman of the Council on Economic Policy and chairman of the CIEP. Rather than creating still a further White House unit, support for the Council on Economic Policy was provided by an executive director who worked with a single assistant and drew on the staffs of existing agencies in the Executive Office of the President and on the constituent departments for council work.

Despite the apparent complexity of the economic policymaking machinery (fortunately no one attempted to draw a formal organization chart), the new machinery was relatively simple. The heart of the coordinating process was a daily 8:00 a.m. meeting attended by its Executive Office and Treasury members, representing all aspects of economic policy. These meetings were informal, but they were successful in permitting those who attended to grasp the interconnections between various economic issues and to form a common view on how to approach those issues.

The bulk of the work of the council was done, however, neither in the daily meetings nor in full cabinet-level meetings, which were seldom held. Rather, many working groups, composed in each case of all concerned departments and agencies, were formed to tackle major issues, such as the separate parts of the administration's legislative program. It was possible, in large part because of the common understanding acquired in the daily 8:00 a.m. meetings, to resolve many issues through ad hoc meetings of those individuals principally concerned.

The very breadth and comprehensiveness of the policy responsibility not only permitted greater informality in operation but also helped to bypass some of the difficulties that had hampered the CIEP experiment. With the Treasury Secretary as the head of the Council on Economic Policy and with the CIEP becoming in effect the international arm of the council, it was possible to coordinate the Treasury's work in international economic policy with the CIEP's and Special Trade Representative's work in the international trade area. Once a single overall structure was in place to resolve broad issues in policy, assignments of day-to-day responsibility for particular issues created fewer jealousies and bureaucratic rivalries.

A wide variety of organizations exist to formulate and administer various aspects of economic policy. Although the advocacy process has produced too many overlapping and competing agencies, any attempt to place all economic policy matters into one organization would be doomed to failure. Each organization has its mission, each its cabinet officer, chairman, or executive director, and each its staff. The path of least resistance and, to a degree, the inevitable consequence of this multiplicity is for each organization to go off in its own direction and to deal with problems from its own intellectual and bureaucratic vantage point.

The flow of economic events does not recognize these jurisdictional lines. The economy itself operates as a system in which the constituent parts are linked, sometimes tightly. The combination of interwoven problems and disparate organizations means that in the process of policy formulation and implementation, some people high in any administration must identify the central ideas and problems and devise some strategy for relating them to each other. Congress needs to give the President sufficient organizational flexibility so that he can establish and rearrange his economic team to suit his taste and theirs and to correspond to the problems of the time. Precisely how coordination is achieved is not as important as that organizational arrangements are in fact developed to encompass the critical ideas and people and that such arrangements are sufficiently flexible to evolve as the agenda of economic problems changes.

CHAPTER NINE

Energy and the Marketplace

WHAT WOULD THE PROVERBIAL MAN from Mars, who cannot understand our language but can observe our behavior, conclude are the objectives of our country on energy? He would observe that our government encourages consumption of energy through a deliberate act of holding the domestic price of oil and natural gas below its world market level. He would see a public quite responsive to this action, reacting, for example, by once again turning to large cars. He would observe a distinct effort by the government to discourage domestic production and privately financed research: by lowering the price and, perhaps more devastatingly, by creating a maximum of uncertainty about the pricing conditions that will prevail when a given energy source comes on stream; by conducting a kind of guerrilla warfare against the oil industry, historically a most creative element in our energy system; and by being reluctant to take the steps necessary to encourage development of our most available sources of supply, particularly nuclear energy and coal-fired energy.

Our man from Mars, observing these things, would have to conclude either that we have no significant energy problem or that we are quite content to become more and more dependent on the importation of energy, principally from the Middle East. Indeed, by requiring the pump price of gasoline to be based on an average of the higher price of foreign crude oil and the controlled, lower domestic price, our government subsidizes and therefore encourages the use of imported oil!

If this is a reasonably accurate picture of what our government is in fact doing and of the conclusions that follow from it, what are the leaders of the legislative and executive branches saying? Almost universally our politicians declare that we have a massive problem and that we must curtail consumption, encourage production, and stimulate research. And above all, they say, we must reduce our dependence on foreign suppliers. Here we witness a massive case of saying one thing and doing exactly the opposite—a case where the political process seems to be unable to permit us to face up to economic and strategic reality.

A Problem in Political Economy

Our problem in the energy field today is not simply, perhaps not even primarily, a natural resource, scientific, or engineering problem. It is fundamentally a problem in political economy. The resolution, or rather the nonresolution, of key energy policy problems demonstrates the role that organizational and equity considerations play, for better or worse, in key government economic decisions.

When the governments of the Organization of Petroleum Exporting Countries (OPEC) increased the price of crude oil fourfold in late 1973 and in 1974, a Pandora's box of energy policy issues was opened. These issues were not unforeseeable or even unforeseen, but the OPEC action forced them into prominence. However complex the technical and business aspects of the energy field may be, the key economic policy issues of the past few years have been straightforward. An obvious question at the time of the OPEC price rise was whether the domestic price of crude oil and its products (particularly gasoline) should be subject to price controls. General wage and price controls were being phased out in late 1973, and the statute authorizing them expired in April 1974. By the time of expiration, however, the petroleum sector had been subjected to comprehensive regulation under new legislation authorizing not only price controls but also mandatory allocation of crude oil among refiners and geographic areas. Indeed, because the Arab oil embargo in late 1973 created an apparent gasoline and heating oil shortage in the U.S. during the winter of 1973-74, public and congressional demands had arisen for the imposition of a system of rationing to accompany the price controls. Although rationing was avoided, the demand for government regulation overwhelmed any possibility for a market solution. That the elimination of price controls and the consequent rise in oil and gasoline prices would gradually reduce demand and increase supply, thereby eliminating the shortage, was lost sight of in the clamor for direct government action.

Concern about the effect of a sudden, dramatic increase in energy price levels on the rate of U.S. economic growth created uncertainty in many quarters, even among government economists, as to the correct economic decision on oil price controls. The fourfold increase in the price of key petroleum imports constituted a sudden but continuing transfer of about 1 percent of our GNP to foreign producers. Although that transfer could be viewed simply as erasing part of one year's increment of growth in the U.S. economy—leaving the rate of future growth essentially unchanged—the more pervasive fear was that the OPEC price rise would have dynamic and far-reaching effects, eventually plunging the U.S. economy into a depression. Many people thought that the risks of these cumulative effects could be offset, or at least diminished, by holding down the price of domestically produced oil and diffusing the full impact of the increased cost of imported oil through a system that would average the cost of uncontrolled foreign oil and controlled domestic oil. This reasoning reinforced the political demand to "do something," and the result was that petroleum product prices in the United States were held below the world market price.

Price controls were, of course, not the only economic policy issue that arose concerning energy. Others included the level of government funding of energy research and development, the use of nuclear and coal-fired energy, the role of the government in promoting energy conservation (through direct limitations on use, subsidies, taxes, and the like) and in negotiating with the OPEC governments on crude oil prices, and the appropriate international monetary policy to deal with the huge and continuing transfers of financial assets brought about by the oil price increase.

Decisions on all of these economic policy issues had to be made in conjunction with decisions in the diplomatic and national security arenas. Few subjects better illustrate the connections between conventional policy fields than do the energy problems that came to the forefront of public interest with the oil crisis. The Arab oil embargo revealed the vulnerability of the United States to economic pressure on such crucial war-and-peace issues as the future of Israel and the relationship between the United States and the Soviet Union in the Middle East. One of the strongest arguments for a large increase in government funding of energy research and development was that such an increase would, by reducing U.S. dependence on foreign oil, strengthen our efforts to deal with the problems of oil prices and with the Middle East in general. The same line of reasoning supported relaxation of oil and natural gas price controls in the United States. Higher oil and gas prices, by reducing U.S. consumption and stimulating exploration and development of oil, gas, and other fuels, would diminish the international political leverage of Arab governments over our Middle East policy.

Drawing by Art Bimrose
The Portland Oregonian

Mideast Diplomacy

Attempts to Deal with Emerging Problems

Although there was no necessary inconsistency between the energy policies that would be optimal from economic, diplomatic, and national security perspectives, these interconnections were the source of intellectual confusion. They led to repeated failures in the executive branch, in Congress, and in public discussion to grasp the essential nature of the energy problem.

The first major attempt to grapple with energy issues in the Nixon administration was the creation in March 1969 of a Cabinet Task Force on Oil Import Control, which I (Shultz) chaired while then serving as Secretary of Labor. The problem for the task force was to assess whether or not the national security interest in encouraging exploration and development of secure U.S. oil sources was effectively being served by the oil quota system and was worth the cost to U.S. consumers of the higher domestic prices induced by this self-imposed restriction.

From a simple economic perspective, the case against quotas was straightforward. Quotas limiting imports of oil resulted in domestic U.S.

prices about half again as high as prices on the world market (about $3 versus $2 per barrel) and hence were costly to U.S. consumers. Quotas also made the world oil industry less efficient. Unless powerful counterbalancing considerations could be shown, they should therefore be ended.

The national security justification for the oil import quota program generally focused on national defense, and thus the crucial question at that time was what the impact of increased imports stemming from abolition of quotas would be on the capacity of the U.S. defense establishment to wage war. In its report published in 1970, however, the task force did explicitly consider the hypothetical case of a year-long Arab oil supply interruption, questioning the probable scope and duration of any boycott but stating that "the possibility of a prolonged and virtually total boycott cannot be ignored." In 1973, when the Arab states, in support of their military struggle with Israel, limited production and attempted to embargo all petroleum shipments to the United States, this possibility became a reality.

Although the 1970 cabinet task force report recognized the possibility of an oil embargo, it, in company with most other observers, underestimated the ability of OPEC to raise the world oil price over a period of time. The error here lay in underestimating the rapid growth of U.S. and world demand for oil, which by 1973 created a situation where petroleum production capacity was for the first time fully utilized in both the United States and the Middle East. The task force's estimates of consumption were, however, at the upper edge of the range of private estimates at the time and, on the crucial issue of oil imports, the report correctly forecast that they were certain to rise during the 1970s.

Despite the shortcomings of the 1970 task force report, its recommendations, had they been promptly and fully implemented, would have placed the United States in a stronger position at the time of the oil crisis. Both the proposed management system, which would have involved continuous monitoring of domestic petroleum production, consumption, and imports by a high-level Executive Office staff subject to interdepartmental review, and the proposed substitution of an import duty system for a quota system (finally implemented in 1973) would have permitted a more careful and calibrated approach to the control of imports. The proposed management system (which was implemented in form but not in substance) would have made possible a serious ongoing assessment of the U.S. strategic position. Such a management system would, for example, have brought home to top-level officials the supply consequences of the seemingly endless delays in the construction of the Alaska pipeline and would have called into question the assumption that oil and gas would soon flow from the Canadian Arctic as well as from northern Alaska. Thus, it might have led to a timelier recognition among top officials that consumption and production factors were rapidly creating a highly favorable situation for the exercise of market power by the OPEC countries.

Prompt replacement of the extraordinarily complex quota system by the proposed import duty system would have permitted an earlier straightforward debate on the appropriate level of imports and would have eliminated the quota system's specialized vested interests and technical complexities that obscured what was really happening to the demand for imports. The quota system and the absence of an adequate management system diverted attention from the crucial variable: OPEC's ability to raise prices by controlling its production. It was, after all, not the OPEC oil embargo that created the key economic problem. The embargo did not result in an insuperable supply interruption; private oil companies were able to rearrange the flow of oil so that boycotted countries were no more affected than other oil-consuming nations. Rather, it was the restriction of production by OPEC governments that, by facilitating the imposition of sharp price increases on the consuming world, created the more serious and lasting problems.

Spokesmen for the oil industry recognized the nature of the oil problem well before either the public or the government and tried to publicize it, but their statements were heavily discounted because of their interested position. The fact that U.S. oil imports were growing rapidly and would continue to grow as domestic petroleum production and reserves fell was not widely understood by the public or most top-level government officials. Even after increasing U.S. dependence was recognized within the executive branch (as imports grew from 2.5 million barrels a day in 1967 to 6.2 million barrels a day in 1973), the intellectual perception of the problem still produced no action. It did, however, at least force top-level White House attention to the energy problem in late 1972 and early 1973.

Even before the oil crisis erupted in late 1973, it had become clear that policymaking in the energy sphere required new thought and new organizational forms. Before 1973, responsibility for energy policy was decentralized in departments and agencies that had little contact with one another. Oil and coal, for instance, were handled in the Interior Department. Until 1971, when an interagency Oil Policy Committee was established, a subject of such importance to international relations and national security policy as the oil import quota system was the province of the Interior Department. Nuclear energy was in the hands of the semi-independent Atomic Energy Commission. Natural gas and electric power (to the extent that electric power was a concern of the federal government) were regulated by the independent Federal Power Commission. Budget matters concerning energy research and development received no coordinated attention beyond that provided in the general budget process.

The first reaction to the need for coordination of energy policymaking was to create a new center of responsibility within the Executive Office of the President. An ad hoc group headed by Peter Flanigan, as Assistant to the President, was created in 1972. Flanigan was charged with conducting the analysis that would lead to a major presidential message on energy. Before Flanigan's work could fully mature into the planned presidential message (sent to Congress in April 1973), a special Energy Committee was formed early in 1973 under three presidential assistants—for Foreign Affairs (Kissinger), Domestic Affairs (Ehrlichman), and Economic Affairs (Shultz). A new supporting White House staff headed by Charles DiBona, special consultant to the President, was also created. DiBona made massive and creative contributions to the analysis of policy issues and to the April 1973 energy message, a document whose recommendations—including the elimination of price controls on natural gas—hold up well today. The DiBona staff group was christened the Energy Policy Office in April 1973, but because the political importance of the issues escalated so rapidly, the President decided that a leading political figure was needed. Colorado Governor John Love was brought into the White House to fill this role as an Assistant to the President in June 1973.

A small White House office could formulate policy, but it lacked the staff to carry out the administrative tasks created by various presidential and legislative responses to the oil crisis that erupted in October 1973. The Arab boycott and the explosion of oil prices led to the appointment that December of William Simon, then Deputy Secretary of the Treasury, to head a new and larger Federal Energy Office (FEO). (The FEO, originally created by executive order, was later converted by statute into the Federal Energy Administration.) With the creation of FEO and the appointment of the talented and energetic Simon as its head, energy policymaking and administration emerged into the full glare of publicity.

But though Simon represented energy policy to the public, much as, say, the Secretary of Agriculture represents an administration's agricultural policy, energy was so broad a subject area that the FEO was in fact only one of the "players" in the internal struggle over energy policy. The FEO could hardly be delegated the diplomatic responsibilities of the State Department and the National Security Council, or the budget responsibilities of the Office of Management and Budget, or the tax and monetary responsibilities of the Treasury. The Cost of Living Council was responsible for administering price controls that worked at cross-purposes with FEO's goals of more production and less consumption. Ironically, when the responsibility for oil price controls was shifted to the FEO in 1974 in an attempt to resolve this conflict, the FEO proved less able to develop price incentives for oil exploration and development than had been the Cost of Living Council.

The creation of a highly visible and heavily staffed FEO consequently could not eliminate the need for a coherent energy policy that would coordinate economic, national security, and budget concerns and personally involve the President in major decisions. All of these reorganizations and new appointments were no doubt in part a substitute for a coherent policy on energy. But the participants properly believed that a coherent policy could not evolve from the balkanization of policy responsibility just described. The inability to settle on any one new policymaking framework is not so easily defended.

Policy Implications

The 1973 Arab embargo and the OPEC price increases did change attitudes, at least for a time. The wolf was finally at the door, and there was no denying it. With the weakening of the President's influence in Congress, however, the crisis attitude did not prove conducive to the clearest thinking on public policy implications. Several common reactions to the oil crisis are worth exploring because they reveal something about public thinking on policy issues in a crisis atmosphere.

One widespread attitude was that higher prices for domestically produced oil would do nothing to improve the situation. Proponents of politically popular measures directed at artificially holding down domestic oil prices argued that higher domestic prices would not reduce oil consumption in the United States. The implications of that view were that price controls should be applied to both domestic crude and to petroleum product prices and that direct controls—including mandatory crude oil and petroleum product allocation among companies and regions and even consumer gasoline rationing—should be used to spread the misery of shortages. To a large extent, this view reflected the great interest in equity as opposed to efficiency so prevalent in public and political discussion of economic issues. The concern for achieving equity for those who would pay the higher prices was, in this instance, supported by a quasi-economic argument that warrants examination.

Advocates of rationing and controls further maintained that consumption of oil products, unlike other goods, would not be responsive to higher prices because the demand for oil products is more or less fixed. Price, it was said, is not a factor in deciding how much gasoline is used. People have to drive to work, whatever the price of gas.

This position, which may be termed "elasticity pessimism," assumed that the responsiveness (elasticity) of demand for oil products to price was very low. This view ignored the critical variable of time: Changes in behavior take time. The greater the passage of time, the greater the potential adjustment.

Even in the short term, the view that higher prices would not affect

Drawing by Paul Conrad; © 1972
The Los Angeles Times
Reprinted with permission, L.A. Times Syndicate

demand overlooked a number of factors. Although it might appear that most auto commuters' demands would be unaffected by higher prices, many auto commuters did in fact adjust. As prices began to rise, many commuters found that public transportation was feasible after all. Car pools sprang up. As people bought new cars, many shifted to smaller cars consuming less gasoline.

Furthermore, automobile gasoline consumption was only one kind of consumption of oil products. Millions of people found that slightly cooler homes were not at all uncomfortable. In the business world many firms were able to save at least 10 percent of their energy costs by such simple steps as turning out lights after working hours and reducing illumination in areas where intense lighting was not necessary. Still more could be saved, they found, by making new investments in such things as insulation, computer systems to control energy usage, and new equipment that used energy more efficiently than the equipment it replaced.

In countries where consumers paid the world price of oil, elasticity of demand has been seen more clearly: Between 1973 and 1976, oil consumption declined in the United Kingdom (−17 percent), West Germany (−7.6 percent), France (−6.5 percent), and Japan (−5 percent). Over that same time span, oil consumption rose by 1 percent in the United States, where consumers paid a governmentally controlled price that, though increasing, was still well below the world market level. Oil consumption in the United States was muted by these higher, but still suppressed, prices; from 1965 to 1973, oil consumption in the United States had been rising at about 5.5 percent per year. During that same time, oil consumption had been rising annually at even greater rates in Japan (+14.3 percent), France (+10.2 percent), West Germany (+7.7 percent), and the United Kingdom (+5.6 percent). Clearly, even allowing for the effects of recession, demand did show significant elasticity.

Elasticity pessimism about demand had its corollary on the supply side. Here, too, the instinctive view in government was that supply was more or less fixed. But as in the case of demand, pessimism about the response of energy supplies to higher prices was not well founded. In the first place, higher petroleum prices had the effect of making substitutes more attractive. The use of coal, one of America's most plentiful resources, and nuclear power became very competitive. Coal prices responded to the increased demand, making new sources of coal such as the western coal lands financially feasible for investment (although environmental regulations, and particularly delays in resolving environmental issues concerning new projects, were a barrier to immediate development). Research and development on new energy sources also became more attractive. Higher prices thus increased the supply of crude oil substitutes, though in many instances the new supplies would not become available for some years.

Even more significant was the supply response to the petroleum sector itself. The recent pace of development in the North Sea and Mexico, for example, suggests a vigorous supply response to higher prices. What appears to be happening internationally is comparable to the response of the U.S. oil industry to a 25 percent increase in the real price of crude oil from 1947 to 1948. That comparatively minor increase brought forth an 18 percent increase in the number of U.S. exploratory wells drilled during the same period and, over a seven-year period, a doubling in the number of such wells without any further increase in the real price of oil.

Today, however, the supply response within the U.S. to higher world prices has been tempered by the continued application of price controls on domestically produced oil. Oil price control legislation passed in late 1975 actually rolled back most domestic crude oil and product prices and provided for continuation of price and allocation controls for most of the remainder of the decade. Worse than the oil price controls themselves is the uncertainty created by the willingness of Congress to pass (and even a conservative President to accept) price control legislation. If such legislation can pass when price controls are obviously contrary to U.S. economic, diplomatic, and national security interests, companies contemplating long-term energy investments must anticipate the possibility that the controls may be extended and, even if they are phased out, that they may be reimposed if world crude oil prices should rise further.

The refusal of Congress to remove price controls on natural gas contains the same lessons. These controls, imposed by the 1954 Supreme Court *Phillips Petroleum* ruling, have had a negative effect on exploration and production of natural gas. Yet consuming states seem more willing to suffer rationing and even interruptions of natural gas supplies than to pay a free-market price for it. Many representatives of consuming states have even preferred to extend price controls on interstate sales to the previously exempt intrastate sales (thereby redoubling the adverse effect on exploration) rather than pay more for an adequate supply.

The possibility of unregulated intrastate sales has been the principal incentive for exploration and new production. The elimination of the intrastate exemption would eventually require some nationwide allocation system to deal with the self-imposed shortages that would result. Since natural gas is found not only in dry gas formations (70 percent of the additions to reserves in the 1966-75 period were dry gas) but also with oil, the unwillingness to face up to the economic costs of this perverse natural gas price regulation further inhibits the increase in investment in oil exploration.

REDUCER

NATURAL GAS SUPPLY

FEDERAL PRICE REGULATION

Drawing by Don Hesse; © 1973
The St. Louis Globe-Democrat
Reprinted with permission, L.A. Times Syndicate

The Petrodollar Problem

Before asking why the United States has been so unwilling to decontrol energy markets, it is worth examining a set of related markets where reliance on the market mechanism has worked to deal with a crisis.

When the OPEC governments succeeded in increasing the world crude oil price fourfold, there was great concern about the international financial implications. Since the OPEC countries produce the lion's share of crude oil entering international markets and since crude oil constitutes a substantial share of international trade, what would be the effect on world financial markets of the mounting current account surpluses of the OPEC countries? Estimates of these surpluses grew, as one "expert" after another came forth with a higher estimate than the one preceding. Each new estimate was given further publicity by television and the press. For a time, the process resembled an auction in which each "bid" had to be higher than the one before in order to be recognized in public discussion. One of the best publicized bids in this process was a 1974 World Bank estimate that the cumulative OPEC surplus would reach $653 billion by 1980 and $1,206 billion by 1985.

These escalating estimates aroused many fears. One was that oil-exporting governments would acquire such great currency reserves and have so few outlets for their funds that they would buy up controlling interests in American blue-chip companies (which were then trading at historically low price-earnings ratios on the stock exchanges). A more pervasive fear, widely felt throughout Europe, was that the international financial system would be unable to handle the growing deficits of countries that were at the time completely dependent on imported oil supplies.

Another fear was that one or more of the oil-exporting governments might choose to switch deposits and short-term securities holdings suddenly from one currency to another. The belief that the OPEC governments would keep their foreign currency earnings in very short-term obligations was, of course, at odds with the belief that they would acquire controlling interests in industrial companies. But at the height of the panic, the OPEC currency reserve build-up was thought to be potentially so great as to support both fears simultaneously. Occasional bank failures, such as the failure of the Herstaat Bank in Germany in 1974 with its widespread international dimensions, merely underscored the felt potential for disaster.

This set of concerns, popularly referred to as the petrodollar problem, rested on a set of assumptions about how the market works (or, more properly, how it does *not* work). The first assumption, already noted, was that higher oil prices would not reduce consumption or bring forth additional supplies of oil and oil substitutes. The second was that OPEC countries would not be able to absorb increased imports from the industrialized countries (for these developing countries presumably had a limited capacity to support industrialization and many of them had small populations).

As it turned out, the second assumption was even less justified than the first. The hunger of OPEC countries for consumer goods, industrial plant and equipment, and military hardware was radically underestimated. OPEC imports from the United States rose 85 percent in 1974 and another 75 percent in 1975. By 1976 Iran was running a balance-of-payments deficit, and major exporters such as Libya and Indonesia each ran more than a $1 billion deficit in 1975. Sparsely populated Saudi Arabia, the biggest oil exporter, more than tripled its imports between the end of 1973 and the middle of 1975. To the extent that the mounting OPEC oil earnings were spent on increased imports, there would of course be no petrodollar problem at all. By early 1975 it became clear that the dimensions of that problem had been vastly overestimated. One of the first realistic estimates, made by Morgan Guaranty Trust Company in 1975, was that OPEC countries' holdings of foreign financial assets would peak at around $250 billion, a fraction of the estimates of those who had ignored the adjustments that would occur in the marketplace.

In addition to these erroneous assumptions about the capacity of OPEC countries to absorb imports from industrialized nations, and hence about the build-up of OPEC currency reserves, there were other assumptions about the workings of financial markets. To the extent that a major threat to the international financial system was thought to be that OPEC governments would maintain their reserves in very short-term securities, the possibility that the market would work to give OPEC countries an incentive to invest in longer-term debt securities was overlooked. As OPEC currency reserves mounted, short-term interest rates fell while long-term interest rates held relatively firm. The law of supply and demand working through financial markets thus created a strong incentive for OPEC governments to hold longer-term securities. Eurodollar overnight deposit rates fell from 9.75 percent in December 1973 to 5.25 percent in May 1975, while 12-month Eurodollar deposit rates fell from 9.56 percent to 8 percent. Far from collapsing under the weight of the petrodollar problem, financial markets thus worked to solve that problem. The evidence is, moreover, that oil-producing countries' financial reserves have been handled responsibly, as might be expected of countries with a large stake in the orderly functioning of these markets.

Financial markets helped deal with the petrodollar problem in still another way. As mentioned earlier, part of that problem was thought to be how to finance governments that would be experiencing large deficits because of the oil price increases. These deficits were expected to be so large that only other governments, acting individually and jointly through international arrangements, could handle the financing burden. Various schemes were developed for recycling OPEC funds from countries in which those funds were invested to countries experiencing the worst deficits.

While governments were meeting to work out the details of these arrangements, world financial markets were quietly doing much recycling on their own. Countries with large deficits borrowed in the Eurodollar market and from large commercial banks in the industrialized countries with the strongest currencies. This is not to diminish the importance of the intergovernmental arrangements, which of course were indispensable since they provided the underlying security against which private financing could continue to go forward and since they could impose certain conditions on a country's economic management. The point is that private financial markets did not collapse but rather made a considerable contribution to the transition from the pre-crisis to the post-crisis world.

Why Don't We Trust Markets?

If the world financial markets saved the day in the 1973-75 period despite the impediments of energy price controls imposed in the United States, how does one explain the almost universal skepticism in political and governmental circles about market solutions to major problems? Upon close examination of the question, one is led to conclude that the answer lies not so much in doubts about the technical efficiency of markets as in a massive unwillingness to allow markets to work.

For a variety of reasons, governments often are unprepared to let markets do their job. The hesitancy to rely on the free operation of market forces in times of shortage and in times of rising prices is by no means limited to the energy sector. The imposition of general wage and price controls in the US in 1971, as well as the experimentation with price controls and incomes policies at one time or another in numerous other countries, is evidence of this general tendency. Controls in the U.S. have not been the product of bureaucrats' willingness to impose their own judgment in place of market forces or of some economists' belief that controls may be superior to market forces. Rather, as the history of U.S. controls in the 1970s demonstrates, the pressure to resort to controls whenever the rate of inflation is perceived to be increasing has deep political roots.

The pressure from Congress to impose controls, not just on energy but more widely, has been greater than the desire of the executive branch to

Drawing by Herc Ficklen
Courtesy *The Dallas Morning News*

"Is there a Houdini in the House—or Senate?"

oppose them. President Nixon's decisions to introduce general wage and price controls in 1971 and to impose a second price freeze in 1973 were essentially political tactics aimed at wresting the political initiative on the inflation issue from Congress. Against this historical background, it is hard to view the tendency to impose controls in recent times as either a bureaucratic grab for power or as an exercise of professional economic judgment.

No doubt the congressional pressure for controls at times represented merely the influence of elective politics. In the politician's world the horizon is immediate. In the world of economics, surely in the world of energy, the only kind of thinking that really makes any sense is long-range thinking. Policymaking often confronts a problem of lags. One might say that the economist's lag can be the politician's nightmare. After the politician correctly perceives a problem and makes the best long-term decision, conditions don't improve immediately. Where does that leave him while waiting for results—defeated at the polls? The problem of lags is very real for the politician and cannot be ignored. Thus, when the public has not had to endure the consequences of controls in the recent past, a promise to hold prices down or allocate scarce supplies by brute governmental force may be politically beguiling and difficult to resist.

Congressional interest in controls during the 1970s cannot, however, be explained solely, or perhaps even primarily, on grounds of elective politics. Even those legislators who believe that market forces produce efficient solutions and who refuse to pander to misguided popular beliefs on economic matters may nonetheless espouse controls on the grounds of equity. Rhetorically, equity arguments focus on the poor, but in practice their range encompasses a wide variety of interest groups. The importance of equity as opposed to efficiency and the difficulty of keeping the equity focus on those with low incomes was seen most clearly in the oil crisis. The concern extended not just to particular consumers but more generally to the relative effects of shortages and higher prices on both consumers and producers, as was readily seen in the massive public attacks on the "obscene" profits of oil companies.

The demand for equity took on some unusual dimensions. Independent refiners that had previously been supplied with surplus crude oil from the major oil companies demanded continued access to crude oil in the ensuing period of shortage. This demand for what was asserted to be equitable treatment was met through a mandatory allocation program and later, in addition, an entitlements program. The allocation program had two aspects. First, historic supplier-refiner relationships were frozen; sellers of crude oil that had supplied small refiners until the oil crisis were required to continue doing so. Second, a buy-sell program was instituted whereby small independent refiners would be able to buy, and other companies would be required to sell to those refiners at a favorable price, crude oil in quantities determined in accordance with their pre-crisis level of operations.

The equity objective of the allocation program was plain. But the actual operation was extremely inefficient. For some months in 1974 the buy-sell program produced the absurd effect that companies having access to the foreign crude oil required to meet domestic demand would not only have to pay the high world price for that foreign oil but would then be required to sell part of that foreign oil to competing refiners at a price lower than they had paid for it. This lower "formula" price was determined by a weighted average of the foreign oil price and the controlled price for the domestic crude. Any economic incentive for the major oil companies to relieve the domestic oil shortage was seriously impeded by the artificially low price required for sales under the buy-sell portion of the allocation program.

Providing access to the oil did not exhaust the demand for equity. In an effort to soften the impact of price controls on domestic crude oil production, a two-tier pricing system had been established. Old oil would remain subject to price controls, but new oil (oil from new wells) would be exempt. This attempt to reduce the irrationalities of price controls quickly gave rise to a new demand for equity. Was it fair that refiners of new oil should have to pay more than refiners of old oil? An entitlements program was created to equalize the cost of crude oil to refiners. Under the guise of the purchase and sale of entitlements to the lower-priced old oil, some refiners were required to make equalizing cash payments to others.

The equity argument also took on a regional dimension. Since the Northeast had few refineries, that region was the prime U.S. consumer of imported heating oil and residual fuel oil refined abroad. Northeastern interests therefore sought compensation from the rest of the country for bearing the burden of higher world crude oil prices at a time when consumers in the rest of the country received the price benefits of access to price-controlled old oil. This "regional equity" argument acquired even more political force than the "refinery equalization" argument. The entitlements program was extended to permit importers of certain refined products to receive the cash benefits of old oil entitlements similar to those given to domestic refiners. A Donaldson, Lufkin & Jenrette report estimated the regional income transfer to the sections of the country consuming imports to be $5 billion per year, observing that although "the Northeast may be shy of resources, it is not shy of resourcefulness."

This concept of regional equity was rich with irony. Before the fourfold world price increase and during the oil import program period, the Northeast had profited by access to lower world fuel oil prices while the rest of the country paid the higher domestic price. Yet when the tables turned, the demands for equity led to the regional income transfer. The absence of refineries in the Northeast was in part due to local environmental objections. In addition, Northeastern consumers had been strong supporters of continued natural gas price controls, which discouraged new natural gas production for interstate shipment to that region and made it even more dependent on foreign sources. Paradoxically, the higher prices for foreign oil made deregulation of natural gas prices even more unacceptable to the Northeast because, it was argued, higher prices for natural gas would further burden the consumer. Equity, now running wild in the field of energy, had become a synonym for self-interest.

By holding down price increases, the government did not provide any more gasoline or heating oil or electricity but rather simply enmeshed us all in the bureaucratic mire of trying to spread the misery of shortages among various regions of the country and various types of consumers. The artificial suppression of price in the name of equity merely compounded the misery by slowing, if not aborting, the natural economic tendencies to bring about long-term solutions to the problem.

In the aftermath of the oil crisis, the political concern with equity has tended to merge in some people's minds with an interest in income redistribution achieved through governmental action. Gasoline, heating oil, and electricity prices, even though held down by direct governmental controls, have been rising more rapidly than the general price level, and the impact of price rises has tended to be greater on the poor. What has not been widely discussed is that redistribution of income through government controls is much less effective than would be redistribution through a system of direct cash payments to the poor. Any attempt to redistribute income by holding down prices simply means that there is less national income available to transfer to the poor. And the redistribution is not focused on the poor but goes to the squeakiest wheels among the interest groups.

We must meet the legitimate demands for equity in ways that are compatible with efficient solutions in the marketplace. A complete overhaul of the welfare system along the lines of a negative income tax system (as suggested in Chapter Five) would provide an effective means of dealing with the equity problem while letting the marketplace perform its vital function of resolving economic problems. A drastic simplification of our income tax system would also help solve the equity problem. What we need is not a trade-off between equity and efficiency in the energy sector, but rather a trade-*on* in which we allow the market to solve our energy problems efficiently and address the equity problem through the tax and income maintenance systems.

Deregulating all energy prices would provide both the most potent incentive for energy conservation and the most natural incentive for increasing supply—including the development of alternative sources of energy. These alternative sources of energy will become more attractive, and increasingly utilized, as the prices of oil and natural gas rise to reflect their true market value. The squandering of these resources can no longer be subsidized; the development of alternative energy sources must be pursued.

CHAPTER TEN

Tools for a Constructive
Economic Policy

SOME READERS MAY HAVE FOUND this book pessimistic. That is neither our intention nor our attitude. Rather, we have attempted to show *why* and *how*, in the world of economic policy beyond the headlines, the instruments of economic policy are so often misused. We have stressed political constraints on economic policymaking and institutional limitations on the tools available and have argued that, in light of those constraints and limitations, economic policy instruments are best used to establish a stable framework within which private-sector economic processes can unfold.

Both the public and policymakers themselves must maintain a realistic view of the possible. The strong real growth in the economy over the two decades following World War II, capped by the apparent success of the across-the-board permanent tax cut in 1964 and the concurrent emergence, at least momentarily, of low unemployment and negligible inflation generated expectations that government could manipulate the economy in order to eliminate boom-and-bust cycles and achieve broad social goals. But that euphoria has given way to a profound public skepticism that economists and economic policymaking can make a positive contribution to the solution of our economic problems. High inflation and high unemployment have been all too visible.

Paradoxically, this new public skepticism, or perhaps realism, may lead to more constructive use of the tools of economic policy. After all, we do have the tools. Fiscal policy, implemented through the budget and the tax system, and monetary policy, managed by the Federal Reserve, are powerful instruments influencing the general economic environment. And we have the market. Contrary to the view of those who believe that legislators and officials are responsible for rising standards of living, the market system itself has been our most resilient and versatile economic tool—a superior problem-solver, both in satisfying private wants and in achieving public goals. Yet too often governmental economic policy tools have been misused, even abused, in attempting to achieve goals for which they are inappropriate, and market solutions have too often been set aside at precisely the time when most needed.

The Budget, Taxes, and Economic Stabilization

The budget is a powerful tool for allocating national resources, establishing national priorities, determining the relative size of the public and private sectors of our economy, and specifying the role of the national government vis-à-vis state and local governments. But these vital long-term functions of the budget have too frequently been subordinated in the budget-making process to the short-term goal of attempting to steer the economy between the shoals of inflation and unemployment. Such short-term efforts to tune the economy by variations in the rate of spending have not been and cannot be successful; the institutional procedures involved are far too clumsy and imprecise.

Are we implying that, in order to focus on the allocation of national resources, it is necessary to abandon the effort through the budget to stimulate the economy in times of recession and restrain it in times of inflationary boom? Hardly. The budget itself has a built-in capacity for contributing to stabilization that must certainly be identified and allowed to operate. If spending and tax rates are set so that the level of spending is within the revenues that would be generated by the economy at reasonably full employment, the central ideas behind the concept of fiscal policy could be harnessed. When unemployment is high, tax revenues fall and transfers to the unemployed through unemployment insurance and income security systems rise, creating a budget deficit. As the economy expands toward full employment, the deficit disappears. If the economy is threatened with a runaway boom, tax revenues would rise further and unemployment insurance payments would fall further, leading to a countercyclical budget surplus. Budgeting in terms of full-employment revenues is thus consistent with the idea of countercyclical fiscal behavior, and the automaticity of this response of revenues and spending makes it possible for budget makers in both the executive branch and Congress to concentrate on long-term priorities.

Adopting a full-employment budget policy would also encourage greater stability in the funding of particular programs. A focus on short-term manipulation of the budget has led to inefficient on-again, off-again funding for many programs, a practice that frustrates the achievement of the programs' goals. This situation is compounded by the success of advocates of various popular programs in isolating them from the annual budget process through various fiscal devices—trust funds, entitlements, and the like. The resulting uncontrollability of the budget throws the burden of adjustment on the remaining controllable programs.

If the tendency to turn particular programs on and off with counter-productive haste in pursuit of short-term stabilization goals were replaced by a greater concern for long-term implications, uncontrollability of outlays would no longer be an enemy of the budget process but could become a tool of long-range matching of resources to priorities. Uncontrollability is another name for stability. Once the decision is made to create or expand a particular program, the program's administrators can proceed with some confidence in the size and continuity of future budget support. They would know that such budget support would be a joint executive-legislative decision based more on the results of the program itself than on arbitrary, unrelated considerations of fiscal policy.

Recognition of the limitations as well as the strengths of fiscal policy can lead to improvements in the budget process. The 1974 budget reform act creates the potential for remedying one key defect in the budget process. Congress has obligated itself to make conscious choices of priorities by looking at the budget as a whole against the background of a predetermined ceiling. Although it is uncertain whether Congress will be able to make the act work over the long run, the early results suggest that at least the level of total government spending will be a conscious political determination rather than simply the result of a series of unrelated decisions on particular programs.

Growing recognition of how hard it is to change the fiscal thrust of the budget through changes in spending has stimulated greater interest in using the tax system for this purpose. Since tax increases or reductions can be implemented almost immediately upon enactment, the tax system has greater potential as a tool for economic stabilization than does spending, which takes time. Still, examples of effective and timely use of tax changes for this purpose are hard to come by. (President Ford's call for an increase in taxes just before the recession of 1974-75 became clearly visible and President Carter's call for tax rebates at the beginning of 1977 just before statistics showed renewed economic growth are recent illustrations of the difficulties involved. The fact that many well-informed economists supported these proposals at the time they were made only underscores the problems.)

The example to which most proponents point is the 1964 tax cut, proposed after long debate by President Kennedy in January 1963 and finally enacted in February 1964. This was a permanent reduction in taxes on all taxpayers, including—through the investment tax credit—businesses making new investments. The theory was not so much that a larger deficit would provide countercyclical stimulation but that "fiscal drag" (revenues above spending at full employment) would be eliminated. As President Kennedy said in proposing these measures:

> The largest single barrier to full employment of our manpower and resources and to a higher rate of economic growth is the unrealistically heavy drag of Federal income taxes on private purchasing power, initiative and incentive. . . . Our tax system still siphons out of the private economy too large a share of personal and business purchasing power and reduces the incentive for risk, investment, and effort.

Tax reduction, he predicted, would "encourage the initiative and risk-taking on which our free system depends—induce more investment, production, and capacity use—help provide the two million new jobs we need every year—and reinforce the American principle of additional reward for additional effort." Whatever the theory, the Kennedy tax cut worked. Permanent tax reduction, by lifting some of the burden of taxation from the private sector, stimulated investment and consumer spending, providing jobs and raising real GNP. Thus, the 1964 tax cut was not an example of a "quick countercyclical fix." Rather, it showed that the long-range benefits from a permanent reduction in tax rates far exceed the immediate gains to taxpayers, so long as the reduction does not create an unmanageable full-employment deficit.

The overriding function of the tax system is to collect the revenues needed to run the government. Critical defects in the tax system, directly attributable to its use to achieve other economic and social goals, are extreme complexity and high marginal rates that discourage work and enterprise and encourage economically counterproductive tax-avoidance schemes. These perverse incentives operate at both ends of the income scale. People with large incomes seek to shelter them from high marginal rates through investments they would not otherwise make. Welfare recipients seek work yielding income not readily identifiable by the government authorities, since the percentage gain to a welfare recipient from payroll earnings is even less than the percentage gain to the wealthy from extra income under the positive tax system. Increasingly, too, barter is spreading at all income levels as people perform services for one another outside the money economy and therefore, they hope, outside the reach of the tax system.

These developments are powerful arguments not just for reduction in the burden of taxation and in counterproductive high marginal tax rates on income and welfare payments but for drastic simplification of our unbelievably complex tax and welfare systems. The problem is more than financial, more than one of rearranging and strengthening essential economic incentives. Even those who spend their lives administering, interpreting, and enforcing the tax and welfare systems do not really understand them. Under these circumstances, can the American people believe that these systems, so central to our economy and social fabric, are fair? The answer, increasingly apparent, is that they cannot. A comprehensive restructuring is needed to refocus the tax system on its vital revenue-collection function. Attempts to achieve social and microeconomic goals of the moment through the tax system must be abandoned. Equity goals would be better pursued through a comprehensive overhaul of the welfare system along the lines of a negative income tax, which would provide a vital trade-on of equity with efficiency. Such a system would afford a means to deal with inequities and unemployment resulting from stringent inflation-fighting fiscal and monetary policies, while at the same time allowing the market system to operate to allocate goods and services efficiently.

The International Dimension

International trade is now running at a rate of about a trillion dollars a year, and foreign investment (investment in one country by firms or individuals residing in another) comes to about the same amount. No stronger testimony could be offered to the interdependence of national economies, including that of the United States. This large and growing volume of international trade and investment reflects worldwide efforts to achieve the potential efficiencies of a world-scale economy. Without a doubt, standards of living are generally higher as a result.

These flows of trade and investment have grown over the past decade in the face of severe problems—the oil crisis, the resulting petrodollar scare, high rates of inflation, drastic change in the international monetary system, and the end of the post–World War II dominance of the United States in the world economy. Despite restrictions imposed in some degree by all nations, continued threats emanating from international meetings, and some rash responses by governments to the crises and opportunities of the moment, the international economy has been stimulated, disciplined, and saved more than once by powerful market forces and by opportunities for mutual advantage in international marketplaces for goods and money. To their credit, the leaders of many key countries have understood and appreciated the fact that, in the end, markets record and transmit the pressures of reality.

We can safely predict that serious problems will continue to test the international economic system and tempt those in authority to pit the power of government against the forces of market reality. Nevertheless, the acceptance by the major countries of a flexible system of exchange rates and the efforts to negotiate lower barriers to trade in the GATT forum in Geneva provide a basis for continued governmental emphasis on fundamentals and a favorable framework for expansion of the world economy. Trade negotiations, for example, can not only prevent a deterioration of the present open world trading system but may very well bring further progress in reducing barriers to trade. In this regard, patience and pragmatism are essential, and it is well to remember that the perfect can be the deadly enemy of the possible.

In dealing with the evolving problems of the world economy, policymakers in all countries continue to face the problem of reconciling demands for greater and more equitably distributed income and wealth with market pressures for efficient use of resources. The so-called North-South issues, which focus on the relationship between the industrialized countries and the developing countries, provide a good illustration. The high and impatiently held aspirations of the developing countries challenge the existing world economic system—that complex network linking a vast array of publicly and privately owned enterprises and of markets for goods, services, and financial resources. The developing countries demand expanded concessionary aid, moratoria on debts owed developed countries, new and changeable rules for the conduct of business, and international commodity agreements designed to change the terms of trade in favor of developing countries' exports. The old political understandings—defining such essential concepts as debt, the rights of ownership, the intricate idea of control, and the rights of buyers and sellers in international commerce—have broken down and have yet to be replaced by new understandings. To many government officials, both in developed and developing countries, North-South negotiations are a zero-sum game, in which the developing countries can gain only at the expense of the developed countries and vice versa. This view is a tragic oversimplification which, if acted upon, may result in a loss of real income on both sides.

As in international monetary reform, government negotiations and market reality are closely linked. Government actions, however well-intentioned, can, by increasing risk and uncertainty, drive out private firms or induce them to seek safer, more profitable markets elsewhere. Private lenders will not continue to lend if debt moratoria become the order of the day. North-South negotiations will be a disaster for both sides unless these negotiations result in arrangements that contribute to the efficiency of the world economy and operate in a broadly equitable manner.

The Task Ahead

The North-South question thus illustrates a recurrent theme in this book: the driving and relentless interplay between equity and efficiency. In field after field, domestic and international, policymaking at the presidential level and in Congress involves choices between what financial officials, professional managers, and economists regard as efficient solutions and what politicians consider equitable solutions. Alan Greenspan has shrewdly observed, "On energy, there is little division among economists. The division is between economists and politicians." This trenchant comment applies beyond energy to most economic policy issues controversial enough to make the headlines. To be sure, equity is often a euphemism for self-interest expressed through the political process. But it is also true that politicians are especially sensitive, and rightly so, to legitimate demands for fair treatment at the hands of government.

If efficient solutions are sometimes unacceptable to major groups, the recurring elaborate proposals for direct government action to accomplish this or that fashionable goal of the moment are far worse. This kind of government action all too often simply doesn't work. Economic policy itself has too often been the enemy of the market economy. Precisely when important problems confront us, we must abandon the fashionable ideology that the government should "do something" and rely instead on what has repeatedly proved far more practical and effective—the market system.

Policymakers must aim for stability and equity in governmental arrangements. If they can succeed in that most difficult task, they will provide an achievement of tremendous significance: a framework within which individuals and institutions can produce a wealth of goods and services and, not least of all, the spirit of fairness that economic freedom and independence nourishes. With such stability there is reason to be hopeful, even brightly optimistic, about the future. It is, after all, in the economy itself—not in the offices and corridors of Washington—that our hopes for more jobs, stable prices, and growing incomes can be realized.

CHAPTER ELEVEN

A Changed World

THE WORLD HAS CHANGED since we wrote two decades ago, and the changes continue apace in country after country and on a global basis. The political, security, and economic landscapes have been transformed in profound ways, and, for economic policy, new questions arise even as old ones continue to command attention.

The World Has Changed Qualitatively

The changed setting for economic policy stems primarily from four major developments. The first is the end of the political divisions arising from the Cold War. The world economy is opening up on a truly global basis. And the release from the threat of nuclear war, however remote, reduces tensions and opens the way to more confidence about the future. Of course, today's promising economic prospects could be set back, even severely, if the geopolitics of security should take a bad turn.

The second major development is the emergence of the information age and a burst of technological creativity. The world of work continues to change dramatically. Knowledge about almost everything is much more broadly and rapidly available than ever before. Financial markets now operate, in Walter Wriston's phrase, on an information standard, registering important developments anywhere in the world almost instantly in what are truly global markets. The resulting impact on the meaning of borders and of sovereignty has important implications for any nation's international economic policy, not to speak of its economic problems at home.

The third major development is a massive shift in the conventional wisdom about what works in economic policy. From the time of the Great Depression and until the 1980s, the idea of central planning of economic policy reigned over much of the world. That conventional wisdom has gradually been replaced, partly as a result of determined advocacy and empirical research but more fundamentally as a result of common observation of what does, and especially what does *not*, work. More and more countries are expanding rapidly because they have adopted economic policies based on markets, private enterprise, and exposure to the global marketplace. Meanwhile, central planning and the walling off of domestic markets from the world economy have been found everywhere to be a dead end. Openness to international trade continues to increase, and the volume of trade has risen sharply, at a faster rate than domestic trade. The global economy, despite some setbacks in some Asian countries, continues to expand rapidly with profound implications for every country.

The conventional wisdom has also changed about inflation. Once viewed by some as a lubricant of the economy, inflation was a preoccupation during the four decades following World War II and the subject of a major fiasco (wage and price controls) during the Nixon presidency (see Chapter Four). Inflation is not a major problem in the world right now, and there has been a return to classical thinking about the importance of a reliable currency to savings, investment, and growth and to a stable currency in international markets. Monetary authorities are being accorded more responsibility for keeping inflation under control and increasing leeway to do so. The New Zealand experience is especially noteworthy. For now, at any rate, the subject is quiet, but experience suggests that the price of stability is eternal vigilance by strong and sensible central bankers and tolerance at least from political authorities.

Finally, huge demographic changes are taking place in the world. To an important extent, demographics is destiny. In economic terms, demography affects growth rates, intergenerational distributions of income, the structure of markets, the balance of saving and consumption, and many other economic variables. The demographic outlook varies radically among countries, particularly between high-income- and low-income-per-capita countries.

The result of these four major developments is that the agenda of economic policy has changed in important ways over the past 20 years, and new issues for the future are still emerging. This changed agenda, which is already making its way into the headlines, presents important opportunities and deep and difficult problems, with long-term consequences and intricate interrelationships among policy issues. We will make a few comments on some of the leading issues, showing in the process how economic problems, each discrete and often considered to be self-contained, nevertheless have also the character of a seamless web; measures taken to deal with one problem affect most other problems and policies. This observation returns us to the themes of Chapter One, particularly the section on interrelationships.

The Compelling Economics of Demography

We in the United States live in a rapidly aging society, with relatively slow economic growth. This phenomenon is even more true of most other high-income-per-capita countries, particularly Japan. The Japanese have done a good job of saving and investing—including investing in other countries—to provide for this looming and inevitable rainy day, but their problems remain daunting and largely unaddressed. The aging countries have relatively high incomes per capita and an educated female population. As seen in country after country, this combination of increased income and educated women corresponds with drastically reduced birth rates.

The low-income countries of the world generally have young populations. Despite reduced birth rates, most of these countries, including India and China with their already large populations, are experiencing relatively rapid economic growth. This contrast means that the two sets of countries will have quite different economic issues to face over the next 20 years and beyond. In interesting ways, the differences can lead to complementary interactions between high- and low-income countries.

Let us look at the situation in the United States. Problems arising from demographic changes are already entering the political discourse. But politicians are nervous. The subject is still referred to as a "third rail" that most are currently unwilling to touch for fear of being fried. Nevertheless, the facts are too compelling to ignore.

Life expectancy has risen dramatically since the notion of "65" as the age of final retirement from the labor force was implanted in institutional arrangements, social insurance, and common thinking. We not only live longer, but we remain healthy and able-bodied to far more advanced ages. Furthermore, the large cohort in the age distribution of our population born in the two decades following World War II—the 76 million baby boomers—will soon be moving into retirement age, while the families of younger people are smaller than in earlier years. Peter Peterson, in *Will America Grow Up Before It Grows Old?* identifies various ways of stating the result of these developments: whereas in 1955 there were 8.6 people paying social security taxes for each person receiving benefit payments, the number of payers had fallen to 3.3 by 1995 and is headed to no more than 2 by 2040. In 1995, revenues paid into the social security system exceeded payments to recipients by $29 billion, but, by the time another 25 years have passed, that surplus will be a deficit on the order of $230 billion and rising rapidly. Still another way of putting the issue is to ask what the unfunded liability would be if this were a private pension plan instead of a government pay-as-you-go system. The answer, according to Peterson, is a staggering $9.5 trillion, or "about 300 times the combined unfunded liabilities of *all* private pension plans in the United States."

To put the matter more generally, changes in life expectancy and in birth rates mean that, unless the basic system is changed, the number of people working per person retired from the labor force will decline—to around 4 as the next century reaches its 20th birthday.

Younger working people raising families have plenty of ways to spend their earnings other than by supporting older generations. So we see in the demographic challenge a variant of a recurrent economic problem. What can be projected from reasonably foreseeable trends cannot in fact be allowed to occur. The numbers and the current political dispositions do not jibe. Something will have to give, and the numbers as they stand are relentless. The political process, sooner or later, must face up to the need for a change. The demographic challenge common to all high-income countries is now only creeping toward the headlines but is bound to find its way to the center of debate about economic and social policy in the years not too far ahead.

What can be done? What will be the shape of the debate? Here are a few subjects to watch.

We are likely to move toward greater privatization of the management of the financial flows arising from savings for pensions. Individual Retirement Accounts (IRAs) and 401(k) and 403(b) plans are growing in importance as changes in tax policy make them more attractive. The example of other countries will be studied carefully. In Chile, for example, the same type of compulsory payroll deductions as in our system have been converted into accounts identified with each participant in their system. These accounts are then managed by a private investment company chosen by the recipient from a list certified by the government. This "defined contribution" approach eliminates the problem of unfunded liabilities characteristic of our present "defined benefit" social security system and, perhaps more significantly, involves individuals far more personally in the way the system works, encouraging the notions of saving and investing. We are already moving rapidly to a defined contribution approach in private pension plans. But any move in this direction for social security will involve huge, though not in the end insurmountable, transition problems. The case for conversion to a privately managed system is compelling. Martin Feldstein, writing in *Foreign Affairs,* has shown how the transition cost can be reduced to a tolerable level. The debate will undoubtedly be fierce, but the shift is clearly a necessary one.

Benefit levels under our current plan are adjusted according to the consumer price index published by the Bureau of Labor Statistics (BLS). For many years now, economists have known that this index overstates the rate of increase in the cost of living. Since the object of indexing is to protect retirees from inflation, the result of the current arrangement is to overdo this protection. In 1995, a bipartisan commission of eminent economists, chaired by Stanford economist Michael Boskin, was appointed by the Senate Finance Committee to examine the upward bias in the index. The Boskin Commission estimates overstatement at more than one percentage point. A correction would make a large dent in the size of unfunded liabilities by eliminating the overindexing of benefit levels. It would also ease problems in a transition to any new system. If a politician touches this clearly justified change, will he or she be touching a third rail? So far, most politicians seem to think so, but sooner or later the answer must be no.

And then there are the twin questions of the age when a working recipient receives full benefits, and the age of retirement when full benefits become available to someone not working (now 65). Longer, healthier lives mean that those Americans who can work to later ages must be encouraged to do so. There is no reason why they should be discouraged from continuing to contribute their skills, time, and energy to productive activity. Simple personal economics will cause most of them to do so. The law must change to allow, indeed to encourage, them to do so. Not only must we have more production from those now artificially induced to retire, but we must delay the now-outmoded age-65 retirement even beyond the two-year extension scheduled to be phased in early in the next century. The limit on the amount of earnings permissible before social security benefits are reduced or eliminated will be seen for what it is: an obsolete holdover from the Depression-era thinking that wanted to move people out of the labor force rather than keep them in. The simple fact is that we will need the over-65 contribution to our national output or we will not be able to maintain benefit levels. The age at which Medicare kicks in and at which full social security benefits can be drawn must rise—gradually to be sure, but rise it must. Changes of this kind will not come easily, but they must come ultimately.

We in the United States have an additional, almost unique tool to use in meeting the problems looming on the demographic horizon: our historic tradition of welcoming immigrants. Over centuries, immigrants have helped to populate our country and have brought us people with intelligence, skill, and energy, real contributors to our culture as well as to our economic well-being and to our scientific and defense capabilities. As we move toward the beginning of a new century, many questions are being raised about our policies involving newcomers. Illegal immigrants, who by definition should not be here, are nevertheless present in large numbers and drawing heavily on public resources, especially, but not by any means only, in California. And a considerable body of evidence is accumulating that a growing proportion of legal immigrants are looking not so much for the land of opportunity as for the land of benefits. In reacting to these problems, we must be careful not to throw the baby out with the bathwater. We need the new, young blood, so we must design our immigration policies so that newcomers are strong contributors. That means, for example, that reunification of family members should no longer be the principal basis for immigration. In addition to strengthening our economy—by providing, for example, more engineers and knowledge workers—immigrants can also contribute to the solution of the problem of our aging society.

Comparative Demographics

Demographic contrasts around the world are striking. Two worlds are emerging. The wealthy nations are also nations with aging populations and little prospect of rapid real economic growth. Western European countries and Japan face the greatest challenge. By contrast, many other countries have young populations. These nations, including China, India, Indonesia, Brazil, and Mexico, while relatively poor, are now experiencing impressive economic growth rates. The use of world markets is increasingly central to their economic policies. With their rapidly expanding labor forces and their access in an information age to knowledge about modern engineering and management techniques, there is no reason that their rapid growth rates cannot continue for some time.

The two sets of contrasting countries will provide very different atmospheres for economic activity. A few numbers dramatize the contrast.

In the United States, the ratio of people 65 and over to the total population will rise from about 12 percent in 1990 to 20 percent by 2030. In Japan, the ratio will rise from 12 percent to 26 percent, while the comparable numbers for Germany are approximately 15 and 25 percent. The foreseeable ratios of people of working age to those of retirement age differ strikingly from high-income to low-income countries, as Table 1 shows.

Also striking is the impact that sharply different population developments will have on the labor force, as Table 2 shows.

These stark differences in projected demographic developments have big implications for almost every aspect of national and international economic life. The tables show dramatically where growth in the world labor force will be located. While the U.S., unlike most high-income countries, will show considerable growth in its working-age population, thanks in part to immigration, most of the growth will be in low-income countries. Furthermore, workers in these countries are sure to become more productive as health and educational levels rise and as they are employed in ways that take better advantage of known, let alone new, technology. Assuming

Table 1. Support Ratios: Working Age to Retirement Age

	1995	2020
Germany	4.5	3.3
Japan	4.9	2.4
U.S.	5.2	3.9
Chile	9.7	6.0
China	11.1	6.5
India	13.1	9.5
Brazil	13.4	7.8
Mexico	14.1	8.6
Indonesia	14.5	9.9

working age = 15 to 64 years of age; retirement age = 65+   *Source:* UN population data

Table 2. A Changing Labor Force: Working-Age Population Growth, 1995–2020

	Millions	Percent
Japan	−12.3	−14.1
Germany	−1.6	−2.9
U.S.	+31.9	+18.3
China	+183.5	+22.3
Chile	+3.3	+36.7
Brazil	+40.8	+40.3
Indonesia	+39.2	+47.9
Mexico	+29.5	+53.7
India	+312.2	+55.6

working age = 15 to 64 years of age   *Source:* UN population data economic policy in these countries continues to be market based, then strong economic growth can be expected. These countries, low on the income-per-capita scale, will likely triple the size of their gross product over the next quarter century, growing at a rate two and one-half times that of the wealthier countries.

Large shifts in the flows of trade and investment must surely result from these demographic changes already under way. The worlds of investment, saving and consumption, finance, and international trade will be sharply affected. Many issues will be posed for economic policy in every country. We will discuss just a few of these issues under the headings of productivity, taxation, and the world economy.

Can Productivity Be Improved?

The issues raised in dealing with an aging population are not just questions of economics but of the skills needed in the art of political economy in view of the sharply competing economic and political interests. But one further issue is far more general in scope and far more important in an ultimate sense. How can we raise the productivity of our labor force and of our investment resources? Substantial success in such an effort is the most fundamental way to tackle the intergenerational tensions inherent in demographic developments.

Rising income levels depend on increases in productivity. That is close to an iron law of economics. To be sure, measuring productivity growth is difficult, and the statistics at hand are inadequate. If, as the Boskin Commission estimates, the consumer price index overstates inflation by more than one percent per year, productivity growth has necessarily been *under-*stated to some considerable extent. The reason is that growth observed in terms of current prices is discounted by an estimate of inflation, not limited to consumer prices, to measure real growth, in turn a basis for estimating productivity. And in keeping with the relationship between productivity and income levels, that underestimate of productivity means that incomes in the United States, rather than stagnating, have grown impressively in the 1980s and '90s, even if not so rapidly as in the 1950s and '60s. According to calculations by Boskin and Harvard economist Dale Jorgensen, using a proper measure of inflation would mean that "instead of falling by about 13 percent (since 1973), real average hourly earnings have risen about 13 percent." And "instead of stagnating, real median family income has risen over 30 percent." Bad statistics don't just mislead policymakers, they distort the national political dialogue, which has increasingly taken it for granted that the average working family has at best been treading water the past few decades.

Growth in productivity, then, is somewhat higher than the statistics suggest. Furthermore, as compared with other countries, the United States is well ahead in the productivity of our labor force. Nevertheless, the rate of growth is inadequate in relation to the needs that will be generated by our aging population and to the importance of minimizing intergenerational conflict. Can anything be done to improve our performance? The answer is yes, but to say how is to set out difficult issues that make headlines as soon as they are addressed in the political process.

A pro-productivity policy should aim to reduce regulatory drag. In fact, the deregulation of prices and outputs in a number of industries over the past 25 years has greatly assisted in the introduction in many sectors of new technologies and new business methods, including those now recognized as contributing to greatly enhanced productivity. For example, telecommunications deregulation, even though only partially completed, has been fundamental to the information technology revolution now underway.

Nevertheless, much regulation remains, and new regulations continue to be introduced. Around 60 federal agencies issue over 1,800 regulations each year, and the Code of Federal Regulations runs to over 130,000 pages. State, county, and city regulations create a patchwork that is often contradictory or redundant. It is increasingly recognized that the old-fashioned command-and-control regulation by Washington-based administrative agencies is a problem, not a solution. What is needed are regulatory solutions that specify goals and objectives, while leaving to the private sector the means of accomplishing them.

The creation of a market in pollution permits is now widely praised as a way of reducing regulatory drag on productivity enhancement while still accomplishing our shared environmental goals. Another example is the auction of the spectrum for new telecommunications uses, such as wireless telephony. Auctioning allocates spectrum space to the most efficient users, in contrast to the old method of endless hearings before the Federal Communications Commission, which involved the Commission in weighing all kinds of social goals rather than focusing on the rapid introduction of new technology that would stimulate productivity and higher living standards for all.

An additional example is in the field of energy. Remember the gas lines. Remember that the problem of energy shortages and skyrocketing prices has faded from view. So has the regulatory maze applied to oil and gas in the United States. We may have problems in the future. Have we learned that the way to deal with them is through the operation of markets rather than through their excessive regulation?

Another kind of drag on productivity comes from litigation. The United States has far more lawyers per capita than any other country, and their number is growing faster than the population. At the beginning of the 1970s only 1.3 of every 1,000 Americans was a lawyer, but by 1990 that proportion had become 3.0. The existence of this enormous cadre of human products of seven years of higher education is a tribute to the increasing complexity of our federal, state, and local regulation and taxation as well as to the needs of a high-income society in managing income and wealth. But it is also, especially in litigation, a heavy burden. The problem has reached such proportions by now that it is being addressed in scholarly works. Several serious economic studies show that we have long since passed the economically optimum mark. Stephen Magee concluded that each new lawyer lowered the Gross Domestic Product (GDP) by about $2.5 million. Kevin Murphy, Andrei Schleifer, and Robert Vishny found a significant correlation between the relative numbers of engineering graduates and law graduates in an economy and the growth rate: the higher the proportion of engineering graduates, the more rapid the growth rate, and the higher the proportion of law graduates, the lower the growth rate.

You do not need to do econometric studies to know that there is simply too much litigation for the good of our economy. In such fields as product liability, litigation too often is not just a burden but the creator of a serious risk for companies seeking to introduce unproved technologies. Since new technologies are both unproved and a major source of enhanced productivity, the problem warrants far more attention from our policymakers. Despite the praiseworthy efforts of many leading members of the bar, legal war is too important to be left to the lawyers. Since most legislators at the state and federal level are lawyers, an uphill battle is the best to be hoped for. Citizen initiatives of one kind or another will be needed.

A third area in which policy can retard productivity is taxation. Contrary to conventional wisdom, taxes have become more of a burden, not less. An overall measure of that burden is the percentage of the GDP that is taken by government. The ratio of receipts by the federal, state, and local governments to GDP is now at an all-time high, and despite the widespread public understanding that taxes were reduced in the 1980s, that ratio is significantly higher now than in 1980, the last year of the Carter Administration and before the Reagan cuts in tax rates and the Bush and Clinton increases in rates.

A greater part of the negative effect of taxation on productivity, however, lies in the fact that taxation falls not just on consumption but on investment and on the savings that underpin investment. Some progress has been made over the years in reducing taxes on the returns from savings, by IRAs and 401(k) retirement plans, for example, but it remains true that we are taxing heavily the very things we need to meet the demographic challenge and to raise income levels—namely savings and investment. The reason is a familiar one: since the bulk of investment comes from those with money to invest, serious efforts at reform through a movement toward a consumption-based tax face the political problem that the tax rate reductions apply to those with the highest incomes. Winning the argument that the long-term effect of greater investment and enhanced productivity is to raise incomes generally takes an uncommon kind of political leadership, as in the case of Ronald Reagan. The political problem is that the beneficial effect occurs with a lag, and, as we observed in our first edition, an economist's lag is a politician's nightmare. But a second and somewhat more serious problem is that tax policy has been captured by a combination of special interests seeking special tax breaks on the one hand, and populist appeals to different groups in the society on the other. Almost gone is attention to economic effects, with productivity the loser.

The result is a tax code of immense and increasing complexity with large-scale distorting effects on the economy and with the clear effect of impeding growth in productivity. Negative citizen reaction to all this complexity does seem to be growing. So is interest in drastic change in the tax system, as illustrated by popular support of proposals for a flat tax. These are important issues to watch, even though now beyond the headlines.

The effect of taxation on productivity is a vital subject because higher labor productivity is to a large extent about leveraging the skills of workers by providing them with more and better capital equipment. The difference in productivity levels between various countries is partly about skills and good business practices, but it is also about how much capital is deployed per worker and how efficiently it is deployed. If we tax savings and investment, we harm productivity and thereby harm income levels. This is a particularly serious matter in the United States because of our low personal savings rate—the lowest of any major country in the world. But some progress has been made recently. The movement toward a balanced budget has reduced public dissaving. And as the baby boomers grow older and start facing the prospect of retiring, they may begin to save more. Taken together with foreign investment in the United States, funds available for investment have nearly doubled in the past three years. So productivity pessimism is unwarranted, but economic policy needs to focus more clearly on the goal of higher income levels, and, in the long run, that means more savings and investment.

Taxation in an Interdependent World

A relatively new constraint is now operating on tax rate levels and increases. As global influences take hold on the flows and locations of investment, the realization will grow that key factors of production can move. Capital is increasingly mobile. So too are engineers and other knowledge workers. In the 17th century, Colbert made the classic observation that taxation is the art of plucking the most goose feathers with the least squawking, but, as the *Economist* recently pointed out, people in the 17th century, unlike geese, could not fly. Today mobile workers and capital can and do move quickly in response to incentives. Increasingly, governments have had to lower taxes on capital in order to attract it. Many

European countries, for example, have recently experienced a round of reductions in corporate income tax rates designed to attract direct investment. Nevertheless, levels of taxation remain discouragingly high.

In the low-income countries where growth is strong, some of the same constraints on raising taxes operate. But if those countries are to develop, they must meet the massive demands for capital for infrastructure improvements. Constraints on rates of taxation limit the extent to which these massive demands can be met by traditional public finance. These countries then need to tap world financial markets. This is probably the most important driving force behind the worldwide move toward privatization of traditionally publicly owned systems.

Privatization means that services usually provided by the state in many countries are being placed in the hands of private, for-profit organizations. Sometimes these organizations are from some other country. Whether from outside or from within, the management of sensitive areas like power, water, transportation, and communications will test the skills of all involved. Costs must be controlled, usually cut. Prices, typically heavily subsidized in the past, will often need to rise. Success will require not only careful management by the acquiring organization but also a special kind of political restraint, even support from governments. Issues will be presented within countries but also across borders, in view of the global interest in equitable treatment of both producers and consumers. Privatization, then, is not a one-stop decision for privatizing governments, but an economic policy that requires ongoing skill in the art of political economy.

The World Economy

When we served in government in the early 1970s, we saw the marketplace force an end to the U.S. commitment to exchange dollars for gold at $35 an ounce (in the parlance of the day, "closing the gold window"). This move also brought an end to the Bretton Woods par value system of exchange rates and led to the emergence of a system of more or less floating exchange rates. We also took part in starting both the Tokyo and later the Uruguay rounds of GATT negotiations. But in truth we were dealing with at best half a world. Today the second world of former Communist states and the third world of less-developed countries have become vital parts of a single world market.

Massive changes in world finance, including deregulation in the United States itself, are part of a continuous set of interacting developments that began several decades ago. The move from fixed rates to a floating system in the 1970s has had the ancillary consequence of removing the need to fence off national financial systems and has exposed the underlying protectionist motivations of many regulatory limitations. Most people have forgotten that even the United States had a form of exchange controls in the 1960s in the name of "defense of the dollar." In the early 1970s, we participated in the final elimination of those controls. Today the United States is witnessing as well the slow death throes of the Depression-period separation of commercial from investment banking as U.S. financial companies strive to keep up with foreign competition. And technology itself, with extraordinary reductions in the cost of communication, has transformed international finance. Faxes, which barely existed when as Administration officials we were lobbied on the retention of fixed brokerage commissions in the early 1970s, now constitute one-half of international telecommunications traffic, and electronic communications now move more than a trillion dollars a day in world financial markets.

At least as impressive as the progress in finance have been developments in trade. We have gone beyond trade negotiations on goods in the GATT and now have a new World Trade Organization, devoted not just to extending the liberalization of trade in goods to services, trade-related investment measures, and intellectual property but, even more important, to developing a rule of law governing trade agreements. Though many in the United States feared the extension of dispute settlement mechanisms in the WTO, experience has proved that the United States has been the big winner, finding international support for eliminating free riding on the U.S. willingness to open its market, and winning as well the bulk of the challenges to U.S. trade practices.

Meanwhile, there has been an explosion of trade in various regions of the world, as barriers have been reduced by regional agreements such as the North American Free Trade Agreement. In fact, regional trade has become important even where there are no formal free trade areas, especially in Asia, where the dependence of their exports on the U.S. market is slowly giving way to truly multilateral trade.

Trade between countries is growing twice as fast as world gross product. The result is not just greater efficiency in the world market and growth for exporting companies, but advantages for the U.S. economy as a whole. As Alan Greenspan observed in explaining to Congress the transformation of the U.S. economy in the 1990s, especially its persistent growth without inflation, "Increasing globalization has enabled greater specialization over a wider array of goods and services, in effect allowing comparative advantage to hold down costs and enhance efficiencies." In short, contrary to the normal view in much political debate that exports are good and imports are bad, both play a vital role. Imports help make the U.S. economy more efficient and hold down inflation. In any case, at the end of the day, just as a person works in order to consume, a nation exports in order to import foreign goods and services that its people and its companies want and need.

Yet protectionist sentiment always lurks just below the surface, even in good economic times, and today often takes the form of alarm at competition from low-wage, increasingly competent labor from the developing world. Genuine issues are posed for governments of high-income countries. Our experience suggests that the most fruitful response is to go on the offensive, taking action with respect to our domestic economy to exploit export opportunities more effectively as well as to deal with the problems posed by imports.

Part of any strategy for dealing with trade flows based on differences in wage rates is to recognize that wages are higher in the United States because productivity is higher here and that there is a strong interconnection between trade policy and our policies to further improve productivity. High living standards in the United States, then, depend on the ability of members of our labor force to perform in high-value-added jobs. Education and good on-the-job training are essential ingredients to strong individual worker performance. But the system of precollege education in the United States is sadly deficient, especially for students from low-income families. The need for educational reform, then, is highlighted not only by the strength of emerging global competition but also by the opportunity an expanding world economy provides for us to use the principle of comparative advantage to improve further our own living standards.

Between 1971 and 1973, as noted earlier, we were deeply involved in a fundamental change in the international monetary system from fixed rates to floating rates, a process detailed in our international monetary chapter (Chapter Six). Today, few serious participants or observers in or out of government anticipate a return to a fixed-rate system. Floating is here to stay, even though qualified by the practice of some countries of attaching themselves to another's currency or of attempting to maintain a band of permissible fluctuations around parity. In all too many cases, these efforts to fix currency relationships break down, sometimes dramatically, as happened in East Asia in late 1997.

The move to floating has changed the institutional requirements for the international monetary system. The International Monetary Fund had been a cornerstone of the Bretton Woods system for the very simple reason that any attempt to maintain fixed parities in the face of market pressures requires weak-currency countries to draw on their reserves of strong currencies to intervene in exchange markets. The Fund was designed to provide a supplemental source of reserves by lending them to countries that would otherwise have to devalue. The notion was that advances from the Fund would give such countries breathing time to adjust their domestic economic policies so that their currencies would recover sufficient strength to permit repayment to the Fund while preserving the existing parity.

With the abandonment of fixed parities, the raison d'être for the Fund disappeared. But the Fund did not go away. As good bureaucrats, the Fund's officers and staff persuaded otherwise cautious finance ministries to approve new roles for the Fund. New IMF programs justified under a variety of rubrics became a principal source of budget support for the poorest of the less-developed countries. The developed countries did not object since the use of Fund resources was an easy way to provide increasingly unpopular "foreign aid." The Fund became a way to support with money a presidential objective without the scrutiny of Congress. In the early 1990s, for example, both Republican and Democratic administrations turned to the IMF to support extraordinary aid programs for Russia that Congress was quite unwilling to provide out of appropriated funds. The stated purpose was to provide general budget support as a means to encourage economic reform in Russia. That this money in effect financed the atrocities in Chechnya or the election campaign of Boris Yeltsin did not seem to bother anyone.

Today the IMF and its Bretton Woods sister, the World Bank, resemble each other increasingly. The Bank, which used to focus primarily on providing finance for infrastructure projects, has long turned to sectoral and other forms of finance, which are designed to supplement budgets of developing countries. Nevertheless, an increasing number of studies, including one by the Bank staff, show that loans from the Bank family make a positive contribution to economic development only when sound economic policies are pursued by the borrowers. Yet where sound policies are pursued, an increasing number of developing countries are able to go directly to huge and growing international financial markets, especially to finance promising projects. Today both the Fund and the Bank have increasingly similar functions—they provide general support for countries that lack the policies or the worthwhile projects to be attractive to international financial markets. As a result, forward-thinking policymakers are today faced with serious questions as to whether the Fund and the Bank should merge, whether their resources should continue to grow, and indeed whether their present path of growing resources and proliferating programs may do more harm than good for many of the developing countries that are their clients.

These issues take on a new light in a period of globalization and greatly enhanced financial flows. With these private flows far exceeding those from the Fund, the Bank, and foreign aid, countries that pursue sound policies are able to finance their needs in private financial markets. If financial market participants see that domestic fiscal and monetary policies are unwise, those sources dry up and the local political system quickly learns a lesson. When the Fund, its original mission no longer relevant in today's exchange rate regime, goes into the more general lending business, it undermines this win-win relationship between private financial markets and economic policymaking.

This subject assumed added importance in 1997. The latter half of the year saw both the Bank and the Fund, and particularly the latter, engaged in massive bailout efforts. Against the background of the large-scale "rescue" effort for Mexico in 1994, the Fund returned to the business of saving countries facing financial panics, this time in East Asia. Bankers, financial intermediaries, and others who financed the governments and enterprises of those countries heaved collective sighs of relief. And well they should feel relieved. They put their money at risk for what they assumed would be handsome returns. The risks turned out to be all too real. They will benefit most directly from the Asian rescue efforts. It is the creditors, not just the debtors, who are being bailed out. The total sums of money from the Fund and from creditor country governments will come to staggering levels, far exceeding $100 billion.

The borrowing countries are being told by the Fund to undertake its standard diet of austerity even though some of the countries are more threatened with recession than inflation. Some financial reforms, particularly in the banking sector, will be put in place, but the depth and longevity of these badly needed reforms will probably be less than if they had been undertaken by the local governments out of conviction rather than as a response to demands of outside forces with large dollars on the table.

A major, IMF-generated problem—perhaps an international monstrosity—may well be the result. Against the background of the Mexican rescue and now the much larger East Asian bailout, emerging market borrowers and especially developed country lenders are being convinced by experience and observation that they will be bailed out in case of big trouble. They can say to themselves, "Heads I win, tails you lose." But there are many losers, and not just the taxpayers who ultimately put up the money.

Today's fast-moving system of finance can work well only when transparency and accountability prevail. The IMF and the government officials to whom it is responding are undermining the essential standard of accountability. While the Fund rightly preaches transparency for countries and banking systems, the Fund's operations themselves lack transparency and strict accountability for the consequences of the bailout atmosphere those operations are spawning.

These issues are now making headlines, and well they should. Large sums of money are being committed with consequences that have genuinely negative aspects. Sooner or later, a tough look at the Fund and Bank will be taken by legislators. When that day comes, real and warranted change is likely.

Some Concluding Reflections

The original readers of this book would have been constantly aware of its context. The world then was one of two superpowers in a global contest that often erupted in dangerous regional conflicts. It was in many ways a world of turmoil. Economic policy decisions at the highest levels were taken in the knowledge that the U.S. and its allies were critically dependent upon economic health and strength if the West were to succeed in this contest. And, indeed, the outcome of the Cold War was in large part determined by the vibrancy of the open economy and the stultifying character of the centralized, statist economy it confronted.

The republication of this book takes place in a vastly transformed global context. America and its allies have triumphed. The open market is the economic choice virtually everywhere in the world. There is no major security threat in sight to compare to that of the Cold War.

The security, stability, and freedom that are required for economic progress must never be taken for granted. Yet that may in fact be happening. As our attention turns inward to domestic matters, or attaches to new global issues such as the environment, the danger is that the fundamentals of statecraft may be neglected. These include sound bilateral relations among the great powers of Europe, Asia, and Russia; strong ties to our allies among the democracies; attention to the special character of our own hemisphere; and maintaining the ability, readiness, and will to use our power when war or terror threaten to destabilize the global security scene. This is the new context that we ask today's readers of this volume to bear in mind.

The basic problems of economic policy have not changed. Maintaining full employment, fighting inflation, stimulating productivity, and providing a safety net for the least advantaged of our society remain central goals. But in the 25 years since we served on the front lines of economic policy, the context in which those goals must be achieved has changed. The demographic time bomb means that attention to economic realities and fundamental principles is more important than ever.

When we wrote the first edition of this book, we argued that economic policy must be as concerned with the allocation of resources for the long run as with stabilization in the short run. Today, that long-run perspective has taken on new importance, and not merely because in the mid-1990s this country achieved what would once have been considered a policymaker's nirvana of high employment with low inflation. As we have reviewed in this chapter, what lies right around the corner of this century is a set of resource problems, highlighted by the uncoming social security crisis, that make issues of saving, economic efficiency, productivity growth, and international economic balance and cooperation more important than ever before. Many pundits talk about the challenges of a global economy. They are there in abundance. From the perspective of economic policy, the question is how to harness the new efficiencies, the new financial market resources, and the new opportunities for an international division of labor for the benefit of all of our citizens. Just as the problems are difficult, so the opportunities for a more prosperous world are tremendous and the stakes are high. We see the prospect of a prosperous world and a resulting economic contribution to international peace and security.

Reader's Guide

The literature on economic policy is vast. Much is of limited value to the general reader who is interested in broadening his general understanding of the fundamental problems of economic policy. Either it is too topical, and thus ephemeral, or it is too technical, often mathematical. Perhaps the most rewarding strategy is to read several newspapers and business journals regularly, critically, and over a long enough period of time to become immune to the changes of fashion in journalistic commentary on the economy. We particularly recommend *The Wall Street Journal* (especially the editorial page), *Fortune*, *Business Week*, and *The Economist*. Several of the principal commercial banks turn out first-rate monthly economic letters.

Some of the most useful material is to be found in government documents. Since they are designed to be read by legislators and journalists, they are usually readable, yet specific. The starting place is the annual *Economic Report of the President*, which is sent to Congress each January. The President's Report itself is actually only a brief introduction to the bulk of the volume, which is the Annual Report of the Council of Economic Advisers. Here the three members of the CEA analyze in about 150 pages the major economic issues of the time. Appended to their report are another hundred or so pages of economic statistics which provide a convenient quantitative guide to the past and present of the American economy.

The *Economic Report* is circulated to key officials before publication and therefore provides information on current policy views of the administration. In fact, the publication of these reports is an action-forcing event. The need to take a position in the report on a current issue may compel agencies to come to agreement or to submit their differences to the President for resolution.

Both the Brookings Institution and the American Enterprise Institute (two Washington, D.C., private research organizations) publish a large number of books on current policy issues, and the reader with specialized policy interests may want to obtain a list of their publications. The American Enterprise Institute has recently begun an annual survey of economic policy issues. The first, edited by William Fellner and entitled *AEI Studies on Contemporary Economic Problems*, 1976, sets a high standard, and most of the subjects are treated in a manner accessible to the general reader.

Milton Friedman's *Capitalism and Freedom* (Chicago: University of Chicago Press, 1962) is a classic treatment of the use of the market and enterprise system to solve problems and of the importance of economic organization to freedom. It is not recommended for readers determined to believe in governmental solutions to economic problems. Ezra Solomon's Portable Stanford volume *The Anxious Economy* (Stanford: Stanford Alumni Association, 1974; San Francisco: San Francisco Book Co., 1976) illuminates a number of economic policy issues and develops with exceptional clarity the relationship between economic policy and the flow of economic events.

For budget matters, nothing compares with *The Budget of the United States Government*. Although necessarily precise when it comes to numbers and rather vacuous when it offers reasons for expanding or cutting programs, the budget nonetheless is meant to be accessible to the average reader and it achieves that goal most of the time. For those with bookkeeping minds, the thousand or so pages of the *Budget Appendix* are replete with mindboggling detail, including such interesting tidbits as the fact that the Supreme Court spends almost a third as much for "Automobile for the Chief Justice" as it does for books.

For those seeking a quick overview, a shortened version of each year's budget is published as the *Budget in Brief*. Still another volume appearing at the same time as the budget is the *Special Analyses*, which offers a comprehensive treatment of a number of selected budget topics for the reader seeking detailed information. The best private commentary on the budget is to be found in the annual Brookings Institution budget volumes entitled *Setting National Priorities*.

Serious writing on tax policy has traditionally been the province of the tax lawyer and the public finance economist. The reader who is not at home with the Internal Revenue Code or with supply and demand curves consequently has relatively few places to turn other than the press. The Brookings Institution has over the years turned out some excellent studies of various tax policy topics in its Studies of Government Finance series. Three recent ones addressed to the income tax system as a whole are Richard Goode's *The Individual Income Tax* (Washington, D.C.: Brookings Institution, rev. ed., 1976); Joseph A. Pechman's *Federal Tax Policy*

(Washington, D.C.: Brookings Institution, 3d ed., 1977); and Joseph A. Pechman and George F. Break's *Federal Tax Reform: The Impossible Dream?* (Washington, D.C.: Brookings Institution, 1975).

An excellent introduction to the 1971-74 controls experiment is Marvin H. Kosters' *Controls and Inflation* (Washington, D.C.: American Enterprise Institute, 1975). Arnold Weber gives a comprehensive review of Phase I, the first 90 days, in *In Pursuit of Price Stability: The Wage-Price Freeze of 1971* (Washington, D.C.: Brookings Institution, 1973). *Phase II in Review: The Price Commission Experience* by Robert F. Lanzillotti, Mary T. Hamilton, and R. Blaine Roberts (Washington, D.C.: Brookings Institution, 1975) takes up where Weber's *Freeze* leaves off. Great and often revealing detail is to be found in the three-volume *Historical Working Papers on the Economic Stabilization Program* (Washington, D.C.: Government Printing Office, 1974).

An enormous literature exists on welfare reform, and much of it is quite readable. On the politics of welfare reform, Daniel P. Moynihan's *Politics of a Guaranteed Income* (New York: Random House, 1973) has not been equaled. For more technical approaches to the mechanics and anomalies of the present welfare programs, the 20 or more volumes of Studies in Public Welfare by the Joint Economic Committee are a rich source. The Brookings annual budget volumes mentioned above also normally contain a useful chapter.

The annual *International Economic Report of the President* nicely complements his *Economic Report*. The International Monetary Fund publishes an annual report that reviews events of the year. A useful and highly readable introduction to the international monetary system is Robert Z. Aliber's *The International Money Game* (New York: Basic Books, rev. ed., 1976). Two volumes by Gerald M. Meier, *Problems of World Monetary Order* (New York: Oxford University Press, 1974) and *Problems of Trade Policy* (New York: Oxford University Press, 1973), are especially useful because they include excerpts from many of the key documents.

The confusion in governmental energy policymaking is reflected in writing. Ink devoted to this subject should be measured in barrels per day. A quick overview of the background of energy policy issues may be obtained in Edward J. Mitchell's *U.S. Energy Policy: A Primer* (Washington, D.C.: American Enterprise Institute, 1974). Paul W. MacAvoy's (ed.) *Federal Energy Administration Regulation: Report of the Presidential Task Force* (Washington, D.C.: American Enterprise Institute, 1977) explains and evaluates in detail the FEA's system of price allocation and entitlements regulation.

A general book on government organization is Harold Seidman's *Politics, Position & Power* (New York: Oxford University Press, 2d ed.,

1975). Stephen Hess's *Organizing the Presidency* (Washington, D.C.: Brookings Institution, 1976) is an interesting history of White House organization. Dean Acheson's *Present at the Creation* (New York: W.W. Norton, 1969) is as rewarding for its insight into the policy process as for its examination of diplomatic developments.

NOTES ON SOURCES

Budget numbers throughout (including tax expenditure estimates) were taken from the budget documents cited in the Reader's Guide. Additional sources of data referred to in the text follow:

Chapter Two. Fiscal 1973 legislative proposals: U.S. Congress, Joint Study Committee on Budget Control, *Recommendations for Improving Congressional Control over Budgetary Outlay and Receipt Totals*, 93rd Cong., 1st sess., 1973, H. Rept. 147, pp. 49-50.

Chapter Three. Advisory Commission on Intergovernmental Relations estimate: U.S. Advisory Commission on Intergovernmental Relations, *Trends in Fiscal Federalism, 1954-1974*, 1975, pp. 6-7.

Chapter Five. Transfer program levels: *Survey of Current Business*, July 1974, p. 28, and April 1974, p. 48; *1976 Economic Report of the President*, p. 94, and *1977 Economic Report of the President*, p. 271. Growth of the AFDC program and public housing: *Handbook of Public Income Transfer Program: 1975*, Studies in Public Welfare, no. 20, Joint Economic Committee, 93rd Cong., 2d sess., Committee print, 1974, pp. 170, 243. Food stamp and school lunch program: *1976 Economic Report of the President*, p. 102. AFDC payment by state: National Center for Social Statistics, *Aid to Families with Dependent Children*, July 1976, pp. 10-11. Disincentives in welfare programs in New York: *Income-tested Social Benefits in New York: Adequacy, Incentives, and Equity*, Studies in Public Welfare, no. 8, Joint Economic Committee, 93rd Cong., 1st sess., Committee print, 1973, p. 141. Authorization and appropriations gap: Lawrence Lynn and John Seidl, "Policy Analysis at HEW: The Story of the Mega-Proposal," *Policy Analysis*, vol. 1, 1975, p. 248. Percentage of AFDC families eligible for other welfare programs: Brookings Institution, *Setting National Priorities: The 1975 Budget*, 1974, p. 177.

Chapter Six. Foreign government holdings of dollars and gold: *Federal Reserve Bulletin*, December 1971, pp. A77-A78.

Chapter Eight. President's message on the 1971 Departmental Reorganization Plan: *Weekly Compilation of Presidential Documents*, vol. 7, 1971, p. 547. President's statement on Department of Agriculture: *Weekly Compilation of Presidential Documents*, vol. 7, 1971, p. 1508. Calvert Cliffs case: *Calvert Cliffs Coordinating Committee, Inc. v. U.S. Atomic Energy Commission*, 449 F. 2d 1109, 1111 (D.C. Cir. 1971). Secretary Volpe's testimony in *Three Sisters Bridge* case: *D.C. Federation of Civic Associations v. Volpe*, 316 F. Supp. 754 (D.D.C. 1970), *reversed*, 459 F. 2d 1231 (D.C. Cir. 1972).

Chapter Nine. Task Force Report: U.S. Cabinet Task Force on Oil Import Control, *The Oil Import Question* (1970). Oil imports and production: American Petroleum Institute, *Basic Petroleum Data Book*. Data on changes in oil consumption 1973-76: *Petroleum Economist*, May 1977, p. 208; February 1977, p. 51; February 1976, p. 66, April 1975, p. 160. Historical data on growth rate of consumption of oil: De Golyer and MacNaughton, *Twentieth Century Petroleum Statistics*, 1976, p. 18. *Phillips Petroleum* case: *Phillips Petroleum Co. v. Wisconsin*, 347 U.S. 672 (1954). Dry gas data: American Petroleum Institute, *Reserves of Crude Oil, Natural Gas Liquids and Natural Gas in the U.S. and Canada as of December 31, 1975*, vol. 30, May 1976, p. 121. Petroleum estimates and Eurodollar rates: Morgan Guaranty Trust Co., *World Financial Markets*, Jan. 21, 1975, and Jan. 21, 1976. Donaldson, Lufkin & Jenrette estimate: Donaldson, Lufkin & Jenrette Securities Corp., Research Note (Dec. 2, 1974).

Chapter Ten: President Kennedy's tax proposal: Special message to Congress on tax reduction, January 24, 1963, p. 74, and State of the Union Message, January 14, 1963, p. 13, in *Public Papers of the Presidents: John F. Kennedy*, 1963.

Index

Acheson, Dean, 17
administered-price theory, 76–78
Advisory Commission on Intergovernmental Relations, 45, 48, 61–62
advocacy system and interest groups, 2,
   4–6, 10, 15–17, 61
   balkanization and, 2, 4–6, 21, 150,
      151, 153, 162, 164, 170–73, 186
   in budgetmaking, 37, 39, 62–63, 67,
      161–62, 201
   clientele departments created by, 162,
      164
   Congress and, 39, 40, 62–63, 82,
      84–85, 87, 166
   in countervailing duties issue, 150–51
   executive branch and, 6, 10, 16, 31,
      82, 84–85, 161, 163, 166–67
   government reorganization and, 4–6,
      161–70
   impact on tax system by, 43, 51–52,
      62–63
   in income security issues, 87, 88, 99,
      101, 102
   in wage-price controls issue, 65, 67,
      82, 84–85
African countries, 137
agricultural commodities, 78, 81, 137
Agriculture Department, in government
   organization, 4, 162, 164–65,
   166–67
Aichi, Kiichi, 12
Aid to Families with Dependent Children (AFDC), 90–95, 99, 101, 102
American Selling Price system, 148, 149
annual reports, as action-forcing events,
   160
anticipations and expectations, 2, 67,
   98–99, 199

in policymaking, 2, 8–11, 67, 68, 71,
   76, 81, 118, 153
   statistics distorted by, 9
Arab oil embargo, 180, 181, 183, 184,
   185, 186
artificial accounting losses, 55

balance of payments, 111, 112, 113,
   114, 117–18, 119, 126, 128, 192,
   193
balance-of-trade surpluses, 107, 138,
   191
balkanization of government, see advocacy system and interest groups
Barber, Anthony, 12
Barre, Raymond, 13
basic benefit level, 99, 100, 101
Belgium, 121
benefit-reduction rate, 93–94, 99, 100,
   101, 102
birth rates, 209–10
Boskin, Michael, 211, 214
Boskin Commission, 211, 214
break-even point, in income transfer, 99,
   103
Bretton Woods agreements, 13, 110,
   126, 130, 131, 218, 220–21
Brookings Institution, 100, 102
budget, budgetmaking, 20–21, 23–42,
   199–201
   accounting procedures and, 32
   allocation of resources by, 39, 40,
      200, 201
   annual cycle in, 24–28, 160
   back-door spending and, 26, 27, 29,
      31, 40, 48, 52, 62
   Congress and, see Congress
   as cosmetic document, 31–34

budget (continued)
deficits in, 41, 49, 67, 87, 200
as estimate, 32
executive branch and, see executive branch
expectations gap in, 98–99
federal funds in, described, 49
"full-employment," 40–41, 200–1
impact on economy by, 31, 34, 37–41, 49, 200–1
"legislative," 27
momentum of, 36–37, 40
negative outlays in, 32–33
as policymaking, 161–62
political process and, 25, 37, 39, 41
presidential vs. congressional influence on, 39–40
shortfalls in, 26, 33–34
short-term goals in, 33, 36, 200, 201
social and economic goals in, 26, 28–29, 40, 48–49, 52, 88–89, 90
stabilization affected by, 21, 23, 34, 36, 37, 39, 40, 41, 67, 200–1
tax base and, 37, 39, 40–41, 200
tuning of, 23–24, 36–37, 41, 173, 200
trust funds in, 28–29, 48–49
types of outputs in, 34–36, 39
uncontrollable outlays in, 28–30, 32, 33, 34–36, 37, 39, 40, 48–49, 89–90, 105, 201
see also fiscal policy
Bureau of the Budget, 159, 160, 161, 174
Burke-Hartke bill, 113, 135, 139
Burns, Arthur, 17, 68, 127, 174
Butz, Earl, 169

Cabinet Committee on Economic Policy, 175
Cabinet Task Force on Oil Import Control, 182–83
Califano, Joseph A., Jr., 165
Canada, 121
capital, mobility of, 217–18
capital controls programs, 18–19
Carter, James E., 2, 168, 201
cashing out, 101, 102
central planning, 208
Chile, 210
China, 209, 212
"closet decisions," 10

coal-fired energy, 181, 184, 188
Cold War, 207, 222–23
collective bargaining, 1–2
wage-price controls and, 71, 72, 73, 75
Commerce Department, U.S., 106, 111, 140, 175
Commission on Budget Concepts, 49
Common Market (EEC), 121, 134, 136, 137
Conable, Barber, 63
Congress, 2, 4, 6, 24, 172
advocacy system and, 39, 40, 82, 84–85, 87, 166
budgetmaking and, 25–30, 31, 36, 39, 40, 200, 201
committees of, 26, 28, 29, 39–40, 61
energy issue and, 189, 193–94
income security matters in, 99, 102, 103
monetary policies and, 20–21, 111, 112, 118, 174
organization of economic policymaking by, 174
reorganization plan opposed by, 163, 166–68
tax policy and, 44–45, 47, 48, 50–51, 54, 55–56, 61–63, 82
trade policy and, 134, 135–36, 138, 139, 140, 145–46, 147–49
wage-price controls and, 68, 74, 75, 82, 84–85, 193–95
see also executive-congressional relations; and specific committees
Congressional Budget and Impoundment Control Act (1974), 24, 27–28, 36, 39, 62, 173, 201
Connally, John, 12, 114, 115, 117, 118, 121, 175
consumer price index, 210–11, 214
contract authority, 29
Cost of Living Council, 75, 82, 84, 185
Council of Economic Advisers, 74, 119, 156, 160, 163, 174
Council on Economic Policy, 7, 176
Council in International Economic Policy, 175–77
Council on Wage and Price Stability, 76, 82, 83, 163
counsellorships, 169–70
credit institutions, off-budget, 30, 34–36

"cult of law," 6
currencies, 107, 114, 118, 119, 139
    appreciation of, 113, 114, 115, 117–
    18, 126
    see also exchange rages

Dean, John, 2
Declaration on Trade Measures (1974),
    107
Defense Department, 158
    budget of, 25, 28, 39–40, 112
demographics, 208
    comparative, 212–14
    economics of, 209–12
deobligation of funds, 28
Departmental Reorganization Plan
    (1971), 5–6, 163–68
détente, 136, 146
developing nations, 204, 205
    monetary policy and, 122, 204
    trade policy and, 136, 139, 204
DiBona, Charles, 185
Dillon, Douglas, 17
Dirksen, Everett, 15
dollar, U.S.:
    devaluation of, 69, 74, 80–81, 109,
    112, 114–15, 116, 117, 118, 127–
    28
    fluctuation in supply of, 110–11, 113,
    114
    overvaluation of, 107, 111, 112, 113,
    119
Domestic Council, 159, 160–61
"do something" policy, 2, 50, 68, 75,
    155–56, 181, 205
Dunlop, John, 84

economic growth, 199
    effects of demographic changes on,
    209–12
    energy costs and, 180–81
    stimuli for, 34, 41, 46, 80, 203
    see also GNP
economic policy:
    "action-forcing events" in, 160
    anticipations and expectations in, 2,
    8–9, 10–11, 67, 68, 153
    basic problems of, 223
    changes in conventional wisdom and,
    208
    changing agenda of, 208–9
    controls in, 65–66

effects of demographics on, 208
efficiency vs. equity in, 3, 205
effort required in, 2–3, 17
end of Cold War and, 207
executive branch role in organization
    of, 7, 173–77
government organization of, 174–77,
    184–87
individuals' roles in, 2, 11–14
information age and, 207
interconnections in, 2, 4–8, 11–12,
    19, 21, 28–29, 40, 41, 44–45, 46,
    48–49, 52, 67, 68–69, 71–72, 85,
    87–91, 93, 98–101, 102, 104–5,
    107, 110–13, 115–18, 122, 123,
    126, 135–36, 137, 138, 146–47,
    149–51, 156–57, 163, 172, 174–
    77, 181–82, 197, 203–5
major concepts in, 2–3
professionals vs. politicians in, 2, 14–
    17, 205
public skepticism of, 199
regulators in, 8
reorganization as substitute for, 156–
    58
timing and, 18–19
see also specific issues
Economic Report of the President, 31
Economic Stabilization Act, 75
economists, professional, 14–17, 57
education, importance of, 220
efficiency vs. equity, 2, 3–4, 9, 153, 205
    competition and, 3, 19
    in energy issue, 180, 186, 195–97
    in international trade policy, 133,
    150, 204
    in welfare system, 105, 145, 203
Ehrlichman, John, 185
elasticity pessimism, 186–88
electric power, 184, 187
electronic communications, 219
emergency boards, 1–2
energy, 179–97, 215
    conservation of, 181, 187, 197
    controls on, 180, 181, 185, 186, 188,
    189, 191, 193–97
    environmental issues and, 172, 188,
    196
    government intervention and, 155,
    158, 172, 179, 180–81, 184–86,
    188, 189, 191, 193–97
    market solutions and, 193–97

energy (*continued*)
rationing of, 180, 186, 189
research and development in, 39, 46–
47, 179, 181, 182, 184, 185, 188–
89, 197
tax policy and, 46–47
see also specific energy sources
Energy Research and Development
Agency, 158
entitlement programs, 29, 32, 33, 37,
90, 99
Environmental Protection Agency, 162
equity vs. efficiency, *see* efficiency vs.
equity
Eurodollar market, 192, 193
Europe:
trade policy and, 135, 137
U.S. monetary policy and, 111, 114,
116, 119
European Economic Community (EEC),
121, 134, 136, 137
exchange rates, 81, 107, 110, 111, 114,
127–28, 138
central-rate levels in, 115, 116, 119
fixed, 109, 110, 114, 116, 117, 119,
128, 130–31
market-based (floating) system of, 80,
109, 115, 116, 118, 126, 128,
130–31, 204, 218–20
policy changes for, 107
see also currencies; dollar, U.S.
executive branch:
advocacy system and, *see* advocacy
system and interest groups
balkanization of, 5–6, 170–73
budgetmaking in, 6, 24–26, 27, 29,
30, 31–32, 39–40, 200
energy issues and, 184, 194
fiscal policy by, 24, 28, 31–32
functions altered in, 6, 170–71
government organization and,
see government organization,
reorganization
income security and, 99, 102
judicial branch and, 6, 171–73
monetary policy and, 12–14, 19,
20, 110, 112, 116, 117, 119–21,
123–24
reorganization as policy instrument
of, 155, 158–59, 160–61
self-selection for positions in, 16

tax proposals by, 44, 45, 49, 50, 54–
55, 59–62
in trade policy, 134, 135–36, 138,
139, 140, 141–46, 147, 148–49,
150
wage-price controls and, 65, 68–69,
70, 74, 82, 84–85, 157, 193–94
see also presidency
executive-congressional relations, 6, 21,
27–28, 39–40, 45, 145–46, 147,
148, 149, 170–71, 177, 186
Executive Office of the President, 5, 16,
24, 25, 123, 124, 159, 175–77,
183, 185
organizational changes in, 160–62
expectations, *see* anticipations and
expectations
export controls, 9, 81, 175
Export-Import Bank, 30, 112
exports:
effects of, on U.S. economy, 219–20
subsidies for, 107, 112–13, 150–51
U.S., threats to, 137–38

Family Assistance Plan, 99, 101, 102
faxes, 219
Federal Energy Office, 185–86
federal funds, description of, 49
Federal Power Commission, 172, 184
Federal Reserve Board, 67, 80
independence of, 20–21
monetary policy and, 110, 111, 119,
123, 124, 174
Feldstein, Martin, 210
financial markets, 207
Finance Committee, Senate, 61, 62, 63,
147, 149
"fiscal drag," 202
fiscal policy, 23–41, 67–68, 174, 199–
200
appropriations and spending discrepancies in, 26, 27, 173
constraints on, 21, 24, 37, 41
countercyclical, 24, 36, 200, 202
federal-state boundaries in, 39
income security and, 87, 88–90, 98,
104–5
inflation and, 40, 41, 44–45, 46, 203
monetary policy linked to, 21, 68–69,
80–81
short-term reductions and, 33–36

social policy and, 87, 104, 105
wage-price controls and, 21, 80, 85,
    156–57
see also budget, budgetmaking; tax
    policy, system
Flanigan, Peter, 127, 175, 185
food prices, 8–9, 77–78, 81
food stamp program, 90–91, 95, 99,
    100
Ford, Gerald, 2, 11, 12–13, 14, 40, 47,
    99, 157, 201
forecasting, economic, 36
foreign credit restraint program, 19,
    111
foreign direct investment program, 19,
    111
foreign policy, 113
    individuals' roles in, 12–14, 116, 117
    interconnections in, 7, 11–12, 80–
        82, 107, 113, 115–16, 117, 118,
        122
    oil and, 181, 183
    organizational aspects of, 123–26,
        147, 148, 158–62, 174–77
    presidential authority vs. Congress in,
        146
401(k) plans, 210, 216
403(b) plans, 210
France, 188
    U.S. monetary policy and, 12–14,
        114, 116, 119, 122, 131
freezes, wage-price:
    of 1971, 65, 67–69
    of 1973, 74, 194
Friedman, Milton, 102
Fukuda, Takeo, 12

Gardner, John W., 167–68
gasoline, 179, 180, 186–88
General Agreement on Tariffs and Trade
    (GATT), 106–7, 134, 136, 139,
    204
Giscard d'Estaing, Valéry, 12–14
global economy:
    effects on U.S., 207–8
    effects of information age on, 207
    tax policy system and, 217–18
    see also international trade
gold, in international monetary policy,
    69, 109, 110, 111, 112, 114–15,
    118, 119–21, 128, 130, 131

governmental intervention, 1, 8, 204–5
    to maintain "orderly" markets, 128,
        130, 199–200
Government Operations Committees,
    168
governmental organization, reorganiza-
    tion, 4–8, 152–77
    advocacy system and, 4–6, 161–70
    agencies in, 6, 123–27, 158, 170–71
    bureaucracies entrenched in, 72, 157,
        164, 170
    cabinet officers in, 5, 158–59, 168–
        69, 175
    changes in, as substitute for policy,
        156–61
    Congress and, 147, 148, 149, 163,
        166–68
    economic policymaking organization
        in, 174–77
    energy policy and, 174–77, 184–87
    executive branch and, 4, 155, 158–
        59, 160–61, 165–67, 168–69,
        170–77
    individual's effectiveness in, 159
    interagency committees in, 158–59
    international negotiations and, 123–
        26, 147, 158–62, 170, 174–77
    policy coordinators in, 159, 160–62
    rivalries in, 4, 6, 160, 161, 163, 169,
        170, 175, 176, 177
    self-protection principle in, 167
    self-selection process in, 16, 62
    task force approach in, 159
government power, growth of, 61
grants-in-aid, 32, 34
Great Britain, 168, 188
    trade policy and, 138
    U.S. monetary policy and, 12–13,
        114, 121, 122, 131
Greenspan, Alan, 205, 219
gross national product (GNP), 37, 44,
        52, 68, 181, 202
    income security portion of, 88–89
Group of Five, 12, 122–23
Group of Ten, 121, 122, 128

health sector, prices in, 77
Heath, Edward, 138
heating oil, 180, 188, 196
Heineman, Ben W., 165
Henkel, Lee, 57

housing:
  government outlays for, 34–36, 92
  tax policy and, 46, 47
Hunt, Sir John, 13

immigrants, 211–12
imports:
  effects of, on U.S. economy, 219–20
  protection against, 7, 47, 69, 107,
    113, 115, 117, 134–35, 137, 138,
    145, 148, 149, 150–51
impoundment of funds, 26, 28, 36, 37,
  173
income, definition of, 103–4
income security, 21, 87–105, 197
  budget and, *see* budget, budgetmaking
  cash vs. in-kind transfers in, 95–98,
    99, 101
  complexity of, 89–90, 98–99, 102,
    203
  comprehensive cash program for,
    101–2, 105
  exclusions and inadequate coverage
    in, 92–93, 98, 99–100
  growth of, 88–89, 90, 91, 98–99
  inflation-unemployment trade-off in,
    87; trade-on in, 88
  major programs in, 90–92
  negative income tax approach in,
    102–5, 197, 203
  pensions and, 7, 30, 139, 141, 144
  political aspects of, 88, 91, 93, 98,
    101, 102, 104
  present weaknesses of, 92–99, 202
  professionals in, 91, 98
  program design of, 93–99
  reforms suggested for, 99–105
  states' participation in, 48, 89, 90, 92,
    93, 101, 144, 145
  unemployment and, 87, 92, 104, 105,
    141–42
  worker adjustment assistance and,
    140–45
  see also social security trust fund;
    transfer payments; unemployment
    insurance
incomes policy, 21, 65, 66, 68, 76, 80,
  193
India, 209
Individual Retirement Accounts (IRAs),
  210

individuals, policymaking affected by, 2,
  11–14, 15, 62, 159
Indonesia, 212
inflation, 19, 20–21, 199, 210–11, 214
  administered-price view of, 76–78
  budget policy and, 40, 41, 87, 203
  changes in conventional wisdom
    about, 208
  devaluation as factor in, 69, 80, 117
  fiscal policy and, 40, 41, 44–45, 46,
    203
  income security policy and, 87, 99,
    103–5
  international monetary policy and,
    81, 87, 111, 113–14, 127, 128,
    131
  monetary policy and, 69, 80, 85, 87,
    117, 156, 203
  taxes and, 44–45, 46, 203
  unemployment and, 41, 87–88, 104
  wage-price controls as response to,
    68, 69, 75, 76, 80, 85, 193–94
  on world scale, 81, 127, 128, 203
information age, 207
in-kind transfers, 91–92, 95–98, 99,
  101
interconnections, *see* economic policy;
  and specific issues
interest equalization tax, 19, 111
interest groups, *see* advocacy system and
  interest groups
Interior Department, 172, 184
Internal Revenue Service (IRS):
  functions of, 2, 59, 83
  negative income tax and, 102–3
international finance, 218–19
  see also global economy
International Monetary Fund (IMF),
  106–7, 110, 112, 127, 220–22
  Articles of Agreement of, 121, 126,
    130–31
  Committee of 20 (C-20) of, 122, 123,
    127, 128–30
international trade, 208, 219–20
  see also global economy
investment tax credit, 46, 82, 202
Israel, 181, 183
Italy, 131

Jackson, Henry, 145, 146
Jamaica agreement (1976), 13–14, 130

Japan, 188, 209, 212
trade policy and, 107, 113, 134, 136
U.S. monetary policy and, 12, 13,
111, 114, 121, 122, 131
Javits, Jacob, 118
Johnson, Lyndon B., 1, 44, 67, 165
Joint Committee on Internal Revenue
Taxation, 63
Jorgensen, Dale, 214
judicial branch, 6
in government organization, 170–73

Kennedy, John F., 45, 202
Kennedy Round (trade negotiations),
134, 147, 149
Keynes, John Maynard, 23
Kissinger, Henry, 11–12, 13, 17, 110,
115–16, 124, 135, 138, 146, 169–
70, 185

labor, 5, 105
collective bargaining and, 1–2
effects of demographic changes on,
212–13
protectionist position of, 113, 134–
35, 139, 140
mobility of, 217–18
in wage-price control programs, 68,
70, 71, 72, 73, 75, 84, 156–57
Labor-Management Advisory Committee, 74, 157
Laird, Melvin, 16
Larosière, Jacques de, 13
lending programs, government, 34–36
life expectancy, 209–10
litigation, 215–16
Long, Russell, 63, 118
Love, John, 185
Lynn, James, 169
Lynn, Lawrence, 98

Magee, Stephen, 216
management, in wage-price controls
programs, 68, 70, 71, 72, 75, 84
market system, 3, 8, 67, 71–72, 115,
128, 130, 193–97, 200, 203–5,
208
Marx, Karl, 105
Meany, George, 5
Medicare, Medicaid programs, 89, 92
Middle East, 137, 179, 180, 181, 183

Mills, Wilbur, 62, 118
monetary policy, domestic, 12–14, 20–
21, 104, 105, 109, 111, 114, 116,
119, 121, 122, 131, 174
fiscal policy linked to, 21, 68–69,
80–81
inflation and, 69, 80, 85, 87, 118,
156, 203
wage-price controls and, 80, 85, 156–
57
monetary policy, international, 12–14,
18–19, 20–21, 69, 80, 106–7,
109–31, 203, 220–22
central banks and, 119, 122, 127, 131
"gold window" closed in (August 15,
1971), 109, 110, 114, 118
government organization on, 174–75
national security interests and, 116
oil prices and, 181, 191–93
political factors in, 110, 112–13,
115–16, 117, 118
trade policy related to, 107, 113, 123,
138, 174–75
U.S. controls for, 111–12
wage-price controls and, 80–81
monetary policy reform, international,
106–7, 119–31
control of negotiations in, 123
effects of, 220–22
evolutionary approach to, 121, 130
Jamaica agreements (1976) in, 13–14,
130
negotiating forum for, 121–23
political aspects of, 126
reserve levels and, 126, 130
stability of domestic economies and,
130, 131
U.S. goals in, 119–21, 123, 126
U.S. 1971 initiative in, 110, 114–15,
117–18
U.S. 1972 initiative in, 126–27
money supply, 87, 109
Morse, Jeremy, 127
Murphy, Kevin, 216

National Commission on Productivity,
156–57
National Security Council, 25, 119, 124,
127, 158, 175
natural gas, 172, 179, 181, 183, 184,
185, 189, 196, 197

negative income tax, 102–5, 197, 203
  assets and income in definition of,
    103–4
  labor market affected by, 105
Netherlands, 121
"New Economic Policy," 69
"New Federalism," 29
Nixon, Richard M., 29, 47, 65, 82, 116,
    124, 136, 138, 166, 194
  administration of, 2, 11, 48, 61, 65–
    85, 99, 182
North American Free Trade Agreement
    (NAFTA), 219
North-South issues, 204, 205
notches, in social programs, 94–95, 101
nuclear energy, 172, 181, 184, 188

Office of Management and Budget
    (OMB), 24–26, 28, 33, 48, 49, 59,
    61, 90, 119, 124, 160–62
  legislative clearance by, 159
  management functions of, 160–62
Office of the Special Trade Representa-
    tive, 140, 175, 176, 177
oil:
  allocation program for, 195
  consumption-demand for, 183, 184,
    186–88, 195
  domestic, 179, 181, 183, 186, 189,
    195
  efficiency vs. equity issues and, 180,
    186, 195–97
  entitlements program for, 195, 196
  import issues and, 175, 179, 181,
    182–83, 184
  management system for, 183, 184
  national defense and, 183
  petrodollar crisis and, 191–93, 203
  prices of, 127, 128, 179, 180–81,
    182, 184, 185, 186–89, 191–92,
    193, 195–96, 197
  quota system for, 182–83, 184
  regional equity and, 196
  see also energy
oil industry, 180, 184, 186, 189, 195–
    96
Oil Policy Commission, 184
Organization of Petroleum Exporting
    Countries (OPEC), 180, 181, 183,
    184, 186, 191–93
  currency reserves increases in, 191,
    192

Pay Board (1971), 70, 71, 73, 84, 157
pension plans, privatization of, 210
pension reform, 7, 30, 139, 141, 144
Peterson, Peter, 175, 209–10
petrodollars, 191–93, 203
Phillips curve, 87, 105
Pohl, Karl Otto, 13
Pompidou, Georges, 116
presidency:
  access to, as power, 16
  attitude toward spending of, 31–32
  augmentation of, 5
  limitations on, 6, 36, 37, 149, 170–
    72
  policy formation by, influences on,
    9–11, 31
  see also executive branch
private enterprise, 208
privatization, 210, 218
productivity:
  accurate measurement of, 214–15
  improving, 215–17
professionals vs. politicians, 2, 14–17
protectionism, 219–20

Quadriad meetings, 174

Rambouillet summit meeting (1975),
    13–14, 131
recessions:
  of 1970, 68, 113
  of 1974–75, 88, 92, 201
Rees, Albert, 76
regional trade, 219
Regulations and Purchasing Review
    Board, 156–57
regulatory agencies, presidential powers
    and, 170–71
regulatory drag, 215
Reorganization Act (1939), 168
research and development programs, see
    energy
resource allocation, 39, 40, 200
  misapplication in, 71
retirement age, 209, 211–13
Reuss, Henry, 118
Rogers, William, 127
Roosevelt, Franklin D., 124, 149

Schleifer, Andrei, 216
Schmidt, Helmut, 12–14
school lunch program, 92, 95, 99

Seidl, John, 98
Shultz, George P.:
  IRS "enemies list" and, 2
  as Labor Secretary, 1, 5
  presidential appointments of, 169,
    176, 182, 185
  as Treasury Secretary, 12, 127, 138
Simon, William, 185
Smithsonian agreement (1971), 115,
  116, 118, 121, 127
Smoot-Hawley Tariff (1930), 136, 149
social policies and programs, 14, 140
  anticipations phenomenon in, 10–11
  in budget, *see* budget, budgetmaking
  categorical, 98–99, 101, 102, 105
  dependency and, 95, 99
  economic policy and, 7–8, 87, 88–
    90, 98, 104–5, 197
  fiscal policy linked to, 87, 104, 105
  income security as, *see* income
    security
  tax policy and, *see* tax policy, system
  see also specific programs
social security system, 209–11
social security trust fund, 24, 28–29,
  45, 48–49, 90
Soviet Union, 145, 146, 181
  trade policy and, 135–36, 139, 145–
    47
  U.S. trade agreement (1972) with,
    135–36, 139, 145–47
Spain, 137
Special Drawing Rights (SDRs), 112
stabilization, 20, 75, 205
  budget effect on, 21, 23, 33, 34, 36,
    37, 39, 40, 41, 67, 200, 201
  income security and, 93, 99
  international agreements and, 80–82,
    130, 131, 203–4
  tax policy effect on, 21, 23, 44, 45,
    201
  see also wage and price controls
State Department, 119, 123, 124, 136,
  140, 158, 175
State of the Union Message, 31, 160
statistics, 9, 36, 214
Stein, Herb, 74, 127
subsidies, 10
  direct budgetary, 50, 54
  export, 107, 112–13
supplementary security income program
  (SSI), 90, 91

Sweden, 121, 137

Taft-Hartley Act, 1, 2
tax morality, 56, 57, 63, 95, 202
  audits and, 59
  barter and, 202
tax policy, system, 20–21, 24, 37, 43–
  63, 197, 199–203
  advocacy process in, 43, 51–52, 62–
    63
  aged and, 47–48
  closed rule and, 51, 62
  collection vs. other functions in, 50–
    52, 63, 83, 202, 203
  composition of revenues in, 46
  congressional role in, *see* Congress
  depreciation provisions of, 82
  export subsidies and, 112, 150–51
  on foreign income, 139
  general revenue sharing in, 27, 29, 39
  global economy and, 217–18
  immediacy of, 44, 201
  indirect effects of, 46, 66
  macroeconomic aspect of, 21, 43–46
  microeconomy affected by, 46–47,
    202, 203
  1964 cut and, 199, 202
  personal income tax and, 47, 48, 49,
    54, 56–59
  political aspects of, 45, 51
  productivity and, 216–17
  progressivity in, 47, 48
  reductions as trend in, 44–45, 55,
    202
  self-assessment in, 56–59, 63
  simplification of code and returns
    as concern in, 55, 56–59, 63, 202,
    203
  social policy and, 47–49, 50–52, 54,
    55, 63, 88, 103–5, 202, 203
  as stabilization tool, 20, 21, 44, 45,
    201
  Treasury Department and, 59–61
  welfare programs and, 48–49, 103–
    5, 200
  see also fiscal policy
tax preferences, 46, 50–53
  congressional support for, 50–51, 54,
    55–56
  disadvantages of, 51
  elimination of, 54, 55–56
tax rates, 45, 54, 55

tax rates (*continued*)
  marginal, 50, 51, 63, 93–95, 99, 202, 203
tax reform, 50, 52–56, 63, 203
  minimum tax as, 54
  political demands for, 51, 52
  reallocation of revenues in, 52–54
  unemployment rates and, 45
tax shelters, 51, 55, 56, 63, 202
technology, international finance and, 219
Trade Act (1974), 133–34, 135, 151
Trade Expansion Act (1962), 134, 135, 139–40, 141
trade-offs:
  in cash transfer program, 99–100
  between competing policies, 163
  in efficiency vs. equity policies, 4, 11, 197
  between inflation and unemployment, 21, 87, 105
trade-ons:
  in efficiency-equity policies, 4, 203
  between energy needs and market, 197
  between inflation and unemployment, 88, 104
trade policy, 8–9, 81–82, 107, 112, 113, 115, 117, 133–51, 203–4, 220
  adjustment assistance in, 139–45
  advance authority in, 148–49
  countervailing-duty issue in, 150–51, 175
  generalized preferences proposal in, 136, 139
  Geneva negotiations on, 133, 204
  government organization on, 174–77
  international diplomacy linked with, 135–36, 138, 146, 150–51
  monetary policy related to, 107, 113, 123, 138, 174–75
  most-favored-nation (MFN) issue in, 136, 139, 145–47
  nontariff barriers in, 137, 138, 139, 147–50, 151
  nontrade issues linked to, 80–81, 135–36, 139–47, 203–4
  oil prices in, 191–93
  protectionism and, 134–35, 137, 139, 145, 148, 149, 151, 179, 184

reciprocal approach to, 149
  reform as central issue in, 139
  tariff preferences and, 136, 137–38, 139
  U.S. objectives in, 135–38, 139
  wage-price controls and, 80–82
transfer payments, 37, 47, 54, 87, 89, 90–91, 95, 99, 101–2, 197, 200
  see also specific programs
Treasury Department, 12, 20, 57, 60–61, 106, 111, 119, 123–26, 150–51, 174, 175
Troika, economic policymaking of, 174, 175
Truman, Harry S., 85
trust funds, 28–29, 48–49, 90
Turkey-Cyprus issue, 146

Ullman, Al, 63
unemployment, 19, 20–21, 40, 41, 45, 199, 200
  income security policy and, 87, 92, 104, 105, 141–42
  inflation and, 41, 87–88, 104, 203
  international trade and, 112–13, 117, 118, 133, 139, 140–45
unemployment insurance, 7, 41, 92, 101, 139, 142, 144–45, 200
unfunded liabilities, 209–10
Ushiba, Nobuhiko, 13

value-added tax proposal, 48, 61
veterans, income security payments to, 89
Vishny, Robert, 216
Volcker, Paul, 127
Volpe, John, 171
voucher programs, 90–91, 95, 99, 100, 101, 102

wage and price controls, 21, 65–85
  administration of, 69–71, 72, 74–75, 83–84, 85
  anticipations and expectations in, 67, 68, 71, 76, 81
  continuing appeal of, 65, 75–76, 117, 193–94
  disengagement as problem of, 72–76, 84
  dynamic nature of, 67, 71–72
  econometric studies in, 80

freezes and, 65, 67–69, 74, 194
institutional rearrangements in, 72, 73, 74
interconnections in, 67, 71–72, 75, 78–82, 85, 117, 156–57
large-unit approach to, 76–78
life cycle in, 66
monetary policy interaction with, 80–81, 85, 156–57
1971–74 period of, 66–75, 80, 82–83, 84, 85
oil industry and, 180, 181, 186, 188, 189, 191, 193–97
political aspects of, 68, 74, 75, 77, 78, 83, 84–85, 194
price fluctuations and, 72, 73, 74, 75, 77
public-private interactions in, 67, 71–72
regulatory programs vs., 66
self-administration in, 73–74
supplies affected by, 82–83
support sought for, 69–71, 72
timing in, 69, 70–71, 73, 74
trade relations and, 81
tripartite wage boards in, 70, 84

Watergate, 147
Ways and Means Committee, House, 44, 51, 61, 62–63, 135, 147
wealth, redistribution of, 47–48, 54, 197, 201–3
Weber, Arnold, 160
Weinberger, Caspar, 16, 169
welfare programs, *see* social policies and programs
West Germany, 188
U.S. monetary policy and, 12–14, 80, 121, 122, 131
White House staff, 16, 159, 160, 161
Wilson, Harold, 13
worker assistance, trade-related, 140–45
work incentives, 91, 93–95, 100, 101, 105, 141–42, 202
working poor, 92, 99
World Bank, 221–22
World Trade Organization, 219
Wright, J. Skelly, 172–73

Yeo, Edwin, 13

zero-sum game, 204

About the Authors

KENNETH W. DAM is Max Pam Professor of American and Foreign Law at the University of Chicago Law School, where he is director of the John M. Olin Program in Law and Economics.

Since graduating from the University of Chicago Law School in 1957, Dam has had widely diverse experience in government service, the private sector, the non-profit world, and higher education. Within government, he has served as a Supreme Court law clerk (1957–58), assistant director of the Office of Management and Budget for national security and international affairs (1971–73), executive director of the Council on Economic Policy (1973), and deputy secretary of state (1982–85). He has served on a number of government panels and committees, most recently as a member of the Defense Policy Board.

In the private sector, Dam was IBM vice president for law and external relations (1985–92), and in 1992 he stepped in to investigate and then restructure the United Way of America as its president and CEO after a widely publicized scandal in that organization. He serves as a director of Alcoa and carries on an active practice as an arbitrator of complex disputes.

In the non-profit world, Mr. Dam serves on the boards of a number of institutions, including the Brookings Institution, the Council on Foreign Relations (New York), and the Chicago Council on Foreign Relations. He co-chairs, with Sam Nunn, the Aspen Strategy Group.

In higher education, beyond his several decades as a professor at the University of Chicago Law School, he served as the University's provost from 1980 to 1982 and has taught at the University of Freiburg in Germany. Currently he is a member of the German-American Academic Council and the American Academy of Arts and Sciences. He has written widely on economic policy and international affairs and is the author of books on the GATT, the international monetary system, the development of oil resources, and the taxation of foreign income. Most recently he has been writing and speaking on intellectual property and information security. His book *Cryptography's Role in Securing the Information Society* (co-edited with Herbert Lin, 1996) is the product of a two-year National Research Council study conducted by an expert panel chaired by Mr. Dam.

GEORGE PRATT SHULTZ is professor emeritus of International Economics at the Stanford Graduate School of Business, a distinguished fellow at the Hoover Institution, and director and senior counselor of Bechtel Group, Inc. At present, as throughout his career, Shultz has combined work in government, business, and academic institutions. He graduated *cum laude* from Princeton in 1942, served in the Marine Corps in the Pacific in World War II, and returned to earn his Ph.D. in industrial economics at MIT in 1949.

Joining the MIT faculty in 1948, Shultz taught economics and industrial relations until 1957, taking a leave of absence to serve as a senior staff economist on the President's Council of Economic Advisers under Chairman Arthur Burns in 1955–56. Shultz then accepted an appointment as professor of industrial relations at the University of Chicago's Graduate School of Business, becoming dean of the Business School in 1962. Having served as a consultant to the Labor Department and on various government commissions during the 1950s and '60s, in 1969 Shultz returned to government when he was appointed Secretary of Labor by President Nixon—the first of four cabinet posts he was to hold.

By the time he became Labor Secretary, Shultz was held to be one of the nation's leading industrial relations experts and was highly regarded by both labor and management for his skills as an arbitrator and administrator. In 1970, Shultz was named as the first director of the newly created Office of Management and Budget, becoming the administration's chief troubleshooter on federal management. He was appointed Secretary of the Treasury in 1972. In January 1973, in addition to his duties as Treasury

Secretary, he also served as chairman of the Council on Economic Policy. In this capacity, Shultz served as coordinator for economic policy, both domestic and international.

Mr. Shultz left government service in 1974 to become president of Bechtel Group, Inc. He remained with Bechtel until 1982. While with Bechtel, he maintained his close ties with the academic world by joining the faculty of Stanford University and working on a part-time basis.

Mr. Shultz held two key positions in the Reagan administration: chairman of the President's Economic Policy Advisory Board (1981–82) and Secretary of State (1982–89). As Secretary of State, he played a key role, over a seven-year period, in implementing a foreign policy that led to the successful conclusion of the Cold War and the development of strong relationships between the United States and the countries of the Asia-Pacific region, including China, Japan, and the ASEAN countries.

In January 1989, he was awarded the Medal of Freedom, the nation's highest civilian honor. His memoir, *Turmoil and Triumph,* appeared in 1993.